A LONG WAY FOR A PIZZA

ON FOOT TO ROME

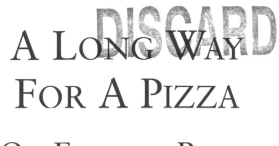

D0762779

Brian Mooney

THOROGOOD

Thorogood Publishing Ltd
10-12 Rivington Street, London EC2A 3DU
Telephone: 020 7749 4748 • Fax: 020 7729 6110
Email: info@thorogoodpublishing.co.uk
Web: www.thorogoodpublishing.co.uk

A CIP catalogue record for this book is available from
the British Library.

ISBN 1 85418 790 2 • 978-185418790-1

Book designed and typeset in the UK by Driftdesign

Printed in the UK by Ashford Colour Press

For Jon Harris – who showed me the way

~

CONTENTS

NOT TO SCALE

ENGLAND

NORTH SEA

B.M.'s starting-point
COGGESHALL

NORWICH
IPSWICH

ESSEX
Pleshey
Loughton

R. Stour & Orwell

R. Blackwater

LONDON

R. Thames

Cobham
Charing
Capel-le-Ferne

CANTERBURY (Sigeric and party)

DOVER

FERRY

CALAIS

FLANDRE

BELGIUM

HOLLAND

AMSTERDAM
(Everdiene, Kees)

ENGLISH CHANNEL

Pas de Calais

Guines

R. Somme

R. Seine

CHER-BOURG

ABBEVILLE

Wisques
Amettes

CHAUSSÉE
BRUNE-HAUT

ARRAS

Picardie

R. Somme

Bapaume
Peronne
Ham

AMIENS

LAON

R. Oise

Coucy-le-Château
Braye-en-Laonnois

CHEMIN des DAMES

R. Aisne

LA MONTAGNE
DE REIMS

REIMS

F R A N C E

R. Marne

Ay

PARIS

Châlons-en-Champagne
Vitry-le-François
St. Dizier

Champagne Ardenne

LAC du DER

Donjeux

TOUL (Nancy): H.B.'s
starting-point

H.B.'s beeline for the Furka Pass

Chaumont
Langres

Franche Comté

R. Salon
Champlitte
Gy

R. Doubs

DIJON

BESANÇON

R. Loue

Ornans

Pontarlier

MOUNTAINS

SWITZERLAND

JURA

Ste. Croix

Chavornay

LAC de NEUCHÂTEL

EIGER,
JUNGFRAU

LAC
LÉMAN

LAUSANNE
FERRY

WILDHORN

GENEVA

LES DENTS du MIDI

Villeneuve

R. Rhône

LES DIABLERETS

ROME

MONT BLANC

Martigny

ALPS

R. Rhône

THE

Orsières

COL du GRAND
St BERNARD

ITALY

AOSTA

Map 1:
East Anglia – Grand
St Bernard Pass,

1100 km.

Map 2:
Gd St Bernard Pass
= Rome,

1000km.

ONE

OUT OF ESSEX

IT WAS ONE OF THE WALKS WE OFTEN TAKE. We had reached the southern border of our hometown of Coggeshall, which by one measurement marks the midpoint of Essex – between Epping and Harwich – though by another it lies closer to the Stour and the county's northern boundary than to the Thames. We were on the Essex Way that leads from Coggeshall's ancient timber framed tithe barn towards Bradwell and London, under a broad oak tree with the River Blackwater down to the right. It was a blustery day in May 2010, and I had a fully laden bright yellow rucksack on my back and was wearing a brand new pair of stout walking boots.

"Where is your next stop?" asked Gail.

"Rome," I replied, savouring the audacity and cheekiness of my reply. What my wife had meant, of course, was: what was my next stage along the Essex Way? But my reply was correct. I was setting out for Rome – on foot.

The lone oak beside the stony track just beyond the barn has often been my beacon. When, as I occasionally do, I walk to Coggeshall from London, its outstretched arms, visible from some distance over the flat Essex country, signal my homecoming. Ten years earlier, in 2000, I had gone out of my way to circle this venerable tree and reverently tap its trunk before heading to Maldon on my first marathon walk – from the shrine at Walsingham, via Coggeshall, to Santiago de Compostela.

The bravado with which I announced my destination this time masked real doubts. I had just hit 61. When I walked through France and Spain to Santiago I was 50, and on my return, as a well trained journalist, I had written up an account of my journey and submitted it to Laurie, another long-distance walker. I had entitled my walk to Santiago *Plain Indulgence* – to emphasise that I had hoofed it all the way to the traditional resting place of the Apostle St James for the sheer fun of it, rather than as penance in sackcloth and ashes to earn an old fashioned plenary indulgence. But Laurie threw my account back in my face.

"You didn't suffer enough," she said. That gave me a lot to think about.

A few days before I began my new journey, I bumped into her outside Moorgate Underground Station, older, of course, and (I noticed) limping.

"This time, I suppose, it's going to have to hurt," I said.

"Maybe," replied Laurie – the first of several maybes.

When I said goodbye to our Anglican vicar in Coggeshall, Father Philip, I couldn't help bringing up the sanguine possibility of the 61-year-old pilgrim conking out along the way.

"Maybe you won't," said Philip, embracing me and giving me a blessing. In due course, as the days of walking totted up and my targets were met, I would come to appreciate his words for the powerful injunction that they were: I might actually have to complete this walk.

I walk because I am an anarchist; I can't abide rules. Walking is practically the last human activity that has not in one way or another been regulated. There are no rules; a walker simply puts one foot in front of the other and, within reason, goes and stops where he or she pleases. Walking is also a means of escape – it allows us to shed all that it is unimportant, and to de-clutter and simplify our lives. It slows us down to the speed at which the first men and women travelled across our planet, and it gives us back time to think; when our feet touch the ground in unison with the pulse of our hearts, the world looks and feels a lot better, and we become once more part of the landscape.

I had long thought about walking to Rome; it was unfinished business. When my mother became terminally ill with multiple sclerosis in 1979, I was working there as a young Reuters correspondent. Summoned home, I sat at her side as she lay dying in the downstairs room of the house of my childhood in Gerrards Cross, with its enclosed view of rhododendrons and silver birches; the book in my hand was Hilaire Belloc's *The Path to Rome*, an illustrated first edition published by George Allen in 1902 which I would 30 years on rediscover in my father's bookshelves when he in turn died. I have it on my desk as I write my own story. But I have never been able quite to finish it.

Even though Hilaire Belloc started halfway down France, his account of his pilgrimage to Rome in 1901 is invariably cited as the benchmark. *The Path to Rome* is in fact one of the few books of his still in print. That's more than a century of successful branding. Everyone seems to know the work and to quote it, but I am beginning to wonder if they, like me, have ever actually got through all 448 pages. Just being able to cite the title and author seems to be sufficient.

Reading it today is not altogether easy; Belloc may set out to walk to Rome in a straight line, but his account meanders; besides, he teases his readers with an imaginary fellow 'lector' who upbraids and admonishes his 'auctor' whenever he feels the narrative is running off course, or the story becoming boring. As a post-modernist ploy that may not be such a bad idea. In any case, I will try to re-read it and let Belloc serve as my 'lector', or at least mentor, as I pull together the threads of my own journey.

I set out for Rome focussed on the many thousands who had journeyed there on foot in the Middle Ages. The sense of following century after century of pilgrim steps – the footfall of prayer, I call it – was attractive to me. It made me part of a continuum; and it was not impossible that there had been others, unknown to me, whether inspired by faith or by a sense of impending mortality, who had made the same journey from Coggeshall to Rome.

On the banks of the River Blackwater in Coggeshall from the reign of King Stephen till the Dissolution of the Monasteries, a powerful and influential Cistercian Abbey of Savignac origin flourished for 400 years, and although its most famous chronicler Ralph of Coggeshall gives no instances, it is hard to believe that at some stage an abbot or monk did not walk from there to Rome. But the Cistercian monks of Coggeshall, either setting out for their mother house of Clairvaux in France or on to Rome, would not have gone as far to the west as I was proposing to go. They would have headed southeast from their abbey to cross the River Thames at Tilbury, or made their way directly to the east coast. But I wanted to reverse history, so to speak, by linking St Paul's Cathedral to St Peter's Basilica, and to do that, I had to walk via London.

I took my first step to Rome from the parish church in Coggeshall, St Peter ad Vincula, just up the road from my own house in Church Street, The Cedars. This fine 15th century flint and stone church, accidentally bombed by the *Luftwaffe* in 1940, has its own special Petrine connection. It is one of only 16 in England dedicated to the chains in which St Peter was supposedly fettered while in prison in Jerusalem and Rome. According to early Church legend, the separate links of chain were brought together, and then miraculously conjoined. They are kept in the 5th century Roman Basilica of San Pietro in Vincoli, the mother of all the churches around the world which hold this singular dedication. That Basilica, not the dome of St Peter's, would be my final goal.

Gail and I parted at the oak. I knew the way into London backwards, having walked from Epping on the edge of London to Coggeshall half a dozen times – five times completing the entire distance in one day. Long days of endurance, they have remained seared into my walking consciousness. The first time I walked from Epping to Coggeshall in one hop I was alone; I didn't initially dare inflict the experiment on anyone else. That was in May 1993; I was in training to climb the North side of Everest, and I covered the distance in 13 hours, averaging 3.19 miles an hour. I never walked it as fast again, but I had some memorable long-haul companions – Eric, a BBC director who wanted to know what it was like to walk more than a marathon in one day and who was all but comatose at the end, the artist and writer Jon Harris whom I admonished for malingering in Ongar and who walks jauntily into my journey a little later, and Jill, a sports masseuse whose feet were nearly broken by the novel experience. Forty-one miles in one day is extreme walking. Setting out on foot for Rome on 28 May 2010, I was older and wiser. I promised myself that I would do no more than 40 kilometres in a day – a kilometre being two thirds of a mile, 12 minutes walking – a promise I almost kept.

It was typical for late May – a cold easterly wind sent clouds scudding across the low East Anglian horizon; between them, a welcome hot sun shone from patches of deep blue sky. I had the wind on my back, for which I was grateful as I was carrying an almost full pack – some 13 kilos of maps and kit. I was soon past the sand and gravel pits at Bradwell and beyond Fairstead church, walking down the stony track at Fambridge Hall into the next valley, where the River Brain rises, and where Jill's feet had nearly given up. Ahead of me lay open country towards Terling, the first big vista of my journey, and I began to sense both the enormity of what I was doing, and the thrill once again of the freedom and pull of the road. My mind slowing in time with my step, I settled into the equilibrium of thinking and walking at three miles an hour. Now eight miles from Coggeshall, I soaked up the simple pleasures of nature; the bluebells carpeting the woods and the white parsley blossom billowing from the hedgerows in the same carefree abandon as the children I passed in Terling, fishing in the ford with their home-made rods.

Keeping to my promise that I would not cover crazy distances, I had arranged to stop for the night at Pleshey, the halfway point between Coggeshall and London. Pleshey has one of the best preserved Norman castle earthworks in England. My previous transits had revealed that though there was a pub, a good stop for my favourite pick-me-up of iced lime and lemonade, there was no licensed accommodation. This posed a problem. It is said that a true traveller sets out in the morning not knowing where he or she will sleep at night. The prospect of arriving somewhere tired and hungry at five o'clock on a wet afternoon to find that the nearest accommodation is ten kilometres down the road, and having to knock on doors or walk on, simply does not appeal to me. Keen on my comforts, I am in that respect not a true traveller; when I am walking I like to know in the morning that a hot bath, a good meal and a comfortable bed await me that night.

During a recent visit to Pleshey I had spotted a sign opposite the *White Horse* public house – the Chelmsford Diocesan House of Retreat. This posed a problem of a different nature. Was I a pilgrim or wasn't I? Officially, yes. I had set out with a pilgrim passport, a little plastic-coated pale yellow booklet from the Confraternity of Pilgrims to Rome, confirming my *bona fides* to stay in pilgrim hostels and which, having filled it with daily stamps recording the stages of my journey, would qualify me when I arrived in Rome for a pilgrim *Testimonium*. All journeys are spiritual, and nobody can really say who is and who is not a pilgrim; but personally I felt a fraud. There was nothing remotely penitential about my journey; or so I believed.

Laying aside these misgivings, I had booked into the House of Retreat. It stands on the site of the castle gatehouse, close to the church, and was given its current redbrick upgrade in the early 1900s when it became, briefly, an Anglican convent. But soon after the diocese of Chelmsford was created in 1914 the nuns fell out with their new Bishop, John Watts-Ditchfield, because he wanted to stop them displaying the Blessed Sacrament in the chapel; and they left Pleshey to found a new convent. Pleshey House was then turned into a place of prayer and retreat – and, of course, the Blessed Sacrament is back in the chapel. The house is Arts and Crafts with a few surprising twists, such as a fine Della Robia *Madonna and Child*. A life-size cross stands on the lawn at the back where the secluded garden slopes down to the moat, bordered by shrubs and flowers. In early summer, dazzling wisteria covered the veranda.

The place exudes calm and prayer, and after the vigour and exertion of walking 21 miles with a full pack, I was virtually flattened by the sense of peace. The warden, Vicky, welcomed me with a cup of tea and showed me to my room. She is head of the Friends of Pleshey and also chairman of the Essex Embroiderers. When I told her that I was on the first day of a walk to Rome I think she must have regretted not putting me in a locked and padded cell, but she took me seriously enough to stamp my pilgrim passport, the first imprint on its pages to mark the start of my journey. "Our prayers go with you ... God speed," Vicky wrote beneath the house stamp.

Vicky also kindly loaned me the key to the Pleshey castle site: it unlocks the gate which guards what remains of it – an arched brickwork bridge crossing the moat to a conical earthen motte. From the summit, all of 59 metres above sea, there is a glorious 360 degree view of the Essex countryside – a rare sighting in such a flat county – and on a good day you can make out the Langdon Hills which rise over the Thames at the county's southern edge. I had a special reason for wanting to stand on that spot on this particular evening – to conjure up the adventurer and author Frank Baines. Frank, who had once owned our house, had brought me there for the first time on just such an evening in late September 1987.

Frank did not drive – he would have regarded driving as a vulgar activity best left to servants – but he had particularly requested the trip to Pleshey. Did he know that he was about to die? Looking back, I think he had some instinctive feeling that he was nearing the end; he was making his own pilgrimage, paying farewell to Pleshey and to its magnificent panorama of open country and, as it happened, passing on a treasure to me, his driver. He died three weeks later. In his younger days, back from his adventures in India and now a fêted author, he had come often to Pleshey, he told me then, to visit a girlfriend – this in the midst of what he himself described as his 'homosexual phase'. Frank was full of such contradictions, and I had got to know them pretty well; indeed I had been living with them, re-living his life in the months when I was contemplating this walk. Just days before tying my boots for Rome I had submitted for publication final drafts of two books by or about him – one, my salting-down of his wartime memoir of fighting with the Chindits behind enemy lines in Burma where he conducted a love affair with his Gurkha orderly, and the other no less extraordinary tale of his brave and irregular life, researched and distilled into a biography. Walking to Rome was a way of moving on from Frank, and watching the sun go down over Pleshey was a good place to start.

Meanwhile, I have begun to re-read Hilaire Belloc's account. The bounder; not only did he start halfway down France, but he didn't even walk it all. I am treating him with the same disrespect. Opening the book again at random, I came across a description of a train ride he takes into Milan. His decision to 'cheat' and board a train was preceded by some hocus-pocus based on which of two candles went out first in a church. He seems to have spent a lot of his journey popping in and out of churches. This man is dangerous. I must go back to the beginning and see what he is really about.

I slipped across the road for dinner at the *White Horse* – cod and chips – and back in my room at the Retreat House I was soon asleep, trying to trace in my mind the 1,300 miles between Pleshey and Rome, and secretly wishing that every day would be as trouble-free as the first.

The next day I tracked through what in 1954 the poet John Betjeman described as lost country: "The deepest Essex few explore, where steepest thatch is sunk in flowers, and out of elm and sycamore, rise flinty fifteenth-century towers," Betjeman wrote, and his words hold good more than half a century on. The magic of the Essex Way, as it snakes south and west from Pleshey towards London, is that apart from the distant snarl of Stansted Airport and the murmur of the arterial roads not much has changed.

The way passes through a mix of open farmland and down green lanes, part of the ancient network of country-wide trails which escaped

being tarmacked and converted into modern roads and which are especially well preserved in deepest Essex. With their hedgerows and banks
harbouring rare and colourful plants, these lanes are invariably covered
by overhanging branches; green tunnels, cut off from the world outside.
Essex, the land of white socks and electronic gates, has 500 miles of
these lanes, more than any other English county except Dorset.

The mid-Essex countryside is still surprisingly empty. Good Easter,
the first village on the Essex Way after Pleshey, is said to be seven miles
from everywhere and on the road to nowhere. I took the wrong path
on leaving the graveyard at St Andrew's, one of Betjeman's flint churches;
the way had been erased in a cornfield, and it took me ten valuable minutes (a lost half-mile) to get back on track. I am a nervous walker and
I hate going wrong – missing a waymark can spoil a good day, and
it's all too easy to do. Failing to spot one at the end of a long day, with
the prospect of adding a few miles to get back on track, can be soul
destroying. Over the years, I have developed a sort of obsessive in-
flight checklist, using compass, the sun, the map and the ground around
me to ensure that I know pretty much all the time exactly where I am,
and where I am heading. On the well-marked Essex Way, which has
been carefully looked after ever since the Campaign for Rural England
conjured it into existence in 1972 by hooking together a chain of
existing footpaths and bridleways, this posed few problems. The lonely
farm tracks and woodland paths in Italy, where waymarks mysteriously
vanished, would prove far more challenging.

The red poppy waymarks and the fingerposts of the Essex Way
carrying the county's logo – three scimitar-shaped Saxon seaxes – were
always a welcome sight, even though each time I passed them I was
reminded of a niggling regret. Jon Harris and I had celebrated Essex
in 2004 by walking around its mainly water-bound borders and we
had turned our shared journey into a book – *Frontier Country*. We
discovered many strange things along the frontier – including the
Broomway on the mud flats off Foulness Island and the hideout of an
ex-soldier living like Robinson Crusoe in the woods near Bishops Stort-

ford, but we forgot to include the story of how the seaxe knives were adopted in 1932 as the county's coat of arms. Walking long distances gives you time to be nagged at by all the things you should have done or that you could have done better. Some days, this became a full-time preoccupation.

As I marched on more south than west, the chatter of the A12 gave way to the increasingly persistent rumble over Stansted, but the views remained timeless. I approached Chipping Ongar alongside the reed banks of the River Roding, with neither house nor farm building in sight. There I intersected with another of the county's long-distance trails, St Peter's Way, which goes due east from Ongar, crossing Essex's lonely Dengie Peninsula and halting, on the brink of the North Sea, at that most exceptional Saxon church – St Peter-on-the-Wall, Bradwell-on-Sea. Built of stone from the lost Roman fort of Othona, it stands on the edge of the shore, a beacon for navigators entering the Blackwater estuary, the river that flows through Coggeshall and past its former abbey. I have often walked around the Dengie on the seawalls in what I call Essex's Empty Quarter. The sight of St Peter – even just in letters on the waymarks – filled me with irrational hope; perhaps I would actually get to Rome, the 'Eternal City' where he is buried.

It was raining hard when I reached another Essex Saxon church, St Andrew's at Greensted, and I took shelter inside its womblike nave of dark upright tree trunks which I saw now for the first time, because whenever I had set out from Epping to walk to Coggeshall it had been far too early in the morning, and therefore locked. I thought of the long distances some had travelled to and from here – about the 'Tolpuddle Martyrs' from Dorset who came to Greensted in 1836 after they were pardoned of alleged rural insurgency and rescued from transportation to Australia, and of the two Crusader knights who lie buried side by side just outside the porch. Greensted is a long way from both Botany Bay and Jerusalem.

The rain didn't stop, and I went on and became lost after Toot Hill and got soaked through traversing a field where the path had been smothered by shoulder-high rape. I was back on track crossing the old Roman road from Colchester to London in the hornbeam forest that leads up to the M11. A pedestrian bridge arches over the motorway here; whenever I drive under it I mentally salute it as a symbol of freedom, although only once have I seen anyone actually walking across it. Reaching the other side, I turned due south for the first time since leaving home and carried on down the hill through Coopersale Common towards Epping and the bridge at Great Gregories Farm. Below me was the M25, London's orbital motorway with its unceasing stream of cars and trucks, headlights ablaze under a blackened sky and pouring rain. Ahead lay the track up Piercing Hill, making the entry through Genesis Slade to Epping Forest, and bringing me within a mile of a waiting friend, and the welcome prospect of a hot bath, dry clothes and a companionable supper over which the spirit of Frank Baines would hover.

TWO

LONDON

THE RAIN MAY HAVE CEASED AS I APPROACHED the forest border between Theydon Bois and Loughton and made the ascent of Jack's Hill, but the trials of the first full day's walk to Rome hadn't quite ended. I had arranged with Chris Pond to stay the night with him and his wife Caroline at Forest Villa, a home from home for me in that, like The Cedars, it has a glazed captain's walk, or belvedere, crowning the roof. Chris had bravely agreed to meet me in a car park off the B172 road. He, knowing every nook and path of London's forest went and waited in the right car park, and I, with my half-scale long-distance map, went to the wrong one. There would have been a lot of bellowing among the dripping trees if we hadn't both used our cell phones to dock.

There he stood, fully kitted – green anorak, walking stick, oversized trainers, gold rimmed spectacles and with his large-scale Ordnance Survey map. That was there for show; Chris knows the forest as well as any ranger. My own links with Epping Forest – owned and run by the City of London Corporation for whom I am a Common Councilman – are tenuous, and the one time I had walked its un-waymarked glades and paths (with Jon Harris) we got lost, so at the end of a hard 27-mile day, soaking wet and tired, I was evidently in need of local guide, and overjoyed to have one.

Chris, a former mayor of Loughton, had chosen our meeting place with characteristic humour; as he explained, it was next to what used to be the City of London's coal duty post, yet safely inside the clearly discernible frontier of his former bailiwick. Epping Forest changes its cut the moment you enter Loughton parish; the trees there were coppiced regularly until 1878, when the City of London took over, whereas in neighbouring Theydon Bois they were left to grow unchecked.

And so, down the Green Ride we walked; it had been cut in anticipation of Queen Victoria's dedication of the forest in 1882 though in the event she took another route. We passed the Ditches, where tank traps dug in World War II are still traceable: a last redoubt to protect London from the north; and then through Hangboy Slade and the Furze Ground to cross the A121 into Monk Wood. An invasion indeed met us in Bellringers' Hollow; thousands of black slugs, brought out by the showers, thronged the floor of the ride. Up to our left, as we descended towards Debden Slade, we could just make out the Iron Age hump of Loughton Camp through the trees. At the bottom, the twisting path alongside Loughton Brook, in sudden spate, brought us to Staples Road Pond where we crossed the lane to Forest Villa.

"We owners of belvederes must stick together," said Chris as he showed me the sights from his high perch over Loughton. To the West, I could see the outskirts of Waltham Abbey, to the east all the way back to the downs that rise up beyond the River Roding towards Hainault Forest. At dinner, while my clothes and boots dried out, Caroline, Chris and I talked about the Baines's – strange father and strange son.

Chris Pond is the author of a book on Loughton and its buildings; he knows the ground well having been a local councillor and mayor. Sir Frank Baines, Frankie's father, was a noted Arts and Crafts architect who tuned his hand to urban development; his career was crowned with a KCVO; he had chosen to live in Loughton, designing and building houses for his somewhat convoluted family (he may have been a bigamist, keeping his wife and son elsewhere, in South London). Chris's interest in Sir Frank, and my own desire to do justice to Frankie, had created a confederacy between us, with many discoveries shared as we went along. Just as I was putting the finishing touches to *Frank Baines: A Life Beyond the Sea* in early 2010, Gail and I had attended the

Loughton Literary Festival to hear Chris hold his audience spellbound in the forest church of Holy Innocents, High Beech, with his account of "twice-a-(k)night Baines", the illustrious father. He has since then generously shared his findings with members of the Victorian Society, which warms to an Edwardian renegade. .

Chris had a surprise for me the following day. The reigning mayor of Loughton, David Wixley, turned up after breakfast, wearing boots and carrying his mayoral chain. David is a serious long-distance walker; his boots have crunched the Pennine Way and the Coast-to-Coast footpath across England, as well as trails in Corsica, Cuba and the Cape Verde Islands. David would accompany us.

Reversing last night's descent, we climbed up the Green Ride and, crossing Earls Path, struck out west by Strawberry Hill Pond. Lincolns Lane took us on to Loughton Fairmead, a deer park created by Henry VIII. From Palmers Bridge, the Red Path took us to Connaught Water; bearing east, we followed the Loughton bank to the boundary with Chingford – I should have been on my mettle.

For it was here that David and Chris staged their hold-up. They demanded that I present my pilgrim passport. For the occasion, ex-mayor Chris had made a rubber stamp, and with it mayor David duly stamped the third box on the first page. It read: Loughton – The Mayor. David signed his name and entered the date. He then covered up his mayoral chain: I was cleared to leave Loughton and enter Chingford.

We walked on together below Queen Elizabeth's Hunting Lodge and climbed Pole Hill to the misplaced Greenwich Obelisk with its plaque to T.E. Lawrence by the three trees, all that remains of the original seven which he planted to mark publication of *Seven Pillars of Wisdom* on a plot where he planned to crown the hill with a mansion. The obelisk marks the old line of the Greenwich Meridian and was raised in 1824 by John Pond, the Astronomer Royal, to indicate True North from the Greenwich Royal Observatory's transit telescope. The plaque recording Colonel Lawrence's links with Pole Hill was added to it in 2008; under the terms in which he eventually disposed of his mansion site, he stipulated that the 18 acres of land should revert to Epping Forest.

I have always felt an affinity for Lawrence of Arabia. A cousin of mine, Colonel Joyce, was his *aide de camp* at military headquarters in Cairo; as a child I used to visit the ageing Colonel at his home in Crowthorne, close to Wellington College, where he would talk affectionately and enthusiastically about his old commander. He once gave me a woven fragment of one of Lawrence's white silk head-dresses, which I still have: to a young boy this was quite the most marvellous treasure.

Pausing by the incorrectly sited obelisk, I couldn't resist teasing the present Mr Pond.

"One of your ancestors no good with his sums," I commented to Chris.

"No relation," said Chris, "but I do think it was more a case of the Meridian line being moved at a later date, than of John Pond miscalculating." Just so: the Meridian was changed in 1850, and the new line of zero longitude, internationally adopted in 1884, now passes 19 feet east of the obelisk.

No wonder the troubled Colonel Lawrence chose this spot. Pole Hill presents the perfect panorama of inner London and the Docklands, a cityscape startling in its scale and boldness. Standing there, on a bright morning clear of the industrial haze that would have been there for Lawrence 90 years ago, I could take pleasure in the thought that as a member of the City of London's Planning Committee I had been responsible for voting through one of the new icons of the skyline – the Swiss Re headquarters, known to everyone now as the Gherkin. The grandeur of the view below me would remain unmatched and unchallenged until some ten weeks later I crested Rome's tallest hill, Monte Mario, and looked down over St Peter's Basilica.

David brought me back to the grass on which we stood. He had prepared a short speech, recalling his return to Epping Forest after walking the Pennine Way and how, no longer weighed down by his heavy rucksack, he had flown up Pole Hill, and how, looking around his 'home' forest, he now realised that in all the Pennines he had seen nothing quite so wonderful.

"I hope that you see many things of great beauty and return with the same thought," said David, as we turned to part at Hawksmouth.

I walked on across the dam of King George Reservoir to join the towpath on the Lee Navigation Canal and headed into London. I had walked part of this way before with Jon Harris when we were beating the bounds of Essex. Some of the sights hadn't changed that much: buddleia was still growing out of the industrial brickwork buildings along the canal. At Lea Valley Road Bridge, on the edge of Hackney Marsh, where Jon and I had continued south to the Thames, I turned westwards to Victoria Park and phoned Marina. My younger daughter was then living close to the western end of the Park, and our last talk had ended with the half-promise of a coffee. Today there was no reply; it was, after all, Sunday morning, and she was probably still sleeping. Victoria Park was in festive mood, East Londoners enjoying their green space and free time on a sunny day. I cut through Hackney High Street and walked into the near empty City of London, passing Broadgate and Liverpool Street Station, gratefully sloughing off my rucksack and shedding my still stiff new boots in my small apartment by the River Thames at Queenhithe.

This had been a short day, only 15 miles, but in view of the long haul ahead I was already observing what a relief it was to unshackle myself from the little yellow monster on my back and unshod my feet. That evening I sorted through the rucksack with greater earnestness than I had given the task in Coggeshall, loading it with the maps I would need as far as Arras; there a friend would bring me a re-fill. It was still too heavy and so I took stuff out, abandoning an extra fleece and a bivouac bag, even discarding the book Gail had given me, *Nothing to be Frightened Of* – Julian Barnes on death. I would carry my Oxford memories of Julian with me, and Evensong at St Paul's Cathedral perfectly wrapped up the subject of death in the words of Psalm 73: "My feet were almost gone; my treading had well nigh slipt."

Before the service began, I had asked one of the deacons to stamp my pilgrim passport, telling her: "I am walking to Rome."

"Yes, dear," she replied, handing me back the duly stamped document and with a gentle pat on my shoulder. I twigged immediately that she had me down for a nutter; she ushered me out of the sacristy as quickly as she could. St Paul's was not used to pilgrims on foot.

As he writes it, Hilaire Belloc seems to have spent a lot of his tramp to Rome on his knees. His account opens with him praying in the mystical church of his soul – no maps or compass needed for that – and it is in front of a statue of Our Lady, which is "so extraordinary and so different from all I had ever seen before", that he makes his pledge to walk to Rome. The man was high on something; I am beginning to warm to him. This is how he records the moment.

> I was quite taken out of myself and vowed a vow there to go to Rome on Pilgrimage and see all of Europe which the Christian Faith has saved; and I said, "I will start from the place where I served in arms for my sins; I will walk all the way and take advantage of no wheeled thing; I will sleep rough and cover thirty miles a day, and I will hear Mass every morning, and I will be present at high Mass in St Peter's on the Feast of St Peter and St Paul."

Born in France in 1870 – his father was French – Belloc served a year in the French army before thinking better of a military career and taking himself off to study at Oxford. He would be starting his journey, therefore, outside his old army barracks near Toul in Alsace, so by the way I had planned my itinerary our paths would not cross for another three weeks. Belloc, then, had a head start on me: fair enough; there is no official start-line for a journey to Rome. There could and should be no rules, except ones that are self-imposed; and even these didn't seem to count for much. On just the third page of the preface, Belloc admits that he only kept two of his vows – the first and last. The others, one by one, went out of the window: walking all the way, avoiding wheels, sleeping rough, covering 30 miles a day and hearing Mass every morning. I am beginning to like him more.

All my other vows I broke one by one. For a faggot must be broken every stick singly. But the strict vow I kept, for I entered Rome on foot that year in time, and heard high Mass on the Feast of the Apostles.

THREE
DOWN TO KENT

JON HARRIS TURNED UP FROM CAMBRIDGE ON CUE at 6.30 a.m., joining me by London Bridge. I recognised his bouncing gait at once; his head bobbing up and down the stone parapet. Everybody has their own distinctive walking DNA, and nobody lollops like that. We had agreed to meet at Southwark Cathedral but I intercepted him at the steps below the bridge, just by Glaziers Hall. Jon was wearing a safari waistcoat over a red chequered short-sleeved shirt and, like Hilaire Belloc, he was carrying a staff; he was ready for business.

Getting him there had been quite a struggle. Six years ago we had gambolled some 500 miles around Essex – fulfilment of a promise we made in our youth at University that we would one day go on a long walk together – and we had twice walked big 40-mile chunks of the Essex Way in one day. Jon has spent a lifetime walking; for many years he tramped East Anglia producing articles on remote villages and striking buildings, sketching as he went, and observing with the keenest eye. He had studied architecture and art history at Cambridge and for one reason and another he never left the University City on the Fens; he still lives in the student digs in Green Street which he first occupied as an undergraduate in 1964. Jon may not drive and he has thrown his bike on the skip, but he takes buses and trains, and he walks. He doesn't do email, but his correspondence by Royal Mail via postcard and letters, with bits pasted on and doodles on the envelopes, will outlive the digital age. I needed his help in negotiating the unfamiliar urban chaos of Southeast London to keep to a timetable: I had agreed to meet another Cambridge friend, Peter, in Arras, and had accordingly booked hotels and pubs right down the line; in fact almost as far as Reims. The schedule meant I must cover 32 miles on my first day out of London so that I could make it to the Calais crossing in three days time. This is pushing it. I am a lousy urban navigator, and Jon was the only person I knew who could steer me out of London without my wasting time and adding miles getting lost in suburbia. But there was a major problem. He was nursing a hernia and, like an injured schoolboy unable to play games, he was more or less off walking.

"I just do the odd four miles now," said Jon. I therefore had to coax him out of retirement, and it was only the day before that he confirmed he was joining me, calling as I walked into London along the Lee Navigation.

"I have set my alarm for tomorrow," he said; he would have to leave Cambridge before dawn.

I, too, set my alarm, and slinging on my now full rucksack I stumbled out of the Queenhithe flat at daybreak.

It was my last night in a familiar bed until I got to Rome – if, fingers crossed, I got there. Queenhithe is a wonderful spot, the original tidal port where the Romans landed to establish their fortified camp on Ludgate Hill. The camp became a temple and the temple became St Paul's, but the hythe remained a simple working port and trading wharf until bombed to bits in World War II. My part of it was rebuilt, first as a swish hotel and then as an apartment block, becoming the pioneer residential building in what is now a little pocket of human habitation on the banks of the Thames within the City of London. Queenhithe is the ward of the City which I represent at Common Council. This is the City's ancient parliament which meets in Guildhall, where occasionally I rise on behalf of our residents when they are unhappy with their lot. We were, however, made very happy when they decided to span the Millennium Bridge across the Thames and land it in our ward on Peter's Hill from where it takes its first miraculous step towards Tate Britain.

I climbed up to Peter's Hill from the Thames Path and there, with a final wave to St Paul's, I was truly on my way from London to Rome – from one great apostle's monument to another. An Afro-Caribbean youth, head tucked in hood, was the only other person on the bridge, leaning over the parapet, gazing upriver towards Westminster, smoking some sweet substance that took me back to my Oxford College.

"Are you high?" I asked, and I made a point of smiling.

"You could say so," he replied.

"Would you be able to manage a digital camera and take a shot of me, please?"

I had thought about this. I wanted a photo of myself walking across the Millennium Bridge with St Paul's behind me. I had purchased an expensive memory stick for my camera to last the entire trip; while I had no wish to lose it to some random head on my first morning out of London, I needed that photo.

Hilaire Belloc did not have this problem. He took a small sketch book with him, filling it as he went with fine pen and ink drawings, many later used to illustrate *The Path to Rome*. I can write and I can point a camera, but I cannot draw.

"Yeah, no problem, no sweat, man."

He took several shots and handed back my camera. His name was David, and I apologised for being so brusque.

"That's OK mate. I just hope the photos come out straight. Everything is whirling inside me."

Thanking young David with a friendly pat on the back, I strode across the Thames and, at Bankside, I turned east for the first time on my journey, heading towards London Bridge. It was the last day of May 2010, a national holiday. The Thames Path was deserted; I had riverside London to myself till I spotted that familiar head on the bridge.

My Sherpa excelled himself. Sharing my frustration at losing one's way down suburban *culs-de-sac*, he had spent time over his A-Z and Ordinance Survey East London maps, and carved me a route which avoided the twin Sargassos of Orpington and Sidcup. What I didn't realise until, greetings over, we locked steps together, was that the week before he had reconnoitred our way as far as Bexley Heath. The result was that, under a grey sulky sky, we eased our way out of town like a purring Rolls-Royce; we even had a light west wind on our backs. We took the Thameside Path as far as Southwark Park, cutting through Rotherhithe to the river at Deptford Creek, where I declined Jon's invitation to walk out to the chalky foreshore of Deptford Point and inspect the statue of Peter the Great.

"The wrong Peter," I said, offering my excuses for not adding another 500 yards to the day by visiting the newish statue of Tsar Peter. It was at Deptford, lodged in the writer John Evelyn's house and living anonymously, that the Russian giant had learnt the ins and outs of the shipwright's craft at the Royal Dockyard. What I didn't tell Jon was that both my feet were hurting – not painfully but smarting sufficiently to tell me that on day four they were beginning to feel the road.

It was a morning of castles, sham castles at least. Jon delighted in showing me a chain of them – Vanbrugh's overlooking Greenwich Park, which we crossed, turning to catch (and snap) a final glimpse of St Paul's, the former Royal Artillery Academy at Woolwich, which hence explains the name Shooters Hill, up which we boldly went, and the elegantly neglected Severndroog Castle, buried high up in the Eltham Common section of Oxleas Wood. My eye, though, was taken by the courtliness of Charlton House, a Hatfield in miniature, which I had no inkling of till it reared up in front of us out of its hilltop suburbia. This is anything but sham; and Jon rates it among the finest Jacobean mansions in England.

Oxleas Wood began with oak and was gradually infiltrated by Spanish chestnut, its southern slopes suddenly opening to a wide vista of the North Downs – my route to Dover. The going underfoot reminded me of Essex, compacted pebbles and leaf mould, ghostly pennants of bluebells (we were just into June) in every vale and dip. The roar of the A2 in its cutting steered us to the 1930s modernist suburbia of Falconwood, and we crossed it and dropped into Blackfen – the first area so far which Jon said was struggling for an identity. We were led out of it along the grass-banked River Shuttle, and through Bexley Woods, with its hornbeam like Epping Forest and so many of the Essex woods, into Old Bexley, East London's surprisingly dignified last outpost. We paused here, packs off, on the benches outside the white clapboarded *King's Head*, for an early lunch – much to Jon's surprise.

"You mean, we can actually stop for a few minutes?"

The halt and the promise of proper Kentish landscape just ahead – steeply rising meadows crowned by the hanger of Joyden's Wood – persuaded my Sherpa to press on with me for a few more miles. Drawing level with Hook Green we left the patchy woodlands behind and at last took to country paths, chalk underfoot. To our north now were views: ahead, the promise of my road to Dover, while at the Thames Crossing rose the distinct pylons of the QE2 Bridge and there once again were the distant Langdon Hills, which I had seen from Pleshey; to the south a bluish bowl rimmed by the North Downs.

Towards Wilmington we picked up the line of the M25. The farmer had driven a clean swathe for hooves and boots between his ripening crops, heading straight for the motorway in its cutting; but the lack of any apparent bridge gave me a horrid flashback to the moment on the last morning of our Essex safari when my companion had attempted a short cut across the M25 just north of Thurrock. In the nick of time, the bridge revealed itself and we crossed it – six lanes of Bank Holiday traffic roaring beneath – and walked on down past the flint church of St John the Baptist at Sutton-at-Hone and into the Darent Valley, traversing little braids of the river and skirting a house called St John's Jerusalem, which kept itself well hidden from view, before joining the Darent Valley Way.

A name resonating with crusading knights and their pilgrim journeys seemed an appropriate spot to wrap up our day's partnership. We sat on a grassy bank outside a neat brick bungalow on the outskirts of South Darenth; Jon confessed that his legs would carry him no further.

He had done me proud; he had walked me out of London to the green fields of Kent. His mission was accomplished.

"I've brought something for you to read on your way," he said, and rummaging in his pack he produced a miniature translation of Virgil's *Aeneid*, leather-bound, and a paperback booklet entitled *A Passion for Life*, which on inspection turned out to be a new international version of St Luke's Gospel.

"Not the *Aeneid*," I said, recalling Gail's book on death which I had ungallantly and perhaps foolishly left behind in London. "It's a lovely volume but it's just too heavy. Give it to me if I get back."

"In that case, Luke, then. I found it on the bus seat in Cambridge last night. It's feather light, and I shall inscribe it for you."

He uncapped his rapidograph pen and wrote inside the front cover: "Did St Luke get to Rome? Brian Mooney did and this – handed to him 31.5.10 at South Darenth – went with him! With JH's love and best wishes."

Jon had given me a travelling companion, and there was no way I could leave him behind. I squeezed the slim volume into my rucksack; and thus the Gospel of St Luke travelled on my back every step from Kent to Rome. It was the random nature of the choice above all which appealed to me; fitting, too, to have someone with me who for several centuries was incorrectly identified as an icon painter and who was therefore mistakenly recruited as the patron saint of artists. Accidental companion or not, I was to grow enormously fond of reading Luke.

But now I had another eight miles to go. Knowing that Jon would find a train at the far end of the Darent viaduct, I left my Sherpa resting on the grass verge and walked on through Grubb Street, along the B26 to Longfield and up to New Barn; then cutting across fields and woodland to the hopfields of Sole Street. Almost there: a farm track led me past Cobham College and the 12th century church of St Mary Magdalene to the hotel where I had booked my room for the night, just as Charles Dickens had 170 years before.

I bet he got a squarer deal at *The Leather Bottle*. I was put in a room under one of the steep gabled roofs, and by the time I had unpacked, sorted out my maps and clothes and plugged in chargers for my phone and camera – I became an expert in locating sockets in hotel rooms and could write a generally negative treatise on the subject – written up the day's log, bathed and rested, it was gone seven thirty. I went down to join the happy throng of evening drinkers in the main panelled saloon eager for supper, only to be greeted with news that the dining room was closed on Mondays, Bank Holiday or no, and that last orders for bar food were at seven. This seemed to be taking to an extreme the notice chalked on the huge timber beam over the room – "Our food is not fast food. It is worth waiting for." Under protest, and only because I was a guest, a most unpalatable plate of lamb chops and chips was produced. This unsinkable repast I rinsed through with a bottle of virtually undrinkable Rioja.

Dickens used to stay here and the inn itself, the same massive oak scantlings, features in *The Pickwick Papers*. A large leather case in which the author carried material for his readings is on display in the dining room. I got to see it the following morning at breakfast, served by the landlord, Bryan Treleavan. He was keen to tell me about *The Leather Bottle's* ghosts, and offered to show me a video of a book flying off a shelf by the reception desk, unbidden, in the middle of the night.

Tempted as I was, a long day lay ahead. Besides, my early dip into Luke that morning had opened up all sorts of questions about reality. When is a fact not a fact? Is something which appears true always necessarily true? Luke is onto this from the first verse:

> Many have undertaken to draw up an account of the things that have been fulfilled among us, just as they were handed down to us by those who from the first were eye-witnesses and servants of the word. Therefore, since I myself have carefully investigated everything from the beginning, it seemed good also to me to write an orderly account, most excellent Theophilus, so that you may know the certainty of the things you have been taught.

Leaving aside the identity of Theophilus, this is a cunning opening paragraph. All the key words and phrases are there: orderly account, eye-witnesses, carefully investigated, certainty of the things taught: the reader is lured into a comfort zone of belief. Luke has investigated everything himself and crossed- checked with eye-witnesses, therefore it is all true. I, too, took notes on my journey and so was I my own witness, and I also talked to many people and read lots about many of the places I visited; yet the journalist in me hesitates to claim that I will have told the whole truth. A story is only as good as its sources, and no narrative which claims to be factual can escape from that fundamental constraint. Perhaps, therefore, it is at times easier to get to the truth in fiction.

As with Peter the Great, I cut out the beckoning diversion, resisting the temptation to walk through the woods below Cobham Hall, and set off on June 1ˢᵗ down Kentish Lanes as far as Lower Bush near Cuxton, and at Mill Hall Wood joined the North Downs Way. The forest path led up to high ground by Ranscombe, and here, beneath seagulls circling over open fields, I sighted the expanse of the River Medway and began my descent to its shore.

The tide was out. A mist was rising from the muddy riverbed and merging almost seamlessly with a band of low cloud above. I crossed by the side of the M2 on a footpath with a fingerpost to Borstal. It's an innocent agricultural place name, replicated elsewhere, but this one, outside Rochester, was the prototype of the network of secure reformatories for juvenile males. Passing beneath its buildings, which are layered into the side of the hill and at that distance resembling a battery farm, I found myself once again on the path I had chosen in 2000 for my walk to Santiago de Compostela. Then I had crossed the Thames at Gravesend and stayed the night in Rochester. Ten years ago, this part of Kent was being ripped up to install the new high-speed railway from the Channel Tunnel to London. Now the line and its overhead wiring was comfortably bedded down in deep cuttings on the lower slopes of the North Downs, and crossing the footbridge just after

Nashenden Farm, it seemed as if it had always been there.

I said goodbye to the chalky heights. The ridge at Ivy Cott offered me my first open view of the Weald below. From here on, short hills would shape my day's walking. Avoiding my mistake of 2000, when by missing a waymark I wandered off course to the edge of the M2, I found my way to the wonderfully named Kit's Coty House – three huge menhirs supporting a cap-stone, the gaunt remains of an earthen burial chamber; the feature is sometimes called the Kentish Stonehenge, and it has a Neolithic outrider, White Horse Stone, soon after which the North Downs Way rises for the first time to 600 feet and to continuous Wealden views as stimulating for me as they had been for Charles Dickens. He declared the route I had chosen to be "... one of the most beautiful walks in England."

As well as unfailingly picturesque, it is also pilgrim country. An ancient pilgrim route follows the valley floor, and the North Downs Way comes down to intersect it in the villages. But these days a pensioner is more likely to receive a warm welcome than a pilgrim. At Detling, I tried to get a glass of water at the *Cock Horse Inn* but was told to wait my turn in the queue behind a group of OAPs ordering their lunches one by one. Rain had been lashing down, and I did not fancy standing inside, dripping with wet and getting cold, so I took my thirst elsewhere to the *Dirty Habit* at Hollingbourne – Kentish pubs have such wonderful names – where I downed a pint and a half of lime and lemonade at a standing sprint. I pressed on past the curvaceous, Botero-esque statue of the pilgrim at Harrietsham – who I noted, with some envy, was seated – and the war memorial carved into the chalk of the down at Lenham, arriving at my night's resting-place, the *Oak* at Charing, at six thirty, 11 hours after leaving Cobham. After 30 miles of ridge and valley, latterly in the pouring rain, I was wet and tired. "A very tough day," is how it went into my diary.

I had checked in here on my Santiago walk; and in the intervening ten years the hotel has been transformed from a rather pot-luck country hostelry into a foodie destination, the bar area opened out into a light, spacious dining room, and the bedrooms made over. While my clothing was laundered and dried, I feasted on a pilgrim fare prepared by the chef Simon Desmond himself – his asparagus and poached egg given just that little edge with bacon; this blended splendidly with a lively Fleurie wine. Simon comes from an island of only 12 inhabitants off the south coast of Ireland. They must eat well there.

Next day's weather threw a new challenge at me – heat. I spent it clambering up and down ridge paths, often through fields of daisies and buttercups, with panoramic views enhanced by the bright light. Beyond neatly manicured Eastwell Park with its showy château-like house, at Boughton Lees, the North Downs Way forks – one spur following the Great Stour north to Canterbury, the other making a beeline for Folkestone and then along the cliffs to Dover. The modern pilgrim route to Rome – known as the Via Francigena and which is almost impossible to pronounce in English (in Italian it sounds like Franchee-gena) – officially starts in Canterbury.

The Way broadly follows the route taken in 990 by Sigeric, Archbishop of Canterbury, who left a written account of the various stages of his journey back from Rome to Canterbury. Sigeric, in Rome to be vested in his pallium or cloak of office by Pope John XV, was evidently following in the steps of his Saxon predecessors, from Augustine onwards, and of many thousands of English pilgrims who over the intervening half-millennium had made the journey to the City of St Peter, as medieval travellers called Rome. Sigeric was educated at Glastonbury, and there he took holy orders; on his appointment to Canterbury at the end of 989 or at the beginning of 990 he advised King Aethelred to pay off the North Sea raiders with tributes – a state protection levy that came to be called Danegeld. He was known as Sigeric the Serious, either from the transliteration of his name in Latin – *Serio* – or because that was indeed his nature. His most solid memorial is the detailed record he had one of his clerks make of his journey back from Rome, and this travel journal, *De Roma usque ad Mare* (From Rome to the Sea), is now in the British Library and forms the template of the reborn Via Francigena. Francigena denotes Franks or people from France, and was the term used in Italy to describe foreign pilgrims coming from north of the Alps on their way to Rome, as well – of course – by the Saracens as a term for their foes, the Crusaders.

The revival of interest in the Via Francigena has led to it being classed as a 'European Cultural Itinerary', and I couldn't help wondering what that would be. Canterbury is 'kilometre 0' of the way, having been made an honorary part of France to give the Via Francigena its starting point in England, but I decided to postpone my enquiries as to what this Euro-Cultural Itinerary classification might mean until I was on authentic French soil. Having done my pilgrim bit in Canterbury ten years before, I had written it out of my journey to Rome, and so I took the eastward fork, crossing the Great Stour and walking on through the market town of Wye.

I skirted its nationally known Agricultural College and left town on Occupation Road by the Department of Biological Sciences. As I pulled away up the steep hill which leads to the Wye Downs, a young boy, out with his parents, raced ahead of me; even climbing to a mere 170 metres I was plodding under the weight of my rucksack, and beginning to welt in the heat of the day. I stopped at a bench on the brow of the hill and enjoyed the open view down the steep valley to the town below, gathered round the square flint tower of St Gregory and Martin's church, and beyond to the woodland coverts and fields of corn and rapeseed and the distant ridge on which I had begun the day's walk. I knew there was a chalk crown hereabout, cut in the summit turf, to commemorate the coronation of Edward VII in 1902, but decided to give the royal monument a miss. For this act of Republicanism, I was immediately punished; slipping on a small branch, I tumbled forwards, propelled by the weight of my rucksack, and landed sharply on my chest; my rib cage hurt for days.

On Broad Downs in the Wye National Nature Reserve, the way-marks gave out. If that were not enough, I now encountered a hazard that would prove a frequent irritant once I got on to the European mainland: nobody seemed to know how the path continued – not even the pair of reserve wardens I met who were working a broad-footed horse to haul felled trees. They were using medieval methods in accordance with the green dictates of the 21st century.

Locals never know. There is a profound issue at work here: people generally do not know the area in which they live and work. Asked for the name of a nearby street or, more ambitiously, for directions to a local footpath, fully paid-up locals throughout Western Europe will invariably shrug their shoulders. Put a map in their hands and they will treat it like a rattlesnake, an object of bewilderment and terror. Propelled hither and thither in cars and buses, people operate within their familiar domains; three blocks away in a city and two lanes yonder in the country is another universe – as is the path which crosses the woodland slope up which a horse can drag a log in a nature reserve.

I questioned my 1:50,000 rattlesnake diligently, re-found my way and continued at a good pace, mostly along a downland spine, above ground scalloped into hollows with names like the Devil's Kneading Trough; open country below me and the sea now shimmering in the far distance. Approaching Etchinghill, the ridge, here called the Pent, sails above the square-built hamlet of Postling, set to perfection in green fields around its church of Saints Mary and Radegund. This is Dickens country no longer. It is where Joseph Conrad wrote many of his major novels, *Lord Jim* included.

The approach to Folkestone winds round the rim of Cheriton Hill high above the Eurotunnel Terminal – its string of platforms with their loading and unloading bays laid out below in neat rows like uncoiled warp on a dockside – and in the time it would take you to walk from one end to the other, cars and trucks will have been whisked away under the sea and deposited in France. I knew this tunnel well, from both ends, so to speak. In my Reuters capacity as UK chief correspondent, I had been with Prime Minister Margaret Thatcher when she and French President François Mitterrand signed the protocols and treaties in Canterbury and Lille which brought this cross-Channel enterprise into being. Writing about it at the time, I recall my amazement at learning that the land bridge between France and Britain had only been breached 8,000 years before – in human span, not long ago, though a mite before Irish Bishop James Ussher's calculation in the 17th century that God had created the world on 23 October 4004 BC.

My day ended in a series of gruelling climbs north of Folkestone, up small sharp humps, over Caesar's Camp and Round Hill, along the sides of Sugarloaf and Wingate Hills; I trudged the span of Creteway Down and finally made the long haul up Dover Hill to East Cliffs and Capel le Ferne, where, at the top, sits one of the most evocative of war memorials. It is to Churchill's 'Few' – an airman in his flying jacket and boots sculpted out of sandstone by the Cambridge Carving Workshop, arms clasped around knees, at the hub of a giant turf-cut propeller commemorating the Battle of Britain. He stares out to the sea, above which he and his fallen comrades fought the German *Luftwaffe* in the summer of 1940, so staving off German invasion.

I had knocked on several doors to refill my water bottle during the day and also stopped in the Stowting *Tiger* for a cool summer drink: even so I reached the *Lighthouse Hotel* ready to consume its entire supply of lime and lemonade, and a good barrel or two of its Kentish beer, as I bet Hilaire Belloc would have done. My room looked out over the Channel which was dappled in shiny light and translucently blue in the glaze of the westering sun. I dumped my kit and boots and sat on the window ledge and devoured a litre bottle of ice-cold mineral water. I thought about the seventy summers since the Battle of Britain, and how fortunate my generation had been to have lived in peace through almost all of them.

It was just hot enough to eat outside on the terrace, and while I was waiting for an indifferent plate of pasta – cooked by a Polish student – I called Jon Harris to let him know that I had arrived in fine fettle at the Channel.

"All thanks to you," I said. "It was that smooth exit from London which set me on my way."

"How are you getting on with Luke?" he asked.

"Well, it's an amazing story," I replied. "I am only on page three, and there have been lots of angels, and already a barren woman and a virgin are pregnant!"

It was good to wake on June 3rd within sight and sound of the sea and, after covering close to 90 miles in three days, to savour the prospect of walking a mere 15 miles, with a relaxing sea cruise in between. Those mornings early in my journey were a struggle. I would stir virtually unable to move; I could only get out of bed by using a wall or table as a crutch. For a few moments, while my stiffened legs got used to standing again, I was paralysed. I would shuffle some steps like a match-stick man, usually to the bathroom where I would try and put some order on the day while my limbs gradually kicked back into life. Getting ready was always a slow process; I never rushed, rather enjoying the slow, contemplative process. These were the moments of stillness and reflection before the hard work of the day. I would methodically repack my rucksack, going through a routine check list – water bottle filled with hot tea made from the kettle in the room, both national and pilgrim passport, credit card, battery chargers, maps, diary, camera, compass and, perhaps most important of all, my BlackBerry. Before closing the lid, I would sit or sprawl on the bed and read a few lines of Luke. I would then go down to breakfast and try to head off by seven. With just a short walk into Dover and anxious to catch an early ferry, I left Capel le Ferne without breakfast, making do with my own room service of tea and biscuits. On this morning, my seventh, I stepped across the road from the hotel straight onto the cliff top path and was on my way at 5.45 a.m.

The notes in my diary summarise two hours of glorious early morning walking.

Brilliant blue sky, ships to sea and France in view, good going up and down the grassy path on the edge of the cliffs weaving in and out of alleyways of gorse and hawthorn. Magnificent views back to Folkestone and out to sea. Lots of old gun emplacements and pillboxes on the cliff tops, sheer drops to the sea on one side, and the whoosh of the A20 below on the other.

Approaching Dover, the path follows the undulating contours of the sheer cliffs, revealing great swathes of their chalky flanks, a close-up of the view that the American songwriter Nat Burton could only have imagined when he wrote the lyrics of the wartime hit: *There'll be bluebirds over the White Cliffs of Dover*. What he had never laid eyes on, Julius Caesar certainly had: he came this way when he invaded Britain in 55 BC, leaving an eyewitness account. It's fair to suppose that William Shakespeare had also seen and remembered the sudden edge of the realm when he had the blinded Gloucester describe Dover cliffs in Act 4 of *King Lear*: "There is a cliff, whose high and bending head looks fearfully on the confined deep. Bring me to the very brim of it ..." These few lines earned the Bard pole position; the cliff west of Dover is known as Shakespeare Cliff.

Dover surrenders its charms with some reluctance. After hauling up the final cliff top, from where the port appears to be just a stone's throw away, the North Downs Way strikes back inland to go under the A20, and then scales the Western Heights to track round the upper ramparts of Drop Redoubt Fort – no hill here left unclimbed.

Under the eager cry of seagulls, Dover was still half asleep; a few vagrants sharing the pavements with the street cleaners sweeping up the night's fast food wrappings in the town centre, a couple of large early morning joggers burning off their side cars along Marine Parade. I needed a stamp for my pilgrim passport but at 7.45 a.m. the tourist office wasn't going to be open. A sign in Market Square, beckoning me to the *Dover Discovery Experience*, led to a modern office complex housing the library. To my amazement, the door was open; an elderly porter at the desk. At first glance he took me for an illegal immigrant, and told me to come back when the offices were officially open at nine o'clock. But I explained my harmless business and eventually coaxed

him into bending the rules. Out came the necessary equipment; my pilgrim passport was duly stamped: Dover Library Tel: 01304 204241.

I would pick up three more stamps that day – one on the P&O
Ferries *Pride of Burgundy*, another at the *Office du Tourisme* in Calais,
and the third at Guînes, at the end of the first short stretch in France.

FOUR
PAS DE CALAIS

MORE THAN THE CROSSING ITSELF, THE TRAMP FROM the ferry terminal to the *Office du Tourisme* in the city of Calais put me in a reflective mood. This was my third time walking across France – between Santiago and this journey Gail and I had, for pleasure and companionship, followed the Canal du Midi from Bordeaux to the Mediterranean. I enjoyed the country, understood its culture a little and spoke its language. I also savoured its food and wide open spaces.

My first human encounter this time on French soil was with a large congregation of Somali refugees, graceful East African features unmistakable, milling around the old railway line that follows the Bassin Carnot to the inner harbour, some squatting on the sleepers and tracks: these ones would be doubtless dreaming of hitching that ride which would take them all the way to the rich pickings of Britain's welfare state, and they were engaged in animated discussion. I cut a path through their midst, thinking how quickly they could close ranks around me, and strip me of passport, cash and credit card. But I also considered how far they had travelled and the difficulties they must have endured for such an uncertain outcome. And yet, despite personal hardship and all efforts to close off the Calais gap, more would come. Passports and frontier controls don't stop the tide of migration; they just slow it. The great population movements in history have all happened because the forces behind them – persecution, poverty and famine – are stronger than the impediments against them; isn't that the case for abolishing frontiers altogether, and just letting the internal markets determine who stays in a country?

Down Rue de la Paix, I passed the brick-built church of Notre-Dame, which was partly constructed during the English occupation in the 14ᵗʰ century, and, with its fine turreted steeple and tall tower, has a familiar air of English Gothic. The church, the oldest surviving monument in Calais, is where Captain Charles de Gaulle married the young Calaisienne Yvonne Vendroux in 1921; it had hugely impressed me when I first walked through Calais in 2000, and now it became the final shared waymark of my routes to Santiago and Rome. Instead of striking due south, as I did on my way to Spain, from here on I would head east and south towards Italy.

For the new country I had already switched mentally from miles to kilometres, and tonight's hostelry was in Guînes, just 12 kilometres ahead. Marvellous: for the first time in my many visits to Calais, I could linger outside the Hôtel de Ville and take in the force of the six life-size bronze figures of Rodin's sculpture of the Burghers of Calais. His monument depicts the moment in 1347 when Eustache de St Pierre and five other prominent burghers, after 11 months of siege, resigned themselves to surrender the keys of the French city to England's King Edward III: having offered their lives to save Calais from massacre, the crestfallen men stand with shaven heads and halters round their necks, fully expecting to be executed. In the event their heroism moved the King's French wife Philippa of Hainault to engineer their pardon, and Edward spared the six men and their fellow Calaisiens.

Calais was reduced to rubble by World War II, bombed by both sides; and I walked by one of its more unusual war monuments at the Bassin de la Battelerie, a tiny fragment of the wall erected by the Germans around the port to demarcate it as a closed military zone; anyone found inside risked being shot. France is studded with many such roadside mementos of war, often only apparent to the pedestrian. Cars and buses whiz past too fast for anyone to notice them.

The Via Francigena is making its mark in the *Pas de Calais*, as this part of Northern France is known. A seemingly helpful girl at the tourist office opposite the Hôtel de Ville knew all about it, and she gave me directions to the canal towpath which would lead me all the way to Guînes. Leaving the city centre along the Quai du Commerce, I set off for the French interior in good heart; but a few kilometres later, at the Pont du Cologne, I discovered that I was on the wrong canal, heading for Ardres! But with a good look at my map, a short walk on the lanes across the former marshes took me to the correct canal. But I was angry with myself. If I couldn't navigate my way out of Calais, how in Purgatory's name was I going to get to Rome? I managed, though, to dilute my self-laceration with curses at the girl at the tourist office who had sent me in the direction of Belgium. Or was this some Protestant plot?

In the end, the afternoon's walk worked out at 16 kilometres, which, with the early morning's eight, made for a total of 24 kilometres for the day, my shortest leg since Coggeshall. The *Hôtel Colombier* at Guînes, set in the courtyard of a Norman manor house with dovecote tower, was at the town's edge; arriving at four o'clock gave me the time to settle in and explore – how better to enjoy the first of many summer evenings in France? I tried to imagine a moment of great pageantry nearly five centuries ago: this place, far less knocked about than Calais, was where in June 1520 Henry VIII and his entourage encamped on the edge of England's slice of France to hold a summit with François I, known as the Field of Cloth of Gold, each monarch challenging the other with displays of splendour and chivalry. Nothing came of it, and 38 years later, during a period of counter-Reformation, Henry's Catholic daughter successor Mary Tudor surrendered Calais and its townlands, including Guînes, back to the French. The place to think about all this was beside the bustle of the main market square, Place Foch, with a glass of Leffe in my hand. As Guînes was a stage on Archbishop Sigeric's route, at the *Office du Tourisme* I also acquired my first official Via Francigena pilgrim stamp. It displayed a cowled medieval pilgrim, bag over his shoulder, staff in his hand, seen side-on. This unknown pilgrim has become the logo of the Via Francigena, and many weeks later in Italy, I was to come face to face with his spitting image.

I returned to the hotel for a meal of roast pork with honey, served on the terrace in the warm summer twilight; but the atmosphere was wholly spoilt by two loud English Crystal Lakes geeks from an adjacent campsite; exchanging technical information about the latest model Winnebagoes. Henry Tudor, who erected 2,800 tents close by for his less distinguished hangers-on, would perhaps be patriotically pleased that his kinsmen are still camping in Guînes. But what would a king, whose party did things on a grand scale by consuming 2,200 lambs, 1,350 crumpets and 70 jars of strawberry jam, have made of their lack of style?

Hilaire Belloc set out from Toul, like the medieval Francigena pilgrim, with a shoulder bag carrying "a large piece of bread, half a pound of smoked ham, a sketch book, two Nationalist papers, and a quart of the wine of Brulé". At first he kept to his vow, sleeping rough, in the open, and walking at a cracking pace, covering 50 miles in the first 24 hours, where lesser mortals would do 40 at a pinch; but he soon re-discovered the comforts of a bed and also the importance of eating and sleeping well. Wine was his staple drink; he drank it with every meal, day and night, and always contrived to carry a supply with him. He wrote constantly about drinking the stuff, rarely mentioning water.

I do wonder about Belloc. What thought did he give to packing? Third time across France, I knew what my solid staples were: nuts and dried fruit. The essentials were water, maps and guide-books. The *Institut Géographique National* has France diced into 76 topographical areas, reducing the country to maps of one centimetre to one kilometre – i.e. 1:100,000, vast in comparison to our Explorer maps, providing clear detail of the lie of the land, and accurately showing the distances between places. I have never known them to be wrong. I needed eight to get across France diagonally, although I did not carry all at once: my friend Peter would bring a fresh supply to meet me at Arras. I also used the three-volume Lightfoot Guide to the Via Francigena. Lightfoot, my foot; in total it comes to more than 600 pages, and weighs nearly one kilogram! The first volume, from Canterbury to Besançon, I carried with me; Peter would bring the next two. Paul Chinn, the author of the guide, has painstakingly mapped and described the farm tracks, footpaths and minor roads that comprise today's official route of the Via Francigena. The book carries helpful information about hotels and other facilities on the way, but often the route it plots meanders and makes lengthy deviations to avoid, where possible, secondary roads. I am quite happy to walk on macadam – particularly French Departmental 'D' roads where traffic is generally quite calm and on which distances can be achieved in rapid time – and so I tended to ignore the detail of the official route to carve my own direct way through France.

Here, Hilaire Belloc and I converge. Belloc determined to walk in a straight line; to his credit this meant going directly over some of the hills of Eastern France and Switzerland, rather than round them, although he was to meet his match with his 'beeline' in the Alps.

> … this mixture of roads and paths and rock climbs that I had planned out, I exactly followed, so as to march as directly as possible towards Rome, which was my goal. For if I had not so planned it, but had followed the high-roads, I should have been compelled to zig-zag enormously for days … It is only by following the straight line onwards that anyone can pass from ridge to ridge and have this full picture of the way.

So it was that I walked out of Guînes along the D125, forsaking the right-hand side of the road for the left, face-on to the early morning traffic and once more entrusting my life to the attentiveness of French drivers. France's roadsides have been good to me; as a student I hitchhiked the length and breadth of the country many times without a major mishap, and on my Santiago walk I spent many carefree hours sauntering down minor roads as I made my way south from Calais to the Pyrenees.

A few things had changed in the intervening years: the old stone kilometre posts had been replaced with plastic and fibreglass replicas, and the trucks were now larger and, of course, there were more cars. Even so France still offers a network of quiet country roads that for serious walkers probably has no match in Western Europe. You have to wonder, though, what happened to the old Napoleonic era markers. In conservation-minded Britain, they would be listed monuments and retained. Are they gathered in some centralised park, the equivalent of the thousand warriors?

I was soon into open country, under a bright canopy of blue sky. It was exhilarating to be free and walking, and to have the whole of Eastern France at my feet. It was good, also, to be back in a country where distance is measured in steps; it is psychologically easier to walk 1,000 metres, the length of a kilometre, than 1,768 yards, the length of a mile. Kilometres pass more quickly, their markers come into sight some 500 metres away with pleasing consistency every six minutes or so, and they can be ticked off and accumulated on the day's mental chart in easy regular increments, the way a batsman in the game of cricket steadily knocks up runs one by one to build his innings.

I tuned in to the morning birdsong, which was lightly orchestrated by the rhythmic throb of a diesel tractor working a nearby field and by the intermittent far off hum of the Calais to Lille TGV. After crossing the railway, the D215 climbs up from the coastal plain into the Bois de Licques and the rolling chalk hills around Tournehem-sur-la-Hem, thickly forested with tall beech and billowing ash. It took me just two hours to reach Licques, which in Chinn's guide is a whole day's stage; I was already motoring.

Drinking a refreshing *citron* in the Relais de Fôret in Quercamps, I learned from the *patronne* of another pilgrim. This German had come by only a few hours before; his French was non-existent, but she had managed to work out that he was heading for Rome. I knew that sooner or later I would meet up with him.

But not as I expected; and nor within minutes. I was just getting my pace back when I caught sight of something moving rapidly in the distance; a wheel driven by two thrashing pistons approaching me on the opposite side of the road. The outline of a man emerged between two frantically waving sticks. They were Leki poles, which are favoured by many long-distance walkers as an aid to propulsion. Face to face on the empty road, we inspected each other. He was in shorts and trekking sandals, his grey hair cropped and face unshaven and beaded with sweat. Carlo Carapacchi, he said; he was Italian, of course, not German, and he was heading for Italy, but not to Rome.

"I walked from the Grand St Bernard to Rome two years ago," Carlo explained. "So now I am filling in the missing part – from Canterbury to the Alps."

"But why are you going backwards?" I asked. "You are walking away from Italy back to England."

"I went wrong," said Carlo. No wonder. He had with him a few photocopied sheets of a route that he had printed out from a website in Italy. "I'm heading for Lumbres, but I missed the turning."

A retired tax auditor from Rieti and now a serial long-distance walker, Carlo gave a sigh for the kilometres so painfully wasted by mis-reading a map and steamed off to find his turning. Why did he want to go to Lumbres, I wondered?

Leaving Carlo to find his Lumbres, I walked on through a hot afternoon, crossing the A26 Motorway at six kilometres an hour, reliving the many times I had sped under that bridge at over 140 kilometres an hour driving to Paris and points south. Now appropriately named *L'Autoroute des Anglais*, the motorway intersects the D206 at the Kilometre 28 post, between Boisdinghem and Liheuse, in expansive undulating country which from a speeding car had always looked so inviting; now that it surrounded me, its sheer emptiness was also apparent. Passing through Zudausques, the first real town since Licques, to arrive at the gates of the Abbey of St Paul, time was on my side. I peeked into the wooded park.

The Benedictine church was obvious, the monastery more like a peaceful château, with its own magnificent round tower, 15th century, all set well back from the road. The Order's occupancy here has had a disturbed history in modern times; that goes for all France and her monastic houses. Suppressed after the 1789 Revolution and reopened in 1833, the abbey shut down in the face of increasing anti-clericalism in 1905. The Benedictines returned again in 1920, only to be scattered, some even imprisoned, 20 years later when the German army took possession during World War II. Miraculously all survived the war and returned in 1945 to resume their Benedictine life of work and prayer. Well placed on the path to Rome, they offer accommodation to today's pilgrims.

"Will you be staying with us?" asked the brother attending the monastery shop in the gatehouse. He had just stamped my pilgrim passport while I examined the goods on sale – locally produced honey, candles, and lavender soap, and some books on prayer.

Now, I had spent eight years at Benedictine schools and, though I admired the Order for its open-mindedness, worldly wisdom and hospitality, two reminders of institutional life just didn't appeal to my pilgrim's sense of freedom. I would have to eat alongside the monks in a silence leavened with a polite drop of red wine; and later there would be the long traipse from the guest cell to showers and ablutions. But I could safely, and without offence, say no. When looking on the internet I had decided that a hotel called *La Sapinière* in Wisques was more my sort of space. My room there was booked, and it left me just two further kilometres to walk.

"No," I replied in all honesty, "Thank you, but I am walking on."

My day's total of 36 kilometres had been comfortably achieved, and any sense of duty betrayed through not billeting with the monks melted as I sat looking at the view from the terrace restaurant; the landscape fell gently away to the south, lit by the slowly setting sun. I ordered a fresh local rabbit and treated myself to a bottle of Beaujolais. Down there was the beginning of tomorrow's walk.

The next morning, June 5th, I left Wisques, descending forest to re-cross the A26 to Esquerdes and Thérouanne, an ugly sprawling town of red brick houses which straddles the nice sounding River Lys. From here a dead straight road leads all the way to Arras. Now the D341, this former Roman road is almost certainly the route that medieval pilgrims would have trodden on their way from England to Rome. It is known as the *Chaussée Brunehaut* – Brunhilda's Causeway – the powerful Visigothic Queen of Frankish Austrasia around the year 600 AD: rapacious, warlike and ruthless and, so the chronicles tell, accountable for the deaths of no less than ten Frankish monarchs. One legend, of her own violent end, has her being dragged by a wild mare down this very road which for that reason came to bear her name: beyond the Rhine, she would acquire mythic status and a quite different dénouement in the medieval epic poem the *Nibelungenlied*, and, of course, its retelling by Richard Wagner.

The *Chaussée Brunehaut* cuts a surgical line along the linguistic divide of this part of Northern France. To the north, lie Dutch speaking towns and villages with distinctly northern names, to the south Picard or French speaking communities. For a few kilometres more I walked the line, then peeled off to the south into unknown Picardy, taking small roads through deserted hamlets and past isolated houses surrounded, as far as the eye can see, by a rolling terrain of farmland and wooded copses. All over it, once, were coal mines; as in the English Midlands, the slag heaps are being greened over. What remains is farming, done here on an increasingly industrial scale. The peasants in blue overalls, the rural icons of 20th century France, are dead and buried. In a whole day, the one person that I saw working a field was a woman; driving a tractor; and the only shop where I could buy food was a mobile store, whose *vendeur* bequeathed me two free oranges as a 'tribute' to my pilgrimage. France has changed.

The spire of St Sulpice at Amettes stands out several kilometres away as the road slowly dips into the valley below the village. Amettes is a stage on the Via Francigena, and its 16th century church should be on the map of every walker. A glass encasement enshrines the kneecaps of St Benoît-Joseph Labre, born here in 1748 and where he is venerated as the patron saint of mendicants, vagabonds, beggars, hobos and the homeless. St Benoît spent most of his short adult life on the road as a pilgrim, subsisting on charity. In Rome, he lived in the ruins of the Colosseum, dying there of malnutrition aged only 35 in 1783. There he rests; but his kneecaps and the straw mattress on which he expired, made it back to Amettes. Kneecaps mean a lot to walkers; and now you know who to pray to!

Benoît-Joseph was the son of a prosperous local shopkeeper, but something, perhaps those harsh words of Jesus in St Luke, called into question his filial feelings, his status, his national sense, all creature comforts.

If anyone comes to me and does not hate his father and mother, his wife and children, his brothers and sisters – yes, even his own life – he cannot be my disciple ... any of you who does not give up everything he has cannot be my disciple.

He determined from that moment to lead "a life most painful, most penitential, not in a wilderness, nor in a cloister, but in the midst of the world, devoutly visiting as a pilgrim the famous places of Christian devotion". As good as his word, he is thought to have visited all the holy sites of mainland Europe.

Madame Duval, *patronne* of Amettes' one bar, *Repos du Chasseur*, knew about pilgrimage, having been to Lourdes no less than 15 times during regular breaks in her 50 years of attending to customers. That evening, one turned out to be a veteran of the Algerian war.

"Walking, eh you?" said the old soldier. "We used to think nothing of covering 70 kilometres a day."

I finished my beer, content with my more modest stint of 32 kilometres, and made my way to the farmhouse *chambre d'hôte* in the heart of the village where, on arrival, the first person I saw was Carlo, sitting outside in the late sun in shorts and with bare feet, writing up his journal; good to see someone else doing my evening task.

"I knew we would meet again," I said.

The previous afternoon, having at last found Lumbres, Carlo had accepted the invitation of the brother in the gatehouse to stay with the monks at the Abbey of St Paul.

"Not easy, for me, they have a rule of silence."

Now that man loved to talk; a pity because he had a voice like a seagull. Our hosts, Colette and Jean-Baptiste Gevas, seemed visibly relieved that someone had arrived who spoke Italian and could therefore get Carlo to re-tune his logorrhoea into his native tongue. His French was utterly incomprehensible.

And so we sat in the farmhouse inner courtyard, facing the former cow-byre with its proud old timber scantlings nogged, as they do in Northern France, with warm red brick. The wall was festooned with discarded watering cans and buckets hanging like forgotten decorations on a Christmas tree, and punched through at random by three blue-painted doors, all at different levels. Winter logs were piled up to the guttering, and, close by, a straw bale lay abandoned next to a mound of sand and a stack of red roof tiles. There was an air of chaotic and contented neglect about the place.

"There used to be cattle in there, of course," said Jean-Baptiste, "but the new European Union laws have driven the cows out of our villages. Mixing dairy cows and people together has become illegal." Take note Essex! It was good to hear the French moaning about EU laws and regulations. We British are not alone.

"And so, I keep pigeons instead! Do you know, I have just had one come in from Barcelona," he beamed.

So that was what all that flapping and crooning was about: looking up I saw a squadron of pigeons popping their heads out of their loft, or resting on the eaves above. Jean-Baptiste has a fleet of homing pigeons and, like all owners and trainers, the fun for him consists in taking one of the birds a long way off and waiting for it to fly back. Much research has been done on pigeons' extraordinary ability to lock in on their lofts from huge distances and fly home; whether they use earth's magnetic field, atmospheric smell or light to guide them. Literalists believe pigeons do nothing more complex than read the main features below them – hills, rivers, valleys and roads – map readers, in fact, like me.

The Egyptians and Persians first used carrier pigeons 3,000 years ago; as a former Reuters correspondent I knew that Baron Reuter, founder of the news agency, had used them to gain a market edge and send stock prices between Brussels and Aachen, the terminuses of early telegraph lines. Every Reuters correspondent learns on day one the cardinal rule is to get the news back by the quickest and most reliable means. The communications highways of the 21st century have changed all that, but there were times on my assignments when all lines to the outside world were literally cut – in Chile, when General Pinochet toppled Salvador Allende in 1973, and when General Jaruzelski imposed martial law on Poland in 1981 – and then a messenger pigeon would have done nicely.

Jean-Baptiste showed me round the cages in which he keeps his prize pigeons, all tagged and raring to go.

"What do you do with the failures?"

"Eat them," he said.

So that night we feasted on pigeon pie. Colette, who had inherited the dairy farm from her father, takes great pleasure in looking after her pilgrims, to the extent of having had a Via Francigena stamp specially made for their passports; and she has photographed every single pilgrim who has stayed the night, back to 1998. We talked in general about pilgrimage and the network of European pilgrim routes. Santiago, of course, came up. For some strange reason, one particular aspect of my journey came back to me.

"On the *Camino Francés*," I said, "I kept meeting people who were either recovering from cancer or were dealing with bereavement from it."

"I have cancer, myself," said Colette. She had just finished an intensive treatment of chemotherapy.

I woke on the morning of June 6ᵗʰ to the sound of heavy rain on roof tiles. It was lashing down. I thought of Carlo, the early starter. He would have left well before dawn. Walking through rain was part of the deal, though by the time I set off it had eased. Last night Carlo had settled my mind about the route I would take into Arras.

"If you are going for covering long distances, don't waste time on fancy farm tracks when there is a perfectly good road." The D341 would be quiet today; in France, on a Sunday, heavy trucks are not allowed on the roads. So it would be 42 kilometres of hard drill back on the *Chaussée Brunehaut.*

The rain showers never quite let up all morning, and a kind of loom obscured any distant views; I passed Carlo a few hours later, hunkering down in a bus shelter, wrapped in a flimsy poncho. Although our paths would cross once more, we never set eyes on each other again. A few minutes down the road from where I left him, a car pulled up in front of me. It was Colette. She had forgotten to take my photograph.

Almost into Arras, the ruins of the Abbey of St Eloi loomed out of the mist, and soon the scars of war were all around me. Passing the turning to Vimy Ridge, where a battle was fought in 1917 that precipitated the destruction of Arras, I entered town down its narrow lanes of reconstructed Flemish brick and timber houses guided to the centre by the belfry at the side of the flamboyant Gothic town hall. Arras was knocked about again in World War II, and once more rebuilt; they were still putting the finishing touches to its two arcaded squares in 2011. The devastating effects of war would be very much on the agenda for the next stage of my walk, but for now I was just looking forward to a day off.

I had selected the *Hôtel de l'Univers* with care. It holds a lot of history, including fragments of mine. Set around a fine courtyard in the heart of old Arras, it began as a Jesuit monastery in the 16th century and it served as a Red Cross hospital during World War I. My own first stay there was for the 60ᵗʰ birthday of Niel, who later that year joined me for ten days' walking in the French Basque country and over the Pyrenees into Navarre. Gail and I have celebrated New Year there, once with all children, once by ourselves. It's a great break from Cogge-shall – champagne supper and dancing; all highly civilised.

Now, I was happy just to be there: not to have to get up the following day and walk. For the first time since leaving Coggeshall, I could lie in bed in the morning without feeling guilt.

This time, though, 376 kilometres deserved a reward – a body mas-sage. The wonders of the internet; a lady offered deep tissue treatment from her home in the city centre, Rue de l'Ours – Bear Street – a lissom African from the Ivory Coast who must have noticed the way I looked at her because, as I stripped for the massage table, she suddenly announced that she did not "finish".

"I would never have expected you to," I said. "Not in my state."

But as she worked her way up and down my worn legs and over my back, which was starting to feel the strain of carrying a laden rucksack for eight hours a day, imperceptibly, unconsciously, I confess the idea began to tingle at my nerve ends. Under the finger-light and tender care of an exotic non-finisher, fresh impulses were at work in the weary pilgrim. I was undergoing a sensual rebirth.

In the afternoon, I went shopping for a new silk handkerchief and a new waterproof jacket, and found another advertisement for a masseuse. Her apartment was close to yesterday's route off Rue Renoir on the outskirts of the city where I had walked in the previous day, and she was also dusky, but not as deeply black as the girl from the Ivory Coast. This coffee coloured lady was from New Caledonia.

"I come from the Pacific where the ocean is deep," she said as I surrendered to her tactile charms. "You must now prepare to swim far out of your depth."

And so, journeying deeper into *La France Profonde*, I furthered my exploration of the secrets and pleasures of its former colonies, *La France Outremer.*

Back at the hotel, I left the window open onto the courtyard so that I could listen out for my friend's arrival. At around six o'clock I heard the boot of a car closing and the unmistakable pitch of county English coming from the window opposite me.

"Hello Beep," said the woman in the window, glass in hand. "You got here just in time for a G&T."

She was talking to a middle aged, smartly suited gentleman, almost certainly ex-army and ex-public school – institutions where he would have acquired his singular English upper class nickname. This was not my friend.

"Very good crossing," said Beep. "And for once my Satnav actually worked, or rather, I actually managed to work it. I'll be up for that gin in a jiffy."

Just a little later, I heard the distinct tones of Peter Jenkins talking in French; his agitated voice carrying across the courtyard. My friend – bless him – was arguing with the receptionist about the cost of his room.

FIVE
PICARDY

PETER WALKED WITH ME FOR THREE DAYS; OUR business together was war. A trained classicist, Peter is also a keen military historian and he had chosen to keep me company on this part of my journey primarily because it would take us through the World War I battlefields of the Somme. Peter would help me get a better understanding of Private Thomas Mooney, 9358, my paternal grandfather, who had served George V in these fields.

Peter goes back to my prehistoric period; he claims he can remember attending my fourth birthday party in Fulmer, on the edge of the Park Springs woods behind Pinewood Studios, where our respective families were living at opposite ends of the same lane. Peter's had the good sense to stay on in Fulmer, while my father moved us to a swanky new house in Gerrards Cross; but our lives continued to interweave. We ended up together at boarding school where I rose to dizzying heights – captain of the cross-country team – but Peter, one year my junior, put me firmly in my place by trouncing me in the inter-house race and setting a new course record. Then we diverged, Peter to Cambridge and I to Oxford, and afterwards we embarked on very different inter-national careers – I became a journalist and Peter entered the diplomatic service. The bond forged so soon out of the pram persisted, and in middle age, retired, we started walking together for pleasure, spending ten days in the hot summer of 2008 walking canal towpaths from Paris to Chalon-sur-Saône. That was when I introduced Peter, half-French himself, to the charms of France's *Chambres d'hôtes;* at Diou in the Upper Loire Valley we shared an evening with two leathered lesbian motorcyclists. The following year, to help me gear up for the *Haute Route* from Chamonix to Zermatt, we tramped along Offa's Dyke in driving rain, but this time there were no alluring sirens awaiting us at the hostelry in Hay-on-Wye.

In every other respect Peter is a good walking companion, but he does not approve of spending money. I have learned to put up with his penny pinching – a tolerance he does his best to reciprocate when I lure him into an expensive hotel. This evening it was my treat: I took him for a beer in the Place des Héros, the smaller of the two grand squares in Arras, and I then sat him down to a good pasta dinner. But the following morning, incensed by the hotel's fixed charges, Peter went without breakfast. I watched him conning his room bill – rimless glasses removed to ensure that he could spot every decimal point – and saw him flinch when he removed the readies from his wallet. His brow-arch, more pronounced each year, was a furrowed field.

"Being a Best Western, that just gives them an excuse to charge more."

"Maybe," I conceded, "but, admit it, the rooms were jolly comfortable."

Apart from the biological accident of producing my father, what did Private Mooney have to do with my walk to Rome? The answer lies in an astonishing string of accidents. My grandfather had the good fortune to be wounded three times on three separate occasions during World War I, and was lucky each time to survive. To dodge death thrice in such circumstances was highly unusual. I had managed to pinpoint each of the locations where he was recorded as hit or gassed, and they were all more or less on the Via Francigena. To see these sites and to pay my respects to the three near-misses to which I indirectly owed my life seemed the right thing to do on a pilgrimage to Rome.

It was only through the accident of his joining the wrong regiment in Liverpool in 1914 that the story of his war survived. Most soldiers' records from the World War I were destroyed by a German incendiary bomb in World War II, but not those of his regiment. Thomas, a Liverpool dockworker with a good thirst, had been born in Dublin in 1892, and had crossed the sea for work. Family legend, not known for kindness, says that on the crucial day he was in his cups and reported to the wrong recruiting office – a 'Mick' who ended up with a Scottish regiment instead of with his native Irish – though it might well be that the Irish Guards had filled their quota and sent him down the road to try his luck with the Scots. In any case, he enlisted with the Scots Guards on 4 August 1914, aged 21. The battlefields of Flanders, not the post-war world, would be his oyster.

According to the neatly penned records of the Scots Guards, Thomas served in the regiment for four years and 236 days – including three long spells in France amounting to 794 days. From basic training in Caterham he was despatched to France in late November, and so came to take part in that legendary front-line Christmas of 1914 when soldiers from the opposing armies downed their weapons and joined forces to sing carols.

Clearly, he was no model guardsman. He suffered several spells in the army slammer – eight days in London in 1916 for "making an insulting remark to an NCO", and nine in France in 1918 for "conduct to the prejudice of good order and military discipline ... gambling in the field". This episode was perhaps a harbinger of one of his many ventures in later life when he assisted General Critchley in setting up the new sport of greyhound racing in England. In London, he was detained for eight days "for quitting his post whilst on sentry duty", and for four for "loitering with females in Birdcage Walk – contrary to orders". He evidently had an eye for the girls, and was headstrong. The records state that apart from his war wounds, he also sustained an injury to his shoulder – apparently in a fight. The records also chronicle that Thomas Mooney married Ivy Matilda Gossick on 16 July 1917 and that the couple produced their first child on 22 September that same year – Francis George Mooney. Ivy was therefore seven months' pregnant with my father when she married. They had ten more children; two died as infants, but the surviving nine would all grow up to lead successful lives. Thomas himself, despite the greyhounds, never prospered. He died aged 59 in 1951 from alcohol and bladder cancer, rejected by his wife and not much loved by his surviving children.

Without aiming to canonise Thomas, I couldn't help warming to him. Whatever came afterwards, he obviously went through one hell of a war. "We buried him, and that was that," said my father. In fact the family parked him in an unmarked grave at Kensal Rise cemetery – ironic for one who had three times miraculously avoided an unmarked grave in France. Thereafter he was written out of the family script, and even years after he died, my father and his brothers and sister simply refused to talk about him. It was time for his grandson to re-discover him; so, armed with information about how he was wounded and map references pinpointing each incident, I laid the Belloc and Sigeric strands of my pilgrimage aside, and Peter and I walked out of Arras on the morning of June 8th in search of my grandfather's war.

Skirting the Citadelle, whose dried moat was used as a place of mass execution in World War II, we turned left at Agny to visit the British World War I cemetery. Like a commanding officer reviewing troops, Peter didn't want to leave a single tombstone un-inspected.

It was good to have an excuse to linger. I had spent my first ten days pushing ahead for our *rendez-vous*, walking hard to get here in time to meet up with Peter; and now that we were together I was determined to slow down and enjoy his company. As a symbolic gesture, a way of surrendering the compulsion to press on, I asked Peter to take over the navigation; it was for him to pick the route, as well as set the pace.

"I have always been rather good at map reading," said Peter, somewhat presumptuously, as he took over the driving seat. "In fact, I won a prize for it at school."

It was not long before we had mislaid our way. We missed the small turning to the village of Ficheux and doubled back to find the lane leading to it, only to discover as we entered the village that we had gone wrong again. The large agri-industrial complex, which we had spotted on the main road before turning back to Ficheux, was in fact our first destination: the sugar beet factory at Boiry-Ste-Rictrude where Thomas Mooney was gassed on 4 April 1918.

"That cost us a good few kilometres," I grumbled as we approached.

"Well, better than having your lungs filled up with mustard gas," said Peter.

According to his regimental records, Thomas was in the line here when he was hit by gas: his third strike in the war, during his third and longest spell, one year and 198 days, in France. He was evidently not seriously harmed, and was soon back in the line, and in action; he was fit enough three months later to be up on that gambling charge.

Walking along the D919, and passing the Bucquoy Road British cemetery, dug into ground as a field dressing station to which Thomas would have been brought after the gas attack, we came up to the tall white factory, which, with its seven fluted chimneys and towering silo, dominates the flat countryside like a great gothic cathedral, as its more modest predecessor – sugar beet was a new industry then – must have done. Strange to think that it should survive, while all the trenches and earth defences around it are gone, filled in and cosmetically covered with a wooded glade which runs alongside the factory's perimeter fence.

It really was third time lucky for Thomas. By 1918, the war chemists on both sides had refined their gas bombs and canisters and created some dreadful substances to discharge from them. Poison gas was probably the most feared of all weapons in World War I; some 1,250,000 men on all sides were gas casualties and 91,000 were actually killed by poison gas, their deaths usually lingering and painful. Contrary to popular belief, the French were the first to use it. But the stuff the French lobbed at the Germans in August 1914 was a bromide, or irritant. By 1915 the Germans had come up with a real killer gas containing chlorine, and they used it for the first time at the second battle of Ypres in April that year. It was then gloves off – and gas masks on

– as both sides developed nastier cocktails to throw at each other. By the third battle of Ypres in July 1917, the Germans had mustard gas, which wrought horrors on its victims: their skin blistered, their eyes became agonising and they began to vomit uncontrollably. Mustard gas caused internal and external bleeding and attacked the bronchial tubes, stripping out the mucous membrane. This was so painful that most victims had to be strapped to their beds. It usually took four or five weeks to die of mustard gas poisoning. But it also had a more devious side-effect – it was carcinogenic. Thomas may have got out of the gas at Boiry-Ste-Rictrude, but in the end it was cancer that got him.

For the remainder of that day, we strolled down *Routes Départ-mentales,* talking of war and comparing our own peaceful lives; hitherto, that is, because Peter likes to quote Herodotus: "Count no man happy, until he is dead."

The deputy mayor of Hamelincourt – even a hamlet in France has its *adjoint* – stopped in his car to shake our hands and wish us a good journey.

"We are bound together by those who rest in our cemeteries," he remarked. Obviously, even from behind, we looked like Allies.

Despite our earlier misnavigations, and our conversational pace, we would still have 30 kilometres under our belts by the time we reached Bapaume. From their starting line in Albert, 18 kilometres to the southwest, it took the British army eight-and-a-half-months, from 1916 into 1917, to claw their way to Bapaume. When a battalion of Australians finally entered on 17 March 1917 they found, as *The War Illustrated* reported, "a bewildering scene of wreckage". But the devastation didn't stop there. The Germans left behind booby traps, and eight days after Bapaume fell, the Town Hall blew up, killing several of its new occupants.

It had taken us just a day to get there but even so our welcome wasn't quite what we expected: thanks to France's 35-hour week, the *Hôtel de la Paix* was locked firmly against the English; like many hotels in France today, it can no longer afford a full-time receptionist. Longing to shed our boots and soak off the day in a hot bath, we sat in the park outside until they opened for the evening's business.

"Let's do a defence review," said Peter as we marched out of Bapaume the following day in early morning drizzle down the D10 into the *Départment de la Somme*. "Now does Britain really have to spend all those billions replacing Trident?" I forgot to say that Peter votes Liberal Democrat these days, and has sympathy with the party's line that Britain no longer needs its own nuclear deterrent. I looked around at the open rolling landscape, so green today and so kempt, where Britain and Germany had buried so many of their young men, and I began to marshal arguments in favour of a weapon that could strike the enemy from deep below the oceans without having to engage in hand-to-hand combat. But all I could really think about was that my feet hurt. After walking for 13 days my feet were emitting strong signals of protest and each step, particularly at the start of the day, was accompanied by a sharp stabbing pain on the heels and soles. I longed to tell Peter; to invite him to stuff his defence review and concentrate on helping me find ways of softening the pain. But then that cross-country race came back to me, and I fell into line and reflected on his arguments.

Half-coming round to his party's goal of not replacing Trident, I asked: "Well, what about leasing the Trident submarines from the Americans, as a way of outsourcing our nuclear defence?"

Peter liked that idea. "Yes, we already lease the missiles from them, so why not the launch pads? The Americans, though, I doubt they would wear it. They keep some kit secret, even from us."

And so, debating war or ways to avoid or limit it, the two of us reached the Somme, where more than a million men perished in a futile struggle over a few kilometres. It was raining hard when we entered the village of Lesbœufs; sheltering till it eased under the church porch, we descended through a wooded dell to the Guards Cemetery, which stands on a bluff marked by a tall stone cross, commanding views to the east over fields speckled with red poppies. This is country which offers little natural shelter from shells and bullets and it's where, according to regimental records, Thomas Mooney had been hit for the first time, receiving a gunshot wound to his right leg on 27 September 1915. It must have been bad; a week later, on 4 October, he was back in England – he'd "bought a Blighty one".

Peter went straight to the record books kept at the cemetery gates; they explained to the visitor just who is laid to rest here, and why. Faint sun had dried the slate coping of the wall enough for him to perch on it, white sunhat over his slight tonsure, chosen volume in hand; meanwhile I toured the colonnaded shrine and inspected the ranked tombstones.

Where, I wondered, would my grandfather have been hit? The gas attack at the sugar factory had been possible to visualise; and later in the day I would reconnect firmly with him, but from the cemetery bluff I just could not get the picture.

Peter came over to me, his research completed.

"Now look, are you sure it was 1915?" he asked.

I took out my diary and read the note: "Wounded in Action, 27.9.15, G.S.W R.leg. The specific location – Lesbœufs (in the line) – confirmed in an email from Lance Sergeant K Gorman BA (Hons) at the Scots Guard HQ at Wellington Barracks."

"Well that's strange, because there was no action here in September 1915. Lesbœufs was attacked by the Guards Division in September 1916 – a whole year later."

The Lance Sergeant had sent me a photo-copy of Thomas' original records, and there was no doubt about the entry for both the location and the date. Peter's research on the ground had, however, opened up a distinct probability that the records were wrong.

This was indeed the case. The day my grandfather was wounded, the Scots Guards were fighting north of Arras, during the final phase of the Battle of Loos, and it was there, in fact, that he took his first hit. We pondered the confusion, and my ancestor's seeming elusiveness, and concluded that it was amazing that in so much chaos and carnage there were any records at all from World War I – the war to end all wars.

"What I always say about front-line journalism," I said. "With so many conflicting 'facts', it's a miracle how much reporters do actually get right."

"We tried harder in the diplomatic service."

"Yes, but you weren't always writing against deadlines, let alone being shot at."

The British cemetery at Combles didn't have anything to add to the Mooney archive; but leaving the village we stopped on the bridge over the TGV railway line, directly above the track as a Paris-bound train hurtled through. As if under fire, it was hard not to flinch as the train came straight for us and disappeared beneath our feet.

"Good prep for our next stop," I said. We had crossed the *Autoroute du Nord*, parallel with the railway, and we wound our way up to the strategic – and scenic – hilltop farm of Le Priez, where my grandfather was wounded for the second time; no doubt this time about place and hour, hit in the left hand on 22 February 1917, the very day he returned to France after a year-and-a-half back in England. He had spent the whole of 1916 at home, much of it getting into trouble at Wellington Barracks, and towards the end of the year he met his future wife, a London-born girl whose mother came from Wiltshire and father from Suffolk. By the time he got back to France to be greeted by a German missile, Ivy Matilda was two months pregnant.

Cuthbert Headham's regimental history – *The Guards Division in the Great War* – tells the story:

On the 22nd the Germans took to shelling the road near Priez Farm. Two unfortunate salvoes of 'Whizz Bangs', coming over in the middle of relief by the 1st Grenadier Guards, wounded five of the Scots Guards, of whom one died of his wounds.

My grandfather was one of those four surviving wounded. Was he aware of his own luck? We walked into the farm courtyard and I photographed the house; its brick walls and the sharply angled eaves above its garret windows not much changed since 1917. The regimental history continues, laconically:

> Baths allotted to the battalion. Water frozen, so only clean clothes available, without baths. The mid-winter Serpentine bather might regard this as a disappointment, but tastes differ. Three days later it was too cold for outdoor services.

I looked at my left hand and down at my right leg, both still intact – the leg despite the day's long march. I anticipated the pleasures of a hot bath that night, and condensed all this into one long howling, grieving thought for Private Thomas Mooney and for all those millions who had suffered World War I. Maybe now, when we are seemingly disturbed by visions of just a few hundreds of dead in Iraq and Afghanistan, we are in danger of forgetting them. Imagine a TV newscaster opening with the lines: "The British Army lost 19,000 men today" – that would have been the headline for the number killed or fatally wounded on the first day of the Battle of the Somme, 1 July 1916.

Thomas evidently recovered from his new wound, and he went on to serve another 722 days in France, almost without interruption, though with time off each side of 16 July 1917 to marry the by then heavily pregnant Ivy Matilda in Southwark, and two weeks' official leave from 9-23 September 1918. That's the first time he would have seen my father, his first son. Thomas was finally discharged on 14 April 1919; on the face of it a fortunate man.

We touched all the remaining coordinates of the Great War that day, June 9th – the German cemetery at Rancourt, where there are four bodies to each cross, and the nearby French *Nécropole Nationale* where the dead are buried two by two. Even in death, both below and above ground, nations leave their distinct marks – the British and Commonwealth Portland tombstones, each with space for a regimental badge and a few loving words, the Germans with sombre granite crosses, room only for the carved out names and dates of death, and the French with slender back-to-back crosses and metal name plaques. The lawns, too, are different; only the British have the grass cut short enough for a game of cricket or bowls.

We tramped on into Péronne to complete 26 kilometres, Peter still with enough steam in him to want to press ahead and visit the World War I Museum in the château. But as we neared the city centre, closing on the banks of the Somme, he let out a pained shriek: "Oh no, not another Best Western."

Peter had spotted a placard for our intended billet, the *Hôtel Saint Claude*, which proclaimed it was part of the Best Western chain. In an instant, he was straining at the leash, having spotted a sign down a side street to the *Hôtel des Remparts*, which was cheaper but which, I recalled, had failed to respond to my emails. The cold calculus of saving money took hold of Peter; and he shot off down the street.

"You're just penny pinching," I shouted after him.

"But I like pinching pennies; it gives me pleasure."

Peter's departure put me in a fix. The two rooms I had booked for us at the *Saint Claude* were guaranteed with my Visa card.

"We will have to charge you for the second room," said the receptionist. "It is company policy."

I was cross with Peter; to save himself a few euros he was going to cost me a round 100. I began to compose his obituary, and then thought up what I believed would be a plausible and pardonable excuse for his absence; my friend was dead.

"*Mais mon ami, il est mort,*" I explained; but just as I was pronouncing him dead, Peter turned up, resurrected, at my side.

"The *Remparts* is closed."

"Ah, so that's why they didn't answer my emails."

Hilaire Belloc would have taken Peter's side; he, too, was wary of what he called rich hotels.

I turned and found there one of those new hotels, not very large, but very expensive. They knew me at once for what I was, and welcomed me with joy ... Next morning I had fine coffee and bread and butter and the rest, like a rich man; in a gilded dining-room all set out for the rich, and served by a fellow that bowed and scraped. Also they made me pay a great deal, and kept their eyes off my boots.

We spent the remainder of the afternoon at the *Historial de la Grande Guerre* – in differing states of shock. Peter nearly choked with indignation over General Haig's Christmas despatch to the King in which he appeared to justify the slaughter of the last few months on the Somme. For very different reasons, I was horrified by one of the displays – the battledress uniform of a Scots Guardsman, a kilt. Good Lord – did my Irish grandfather go to war in a skirt?

Another unexpectantly imaginative exhibit drew me back into a contemplative mood: a pile of rubbish – detritus of war scavenged by the pacifist writer Yves Gibeau from the *Chemin des Dames*, the front that almost broke the French army, along which I would walk on my own in a few days. Gibeau, whose novel *Allons z'enfants* was turned into a brilliant anti-war film, bequeathed his collection to the Péronne museum, where it resides in a random heap, a bitter, bewildering, monument to both the horror and the banality of war. Every item, once handled by a living being, is rusting, rotting, torn, distorted, exploded, contorted – shoes, hobnailed boots, body armour, an egg beater, wire cutters, a Primus stove, spades, shovels, bottles, pots and pans, ladles, knives and forks, gun-nozzles, bayonets, bullets, shards of shell, rolls of barbed wire, helmets and jerry-cans ... dead objects that talk with eloquence to the surprised viewer.

The next day we were back on familiar terrain, the shadow lands of World War I. Following the towpath of the Canal de la Somme for the 28 kilometres to Ham should have been an effortless stroll. But it rained constantly, and maps and rain don't go well together. We botched our directions twice. The first time was my fault. The rain was by now so bad that we took shelter in a municipal workshop by the lock at Béthencourt where a sympathetic workman assured us it would rain until Sunday – it was only Thursday, and not even St Swithin's Day – but he boosted our morale by suggesting we follow the south bank and cross the bridge at the intersection with the Canal du Nord. When we arrived at the junction, there was no bridge, nor any sign of a barge which could have ferried us across; and as neither of us fancied swimming that meant trudging two kilometres back: in total, four wasted. Canals are not always as easy as they look, and we made a similar error after Buny; Peter misinterpreting the instructions from the lockkeeper leading us to stay on the wrong side and miss the towpath. By the time we reached the large industrial plants on the outskirts of Ham we were hardly talking to each other. Peter, tired and disconsolate, had marched on ahead. It had been a hard day for both of us, and when I caught up with him, he was complaining because the towpath was now rutted, and the jagged bits were jamming into his feet.

"But this is marvellous," I said, using old experience to jolly him along. "This uneven surface is giving our feet a really good massage."

"I don't want a foot massage," said Peter.

The rain lifted, and with it our moods, as we entered Ham. Like almost all others in the vicinity, the town was largely re-built after World War I, but it has a pretty centre and we parked there in a hotel where my clothes and boots dried out under a hot evening sun on the balcony opposite a statue to Ham's most famous son, General Maximilien Foy, one of Napoleon's generals who fought against Wellington both in Spain and at Waterloo. Foy's remarkable career – he was wounded 15 times – freed us from the Great War; Peter reminiscing at dinner about the Napoleonic battles that he has studied on the ground, his marvellous mind mastering the details and tactics of each phase and skirmish with the enthusiasm and passion that he had shared with me since Arras.

I was away by seven the following morning; Peter was still in bed, as he was catching a train back to Arras later that morning. Although

I would miss his sharp intellect and questioning mind, without him and the ghost of my grandfather at my side, I suddenly felt freer. Crossing the River Oise, I walked out of the ugly red-brick town past its huge Alcan steel plant, and I was quickly into country lanes. Contrary to the official forecast and to that prediction by the workman at Béthencourt, the rain held off and the cornfields were alight with red poppies. This was walking in provincial France at its best – warm sunshine and deserted country roads. I could feast on the soft contours of the landscape and cheerfully tick off the villages as they fell to my step, one by one like kilometre posts – La Neuville-en-Beine, Ugny-le-Gay, Le Plessier Godin, and La Rue du Chaumont. The café in the market square at Chauny provided me with a standing lunch – two Mars bars and a glass of lemonade. Chauny had grown rich supplying 19th century France with soda, and that seems to have coloured the way it was resurrected in the 1920s after being flattened by the Germans in 1917. Wherever my eyes rested, as I walked through the centre, the splendour of art deco facades caught the midday sun. It was enough to carry me on to my night's destination, the first hilltop town on my trek through the lowlands of Northwest France.

Dominated by its castle ramparts, Coucy-le-Château-Auffrique stands on a chalk crag 150 metres above the Oise Valley, and it was a sharp pull at the end of a 36-kilometre day. The castle was one of the largest in medieval France, and was partly destroyed by the Germans in 1917; a bit like Parliament's disabling of Corfe Castle in the English Civil War, they blew up the donjon and four of the towers, but enough survives to justify charging five euros to visit. The guide there told me about the eerie archaeology of the World War I in the beech woods above Coucy, where much of the profile of the trenches remains intact; nature, let alone cosmetic efforts, has not yet filled them in.

The town's *Hôtel Bellevue* seemed to have mislaid my booking, or so they said, but they fixed me up with a nearby *chambre d'hôte*, which was actually more comfortable; the *patronne*, Madame Lefèvre-Tranchart, even did my laundry. The only discomfort was that I would have to put up with the noise of television in the room below where the other guests would be watching France play in the World Cup late in the night. Nothing to get excited about; I slept through the whole match.

And so June 12th began with all my garments fresh and dry: always a good feeling. My day's prime objective was to walk the *Chemin des Dames*, the strategic east-west ridge overlooking the Aisne Valley which still cuts deep into French psyche. It has remained a secret wound to French military pride, but that is not the origin of the name; that goes back two and a half centuries to Adélaïde and Victoire, the daughters of Louis XV, who would travel this way to and from Compiègne and the Château de la Bove. The Kaiser's Germans dug in here, making use of old chalk quarries and tunnels to house their soldiers. These underground shelters protected them during the bombardment which preceded the all-out French attack ordered by General Robert Nivelle on 16 April 1917. The defenders, equipped with their new and more efficient MG08/15 machine guns, created carnage, mowing down their assailants as they reached the open ground on top of the ridge. On day one alone, the French infantry and the Senegalese colonial troops fighting alongside them took 40,000 casualties. Within 12 days, French casualties had mounted to 120,000. The troops then mutinied – some even turning their rifles on their superiors, but this rebellion was kept secret from France's allies and was dealt with by stealth and exemplary leniency. Nivelle was replaced by the rising star General Pétain, front-line conditions were improved and only a handful of mutineers – the 28 men who could be proved to have opened fire on their own officers – were executed.

After the morning rain, the *Chemin des Dames* was enfolded in low cloud. Climbing to it by a steep wooded hill, I joined the open plateau of the ridge on the D18 at Malmaison; the fields of sorrel either side of the road giving way to an immense roadside German World War II cemetery, its serried lines of simple metal crosses planted in perfect geometrical rows, broken only by patches of swirling mist and a few random oak trees. That was enough for me. I had had my fill of war, and so less than half way along the *Chemin des Dames*, I dropped off the ridge and headed south, descending the steep wooded slopes of the Aisne Valley to find out what else France had to offer.

That night, 30 kilometres on from Ham, I was booked to stay with a Franco-Polish family. I was intrigued to find them on the internet. I relate to Poland; I worked there in the early 1980s during the Solidarność Revolution and, as a Western correspondent, I played a small part in it. David Kaczmarek and his wife Claire run a *chambre d'hôte* in a converted farm granary in the hamlet of Braye-en-Laonnois which is tucked into the floor of the valley. It was very comfortable. David's grandfather, a miner from Katowice, was a communist; deported from France during the Occupation after firing a pistol shot through a picture of the former local hero Pétain, he ended up in a concentration camp; having a Polish name in German-occupied France was never a good thing. He left behind David's father, who became a skilled operator of a mechanical digger, and his Polish family name. I looked at David and Claire's nine-month-old baby, who was paraded around the house like a prize trophy, and I contemplated the vagaries of history – nothing left of the child's great-grandfather but an unpronounceable Polish name.

The house was an unexpected treasure trove of pre-history. David's father had used his excavator to dig up fossils from the age of dinosaurs – a five-foot tusk, and a tooth twice the size of a glass of wine. Both pieces should have been in museums; instead they were in the open hall of a farmhouse in a hamlet where – apart from the Kaczmarek family's hospitality business – there seemed to be no life left. I commented on the lovely chimes from the church.

"The work of a local enthusiast," said David. "The church is actually closed and it now belongs to the commune. That's probably just as well; the cemetery is full."

There aren't proper livings to be made in hamlets like Braye; so David spends six months a year working as a *plongeur* in ski resorts, washing up dishes in high mountain restaurants. It was St Moritz last winter.

"Excuse me," said David over our breakfast the next morning, June 13th. The sun had scarcely put in an appearance. "Excuse a silly question – do you use a compass?"

"Yes, it's my best friend."

Soon after I left, I took a photograph of my long shadow falling ahead of me under the rays of the early sun; a pointer to the east and a signal of an early start to what would turn out to be a long day. I joined the towpath of the canal that runs under the *Chemin des Dames* ridge and links the Aisne with the Oise, and then turned what I thought was due south towards Moussy-Verneuil. Old walking habits die hard and, out of curiosity, I took my compass and checked. The red arrow, which indicates north, was pointing in the direction I was walking. Good God, pigs will fly! I sat down, I took bearings on the bright sun, and I double checked my map. I still had David Kaczmarek's number, and even though it was early I knew he was up because he had served me breakfast. Feeling silly, I called him: was he sure that the canal went south? Of course, he replied. I told him that my compass was pointing to the north, the way I was going down the towpath.

"In that case your friend is *en panne* today," he said. I never understood what had caused this 180 degree deviation, and it wasn't until weeks later that the needle, once again without explanation, returned to true north.

I crossed the River Aisne at Bourg-et-Comin and got stuck in. David had warned me that driving to Reims they clocked at least 50 kilometres in their car, and that I wouldn't get away with much less. The D22 led me along the south of the canal and then curved away towards the village of Cormicy. It was turning into the hottest day so far, and I was running short of water. As it happened, in the centre of the village, a French-African family were eating lunch on a table in their garden; I asked them for water and they not only obliged but insisted I stay a while to share their meal. Apart from the kindness of some of my official hosts, this was the first spontaneous hospitality the pilgrim had been accorded; it broke my marching routine, but it was a delight. While the father and mother chatted amiably, their two young children stared at me as if I were from another planet. They were from Senegal.

When I left Cormicy, the sloping ground on the southern side of the Aisne Valley began to fill with vines, the young grapes just budding. I emerged from a green lane near Cauroy-lès-Hermonville to find myself in sight of Reims, the city's faint outline gradually sharpening in definition until I could work out the towering silhouette of its cathedral. I walked into the city along the towpath of the Canal de L'Asine et Marne feeling the fatigue of a long march. Monsieur Kaczmarek had been right; it was 48 kilometres.

SIX

CHAMPAGNE

I HAD TO CLIMB INTO REIMS; FROM THE canal towpath, which led all the way into the city centre, I scrambled up repair scaffolding on the bridge at Rue de Vesle, and at the top a kind passerby helped me jump from the contractor's site fence by holding my pack before I leaped onto the pavement.

"Why are there no steps up here from the canal?" I asked him.

"This is France. They have to leave something for you anarchists to do."

Waving him goodbye and re-attaching my rucksack, I walked up into the spacious Place Drouet d'Erlon, named for another of Napoleon's Marshalls; here the terrace cafés were filling with their evening customers. Like a good anarchist, I then turned left down Rue Buirette to check into the Best Western *Hôtel de la Paix*. The spirit of Peter flinched at my side as I strode into its bright marble lobby, but even he might not have begrudged the price of my room given that it looked out over the twin towers of the west front of the Cathedral of Notre-Dame. It had been a hard march, and it was time for a day off.

Despite being levelled in World War I and pummelled again in World War II, Reims has character and elegance. Including the smiling angel on the western portal of the cathedral, it's full of unexpected sideshows. There is a neo-classical library on the Avenue Jean Jaurès which was donated by Jonathan Holden, an English textile merchant, to commemorate Queen Victoria's golden jubilee in 1887. The *Bibliothèque Holden* would not be out of place as a wing of an English stately house. It was the first public library built in Reims, and it is good to think that the English, having burnt alive the great Saint of Reims, Joan of Arc, and having consumed champagne from its nearby vineyards by the lakefull, actually put something back into the city apart from the letter 'h' in their spelling of it.

As portrayed in her effigy in the cathedral, relegated for choreographic reasons from its original position to a side chapel, St Joan looks out of sorts. Here, after all, in July 1429 she completed her remarkable mission by crowning the new King of France. Her statue, cast in Rome in 1901, has her dressed in armour of so tight a fit that it makes her look less the Maid of Orleans and more like an early 20th century pioneer aviator – Earhart or Johnson. Originally the statue stood at the very spot where Joan herself placed the crown on the head of Charles VII. Joan tugs at nerve ends almost 600 years after she met her brutal end – both French and English. The French betrayed her; the English, two years after the coronation, tried and executed her. Her battle tactics are still studied at the French Sandhurst equivalent, St Cyr. Where did this illiterate peasant girl from Eastern France, aged just 17 when she embarked on her quest to save King and Country, find her courage and her military genius? Mark Twain, not one to overstate a case, thought she was "easily and by far the most extraordinary person the human race has ever produced." Hilaire Belloc, who devoted one of his more than 100 books to her, saw Joan as a saviour of Christendom.

I spent the early part of the afternoon at the *Musée des Beaux Arts*. Marriage to an art historian, and with a taste of art history at Oxford, where I studied for a special paper on the French 19th century academics, has given me an appetite for painting. Whenever and wherever I can I escape into an art gallery. I do ask myself, though, what an extra-terrestrial would make of our quasi-religious practice of entering these grand buildings and perambulating in solemn silence, staring at bits of coloured canvas and board hanging on the walls. I get enveloped by the painted surface, drawn irresistibly into the scene before me. Faced with a 19th century seascape or landscape – a beach scene, a snowbound lane, a tree-lined riverside – I am overtaken by a wave of nostalgia, powerfully sucked into a past that is tangible and yet tantalisingly unreachable.

I had arranged a massage for what in England would be teatime, little suspecting that I would be continuing my intimate tour of France's former overseas possessions. A petite young lady from Cameroon, Mireille, turned up at the hotel. She had immigrated to France and married a Frenchman, but for the *Rosbif* at her tender mercies, the rhythm of tropical Africa still pulsed through those knowing hands.

And so a dish of pasta with *Coquilles St Jacques* and a *Salade Ardenois* on the terrace at the *Brasserie Martin* completed a near perfect day. The only thing that had not worked to plan was my laundry; being Monday, the city centre *lavanderie* was closed, so I had to do the washing myself in the shower at the *Hôtel de la Paix* and let my clothes hang out to dry in full view of the cathedral. Charles VII would not have been amused.

Reims was still half asleep when I left the hotel on June 15th. I made a point of visiting the church of St Jacques, touching the trajectory of those passing this way to Santiago from Germany and Poland. That done, with a skip in my step I descended to the Quai to begin my walk out to Cormontreuil. Just before crossing the Pont Albert Thomas, though, I was accosted by an early morning jogger, a middle aged, track-suited woman. Claude was instantly noticeable; she was blonde. She was unusually friendly: most French are wary of strangers, but, in defiance of local manners, she was eager to talk and asked me where I was walking to.

"Rilly-la-Montagne," I said, "on my way to Rome."

"Ah, so you are going over our Alps?"

I knew at once what she meant: the Montagne de Reims, the wooded range south of the city that rises a little short of 300 metres above sea level. We talked about exercise – Claude had jogged the canal sides of Reims every morning for some 15 years – and about the pleasures and rewards of long-distance walking.

"My knees cannot take jogging any longer," I confessed.

"I think I could work on them for you," she replied, obviously a disciple of St Benoît.

"Another time," I replied, planting a friendly kiss on her cheeks and, I am afraid, making her blush.

I turned away to cross the bridge, feeling a distinct tinge in my left knee. It is extraordinary how sensitive parts of the body become the minute they are talked about. Do knees have ears?

The pain soon eased; perhaps it was the thought of entering the region of France that has grown rich on the sparkling wine that came to be called champagne. It was one of Peter's stories that prompted me to go via Rilly. His mother, Monique, came from there; and it was there over a bridge-table during the 'Phoney War' that she met Peter's father, Denys, in February 1940. Denys was stationed at the nearby village of Hautvilliers, where some three centuries before a local Bene-dictine monk Dom Pérignon had been one of the pioneers of sparkling wine. Monique and Denys fell in love, but within months they were separated, Denys being among the last members of the British Expe-ditionary Force to quit France on 18 June 1940, and leaving his girlfriend to tough out the war under German occupation. The Red Cross kept them in touch throughout the war, and in April 1945 Monique crossed the Channel. Their marriage on 30 April pretty much coincided with the last gasp of the Third Reich, the moment Hitler and Eva Braun committed suicide under the streets of Berlin.

The headmaster of the *Collège Paul Fort* was herding his pupils in for eight o'clock assembly – "*Allez! Allez!*" – as I walked past the school gates at the last gasp of suburban Reims. Turning off onto the D409, and crossing the excavations for a new section of motorway, I was in open country. Under a blustery sky, vineyards unfolded before me and Rilly lay ahead, its château outlining itself on the side of the hill. As I climbed, I ticked off the rows of vines owned by the local Champagne houses – among them Michel and François Fagot, and Taittinger: the sign at the entrance to Rilly boasted 70 local *vignerons*; not a bad place, I reflected, for Peter to be descended from.

The village itself was strangely deserted. I could have heard a grape pip drop as I walked up to the centre, the intersection of Rue de Reims and Rue de Chigny. And that's about all there was to Rilly; from then on, nothing but the wall of forest cloaking the ridge above.

"Don't worry," Peter had said, "There's a good track over the mountain, and you'll be able to ask the way."

Yes, but the one person behind the counter in the village *Poste* perfectly illustrated Mooney's First Law. She didn't know the track. In fact, no-one knew. So, anxiously picking my way through the side streets leading up the hill, I came across the faint outlines of a way which looked half hopeful. I dislike walking in forests, at least on unmarked tracks: they are often driven deep into the forest for logging, and end up nowhere. In forests, there are few enough points of reference, and compass bearings may not always help – tracks meander. After one such S bend, a party of school kids came down the hill towards me, led by well kitted teachers, dressed in mountain boots and Gortex anoraks, looking the sort of people who knew where they were going, or at least from whence they had come.

"Is this the track that leads over the mountain to Ay?"

"No idea," one replied. "We are just teachers here."

And so I spent an unpleasant hour winding up the track, trying to divine by inspired guesswork which tributaries to avoid and which to take, all the time keeping my brand new French compass pointing south as much as I could. It was a neat little thing, no bigger than a euro, which I had been persuaded to buy at a sports shop in Reims after tests established that my original compass, my best friend, was indeed *en panne,* standing as it were on its head – tests conducted by the simple method of holding the two compasses in separate hands. At one stage on the woodland tracks, I had both of them in either hand again – one pointing north, the other south. Forests can be such bewildering paramagnetic places.

Open fields and the sound of the railway which runs below the mountain announced the other side. The sun had warmed the early June day; I spent the afternoon in rolling valleys of vineyards and corn-fields, the pure green landscape broken by the occasional grey slate roof of a steeple, all the while I was descending towards the Marne Valley. On the way into Ay, one of those souped up, noisy little Peugeots drew up beside me, and the driver asked whether I came from England.

"Yes," I replied.

"Feerk off, then" he responded, making a bold effort at colloquial English. Oh yes, it was World Cup time, but its tensions seemed particularly to infect the district around Ay.

Installed at the rather classy *Castel Jeanson* in Ay, and after a refreshing swim in the hotel pool, I walked over to the *Vieux Puits* restaurant. It fancied itself, but I should have known better, not so much because of its name – Old Well – but because it was dark and empty. Could I have a *pichet* of white wine? No such thing, I was told by the superior waitress: wine is sold by the bottle or glass.

"But we in the heart of wine country," I insisted. "There must be plenty of local wine."

"We do not sell *pichets* of champagne," she replied haughtily. "If you want a *pichet* of wine go to the *Brasserie.*" And so I jolly well did, the first and only time that I lost my temper over dinner on my entire journey. *Le Resto d'Ay*, with a plate of ravioli and two *pichets* of excellent local wine on an open terrace, restored my humour, and I took stock of my journey. The 30 kilometres from Reims had brought me over 600 kilometres from Coggeshall; I was well on my way to Rome.

Back at the *Castel Jeanson*, the *patronne* shared my disgust.

"We never send our guests to the *Vieux Puits* – far too many bad experiences."

She invited me to join her in the granary across the courtyard by the pool where I had swum in the late afternoon. Under its vaulted beams, the room was heaving with *vignerons* – all local champagne producers; this was after all a *Grand Cru* village, and home of the world's oldest champagne house, Gosset, whose business dates back to four years before the Spanish Armada. One of the *vignerons* laughed at my earlier contretemps.

"They wouldn't serve you a *pichet* of champagne?" he exclaimed. "Pouf, I could fill my swimming pool with the stuff."

As noted, Hilaire Belloc was obsessed with wine-bibbing. He seemed to absorb no other liquid throughout his journey to Rome, even carrying bottles and flasks of wine to drink along the way. *The Path to Rome* is peppered with descriptions of him purchasing and consuming wine, as well as the odd glass of brandy, and among the many random stories that Belloc throws up on drink, one touches on champagne. It is about a man who controlled his habit of heavy drinking by not imbibing wines and spirits made and sold since the Reformation. (Along with whisky, gin and absinthe, champagne is included among the register of post-Reformation tipples; and this I would never have believed had I not walked past the house of Gosset.) Anyway, the heavy drinker in Belloc's parable had it easier than John the Baptist of whom Luke recorded the Angel announcing John's coming as saying: "He is never to take wine or other fermented spirit." That was pretty hard – to be ordered teetotal before even being born. Needless to say, Belloc's story has a moral twist; his man comes to no good when he starts drinking post-Reformation whisky. I was more relaxed about drinking products either side of the Reformation, although, unlike Belloc, during the day I didn't touch anything but water, lemonade or tea. Thirty plus kilometres is, however, good prep for alcohol, and I generally managed a beer or two at touchdown, and a generous carafe of wine at dinner.

This never interfered with my mental alarm-clock. I was always up and dressed, ready for breakfast by seven o'clock. But when I went down on the morning of the 16th, I had to scratch my head as to how to pay my night's bill; the girl who was supposed to produce my breakfast and take my money never turned up. I scavenged in the kitchen for some food and orange juice and filled my tea flask, without setting off any alarm bells, wrote a note leaving sufficient money for the night, and took a photograph of the result as proof of payment. I sent myself an internal memo that in future I would settle my hotel bill the night before.

Crossing the square beside the ornate 15th century west front of Ay's church, which is topped with a tall and slender steeple, I was soon on the haling way of the canal by the River Marne. Ahead I had six ideal days of towpath walking in which I would cover 216 kilometres, at an average of 36 a day. I would be in a world of my own.

Ever since a teenage summer holiday, I have loved these French canals. It was 1962; we set out from Dartmouth in the motor-yacht *Old Walrus*, crossed to Le Havre – an adventure in itself – and worked up the Seine to Paris; from there we locked down the canals and rivers to the Mediterranean. I ended up with huge biceps; in those days, most of the lock gates were manually operated. There were still a few horses pulling barges; the canals were chock-full with commercial traffic. Today the commercial barges are history, but *Voies Navigables de France* do a valiant job keeping the great waterways open for tourism, however sporadic, while the towpaths, or *chemins de halage*, make wonderful cycle ways and walking tracks.

With characteristic Gallic logic, notices at periodic intervals remind users that horse riders are not allowed; a riderless horse towing a barge would, of course, still be permitted. In any case, there are no restrictions for pedestrians, and great distances can be covered cross-country along the banked sides of France's canals with a fraction of the usual effort. All you have to do is put one foot in front of the other.

The *Canal Latérale de la Marne* took me 30 kilometres that day to Châlons-en-Champagne. Starting by the lock at Mareuil-sur-Ay, the first thing I saw was a glorious natural advertisement for the local product. Imagine a bottle of champagne sliced vertically, then laid on its side and blown up so that its outline filled the contours of the vine-clad chalk hill above the canal. From the towpath opposite, the reflection in the basin below completed the bottle – *et voilà*. The delightful illusion made me suddenly aware of the mirror itself, its playful surface scored by the dancing movements of water-boatmen, and momentarily pitted by the 'stoops' of diving beetles and damsel-flies, hunting their food. I could see the indigo shells of fresh water mussels on the muddy floor, and thought of the strange extendable foot with which they move about to feed. But it was the water-boatmen, their rowing legs which never quite break the water's surface, who entranced me the most with the rhythms of canal-side life, and opened me to its quiet buzz and to the gradually changing views around me.

To my right, the canal ran by the gently flowing River Marne and its wetland ponds and lagoons, at times nothing but the banked towpath between the two; to the left it butted up against chalk cliffs and the towering green walls of poplars and planes planted to shade and protect it. The canal follows the contours of the land, taking broad sweeps around the small hills of the Marne Valley and then straightening out again for long stretches; as each new section opened up I would spot a heron perched on a high overhanging branch, ready to dive for a fish, or watch cormorants track low over the water. There was always a counterpoint of cuckoos, and if I was lucky I would be cut across by the shrill nearby tseet of a kingfisher.

Very occasionally a boat chugged by to disturb this tranquil world. When my first working barge passed noisily I reminded myself that this floating metal hulk with its methodically drumming diesel engine was after all in its own domain. The skipper must have been a Sinatra man: it was called *My Way*. The next barge, indeed the only other vessel I encountered all day, was the *Levant*, a prim English canal boat in green livery. I thought back to my own voyage in *Old Walrus*, and many subsequent sailing adventures; with her exposed stern cockpit, narrow beam and shallow draft, the *Levant* must have had an uncomfortable and rather perilous journey across the Channel.

Walkers and cyclists proved a surprisingly rare species. A Frenchman paced towards me, making his way diagonally across his country from Marseilles to Calais. He had taken six weeks to get here. His eyes were sunken, he looked ill.

"I've done all the best bits," he said wearily. "Especially the Auvergne; *en tout cas,* from here on it's flat all the way."

I thought of all those climbs in Northern France, plodding up to 300 metres and then swooping back down into the valleys. Compared to what lay ahead, the North was indeed relatively flat, but by no means the pancake he envisaged.

"Oh, there is a hill or two ahead of you," I said. "There is even a mountain near Reims."

"Nothing beneath 1,000 metres counts in my book," he replied, and he went off cheerlessly into the French lowlands.

Close to the villages and the locks, I would come across fishermen sitting on the banks, rods stretched over the water as in prayer, vying patiently with their competitors, the herons and cormorants. Mostly, but not always, a "*bonjour*" would elicit a half-friendly grunt.

The evening's destination was a city with many claims on history. St Bernard preached his crusade here in 1147, Nicolas Appert, a confectioner and the inventor of preserving food in airtight glass bottles – our Kilner jar – lived here, as did Étienne Oehmichen, the father of the flying helicopter. Although the city lies outside the official Champagne growing region, the association with the name of the sparkling wine persuaded the city's chamber of commerce to undertake a rebranding. In 1988, they reverted the city to its pre-Revolutionary name, Châlons-en-Champagne; the former name, Châlons-en-Marne, even 74 years on, was too redolent of the first major trench battle of the Great War. In the soft and verdant terrain threaded by the River Marne, as 1914 ended, the French checked and repulsed the German advance on Paris, but at the cost of 500,000 dead or wounded. The memory, like that of the *Chemin des Dames*, still cuts deep.

I entered the city over the double bridge spanning the canal and river, which here run side by side, and made my way to the Cathedral of Notre-Dame to get my pilgrim stamp. That, though, isn't the place; I was waved on to Notre-Dame en Vaux, a 12th former collegiate church with two surviving spires.

"Aren't you ever afraid walking alone?" asked the woman in charge of the rubber stamp.

"Good heavens, no," I replied with the same assurance of St Peter. Within hours, the cock would crow, and I would have reason to regret the certainty of that remark.

My next stop was a *pharmacie*. France is awash with them and most have been expensively refurbished to give off a bright, refreshing image, tapping into that sense of wellbeing even before you have come through the door. This one responded commendably to the threefold challenge I presented: I had an irksome tear in my fundament, my feet were raw and painful, and somehow I had lost my glasses. I walked out with a restorative cream, a soothing lotion, and a new pair of reading spectacles. I was instantly back in working order.

Early in his walk to Rome, Hilaire Belloc also had his fair share of aches and pains; and he too found joy in a French *pharmacie*.

First my foot limped, and then my left knee oppressed me with a sudden pain. I attempted to relieve it by leaning on my right leg, and so discovered a singular new law in medicine which I will propose to scientists. For those excellent men have done investigating the twirligigs of the brain to find out where the soul is, let them consider this much more practical matter, that you cannot relieve pain in one limb without driving it into some other; and so I exchanged twinges in the left knee for a horrible great pain in the right. I sat down on a bridge and wondered; I saw before me hundreds upon hundreds of miles, painful and exhausted, and I asked heaven if this was necessary to a pilgrimage. (But, as you shall hear, pilgrimage is not wholly subject to material laws, for when I came to Epinal next day I went into a shop which, whatever it was to the profane, appeared to me as a chemist's shop, where I bought a bottle of some stuff called "balm," and rubbing myself with it was instantly cured.)

I lay snug in bed at the *Hôtel Pot de l'Etain* the following morning conscious of a persistent beating of rain at my window. At breakfast I scanned the local paper – rain for the next two days. The girl at reception said the weather would improve in July, today being June 13th. Well, blow that; I was soon back on the towpath, and getting pretty wet. The canal after Châlons is flanked either side with more magnificent lines of planes and poplars, their leaves all serving as runnels for the rain to cascade down on me. The towpath still had tall grass – it had not yet had its spring cut – and as I brushed through the tangles, water soaked onto my trouser legs and down into my boots. There was nothing for it but to lash my head into the hood of my anorak, eyes down, and march on. Painstakingly I counted down the kilometre posts, common to both the canals and roadsides in France, taking some comfort from the thought that I only had to cover 33 kilometres to get to my next destination, and also from the real relief that the Norwegian formula Neutrogena cream seemed to be giving my feet. Mind you, those feet were probably also enjoying the half centimetre of water sloshing around in my boots; in any case they continued to glide forward effortlessly and painlessly. At five kilometres an hour, I should be able to knock the day off in six and a half hours.

There was virtually nothing else to think about in my lonely tree-lined canyon which dripped like a sub-tropical forest in a monsoon. Nothing stirred, so I thought. Then something moved on the towpath almost at the most distant point of the long tunnel. I thought at first it was someone walking towards me, and began to make out the distinct shape of a man and what appeared to be a dog beside him. I quickened my pace, and, yes, the distance between us started to shrink. But not by much; I reckoned he must be walking very slowly. I sped up and closed the gap a bit more. Soon I was close enough to realise that he wasn't walking in my direction, but rather away from me, and I was following him; and in the instant I worked that out, he and the dog vanished. Was it hypothermia conspiring perhaps with Neutrogena to make me hallucinate? Imagination started to run riot; the rash words I had spoken when my pilgrim passport was stamped in Châlons-en-

Champagne came back to me. I began to concoct all sorts of reasons for being quite fearful and extremely cautious. I totted up the valuables that were about my damp person – cash, credit cards, camera, mobile phone and watch – any of them a perfect excuse for an old fashioned stick-up. Where better to mug somebody than (a) on a deserted towpath on a French canal (b) in the middle of nowhere (c) on a wet day (d) when nobody in their right mind would be anywhere except indoors? I began to imagine my assailant marking my progress from behind one of the large plane trees, or lunging at me from the thick hedgerow. I walked on faster, with more resolve, and stirred my lower limbs into a very deliberate trot as I passed the place where I had last seen my would-be attacker.

It was with considerable relief that I broke cover from the lonely towpath to arrive at the lock, which I knew would soon come, at St Germain-la-Ville. I marked my escape with celebration: sitting on the steps of the lock, I removed my boots and poured a cupful of rain from them, and then wrung out my socks. Have my feet ever been so wet? I warmed myself with a sip of tea – well into June I religiously carried a hot flask of tea brewed and filled at breakfast. The hotel breakfast table also supplied other things ideal for the pilgrim pocket: bread and fruit. I supplemented these with dried fruit and salted nuts. These staples, and the occasional Mars bar and lemonades from cafés along the way, would keep me going during the walking day.

By midday, after a downpour lasting all morning, the rain began to ease. A pair of cyclists was negotiating the towpath by the bridge at La Chaussée-sur-Marne; like medieval travellers we stopped to exchange our stories. They were young Canadians from Montreal, and were heading north towards England. They had come across just one person walking to my particular destination – a Belgian – one more reminder of how lonely is the path to Rome; how different from the hullabaloo of the crowded *Camino Francés*. By choosing to walk the canals, I had in fact steered away from the official Via Francigena route, which cuts across empty countryside directly south from Châlons-en-

Champagne. This was deliberate: it spared me leagues of muddy fields and rutted tracks, but deprived me of stopping by Clairvaux, the Cistercian mother-house of the Abbey of St Stephen at Coggeshall. That, though, is a sad place. The original abbey building, dating back to 1115 (only a few years before Coggeshall Abbey was founded), is now in ruins, and a high-security prison occupies the grounds. I was well content with what I began to see as my own canal, my private route through this region of France, and if I set myself to hum a couple of the still current hymns of St Bernard of Clairvaux, that was sufficient for not tying up all the knots, and indeed the nearest I came to emulating Hilaire Belloc, who would sing aloud as he marched.

The country gradually changed shape as I progressed south and east. The chalk cliffs of the canal's far bank now gave way to a darker, crustier rock; and the River Marne settled into its middle stretches, meandering in lazy oxbows through woodland and open fields. Over the coming days I would follow the river to its source, catching glimpses, through serried poplars, of its bubbling waters in a narrow culvert or looking out from the top of a levée over a wider stretch silvered by the sun, even once or twice walking from one side to the other on a canal bridge. The River Marne sneaks up almost apologetically on the country through which it flows; unless in flood, its presence is never over-stated. I began to see how its gentle course and soft green banks had inspired so many painters – Corot, Cézanne, old Pissarro, even Rousseau (*Le Douanier*) all brought their easels to its banks.

And now in a new geology and after a – not quite envisaged – tough 33 kilometres, I approached Vitry-le-François, an inland waterway junction which connects the Marne to the Rhine and the Saône. In its heyday the waterside bustled with masts and spars of the sailing barges moored on the wharves and in the inner basins. World War II left the town in ruins, and what you see today is largely a 'repro'. In 2006, when driving with Gail and our eldest daughter, Sophia, to Rome in our much-loved BMW convertible, we had chosen Vitry for our first night's stopover. That was in one of the new concrete convenience hotels; we seemed to relish the convenience, while concurring that Vitry wasn't worth another look. Four years on, and after a full three weeks in walking boots, I revised my opinion, warming to its spacious somewhat Italian boulevards. The main Place des Armes is a real urban square, and the church, Notre-Dame, flies the flag for French architecture; not a bad spot from which to bid farewell to Champagne.

SEVEN
BURGUNDY

SETTING OUT FROM VITRY-LE-FRANÇOIS ON June 18th, I switched canals and started at Kilometre 1 and Lock 71 of the *Canal de la Marne à la Saône,* which is now more enticingly rebranded as the *Canal entre Champagne et Bourgogne.* My destination was St Dizier. Nothing stirred all day on the canal, no boat washed over the emerging yellow blooms of water lilies. On the still surface, water-boatmen sculled with such abandon and in such great numbers – creating what looked like myriad drops of water – that I had to consult my sleeves, and then my wrists, to make sure it wasn't raining again. It proved to be a long haul, 30 kilometres down a dead straight tarmacked towpath, and the day would have contracted into two sentences had it not been for three little girls and their younger brother, playing on the canal banks, who took me for Jesus.

I was sitting on a bench by the bridge at Perthes when they spotted me from their play and stole up on me unawares. I could see that they wanted to talk, but they were shy and giggling. I smiled at them and said hello.

"Do you have a home to go to?" asked the eldest girl. Her hair was tied in a pony-tail; she was not much more than thirteen.

"But, of course; in fact I've got several homes."

"But you look so poor, and so hungry," she insisted. "You're like Jesus, we feel pity for you."

"Oh you are so kind," I said, feeling distinctly uncomfortable, and increasingly like Alan Bates in that role as a criminal in the 1960s film *Whistle Down the Wind* in which he is mistaken for Jesus by a simple country girl, played by the lovely Hayley Mills. "I am OK and I am truly not hungry."

But so meek a protest wasn't going to get me off; the four children had come across the bridge with a plan, which they were determined to execute. From behind her back, the girl produced a *paté* sandwich, evidently made by mother, and a bottle of mineral water.

"This is my lunch today and we want you to have it, right," she insisted.

"But no. You must eat it. Otherwise you will go hungry."

"I brought it back from school. I don't need it," she said.

I had no choice. I took the sandwich and bottle of water and gave them all an enormous smile.

Then something totally unexpected happened. The girl, who had been all genuine innocence, now transformed herself into a teenager. Like a growing kitten suddenly baring her teeth, she pouted her lips and swapped her child's pitch for a low purr.

"You wouldn't happen to have a cigarette for me?" she asked.

"No, I haven't smoked for 30 years!"

I offered her money, but she wouldn't take it. She wanted that divinely-offered cigarette, and I had failed her. I harnessed up, and with her water and sandwich in hand, set off half in wonderment, half in shame, thinking of what Luke wrote about Jesus welcoming children: "Let the little children come to me, and do not hinder them, for the Kingdom of God belongs to such as these."

As I neared the end of my long straight trail, St Dizier announced itself with the roar of jet fighters landing at and taking off from the nearby air base and with a new tree species on the canal side, Scots pines, which provided the unfamiliar crunch of needles and cones underfoot. I approached along a street of down-at-heel houses, but the centre itself has class – the remnants of a fine fortified château, and a near perfect neoclassical theatre giving suave grandeur to Place Aristide

Briand. That evening I took a chair on the terrace of a restaurant in the square facing the theatre, enjoying my rewarding *bière*, and casting a sympathetic eye towards the bearded man on the next table anxiously scanning his maps; then I attacked a dinner which culminated in a six-inch-high, home-made *Tarte Tatin*.

It had taken me a little over three weeks to get to St Dizier, like Hilaire Belloc's starting point, Toul, a garrison town. The two places are on the same latitude and roughly the same distance from Rome, about 1,600 kilometres. Belloc chose Toul, 65 kilometres to the east, for his point of departure for no better reason than it was where, as a young gunner, he had spent 12 months in the French army in 1891-92, doing his military service with the 10th Battery of the 8th Artillery Regiment. We would now follow parallel paths to the Jura and over the Alps before converging in Lombardy.

I stayed in St Dizier at the *Hôtel All Seasons*, a comfortable, modern box, and set out early, passing the rare medieval relic of a gothic church, before entering industrial suburbs; these were dominated by a giant MIKO plant, doubtless turning out enough coffee for the whole of Eastern France. The canal towpath as usual threw up its strange encounters. A cyclist overtook me – the same bearded gentleman who had been looking over his maps at the terraced restaurant opposite the theatre in St Dizier the night before. I waved him back; he was Michael, a Flemish-speaking Belgian. A serial Santiago pilgrim, he had cycled there three times. This time he was on his way to Le Puy, and thence to Roncesvalles.

"I won't quite have time to get all the way to Santiago this year," said Michael. "But I am determined to make it six times before I hang up."

"Why so many times?" I asked.

"Each one is different." I think he made a good point.

Nearing the hamlet of Bienville I ran into a serious Pattonista. In a canal-side warehouse, a local businessman, Bertrand Bourgeois, has assembled tanks, armoured vehicles and other militaria from General Patton's Third Army; a tank and a model U.S. Military Policeman guard the compound. Bertrand, himself, invited me inside this treasure-trove of machinery and war equipment, everything polished and sparkling, but to me it was sanitised and somehow out of context. I thought back to the haunting collage, the reality of war, the broken and twisted debris from the *Chemin des Dames* collected by Gibeau, which Peter and I had seen in the Péronne museum. The closest you get to action here is a fingerpost on the canal pointing to Omaha Beach – 511 kilometres away. But everyone is entitled to his enthusiasm, and Bertrand has the heroic and controversial George Patton, who not only led the Allied breakout from Normandy after the D-Day Landings but also thwarted the German counter-attack at the Battle of the Bulge. The general died in December 1945 after being bucked from a military jeep.

"Do you think he was murdered?" I asked Bertrand.

"But of course," he replied. "He was far too big a threat to the establishment."

River and canal were now side by side as the valley hills gradually closed ranks; I was moving steadily towards the hills of Eastern France, burrowing deeper into a seemingly lost world. The chime of bells in village churches would remind me that there was still some life here, but there was little else. The bascule bridges over the canal took me back to childhood; to the painting by Vincent Van Gogh of Langlois Bridge in Arles, a copy of which hung in my bedroom.

I still had a distance to go when the Tourist Office in Joinville rose to the challenge and found me a bed at an inn in the village of Donjeux. This was further than I wanted to go, but the only hotel closer was shut for its weekly day off. Getting to Donjeux meant a 42-kilometre day, and an extra spurt down the towpath at the end; little did I suspect that at the *Auberge du Lion d'Or* in Donjeux I was about step into a broken dream in the heart of rural France.

The three-storey *auberge* is at the edge of the village, close to the canal and river. From it, a narrow central street winds up to the church from whose belfry there is a view over the surrounding fields and wooded slopes. The street is well maintained; one old cottage is adorned with flower baskets and brightly painted coloured gnomes; onto the barn doors of another are nailed the claws of several dozen slain wild boars, never to scrape again. Inside the *auberge* the bar and dining room are freshly decorated. The pleasant atmosphere is thanks to the couple from Belgium who have invested their life savings here. When the previous *patron* died of a heart attack, leaving the establishment empty, Jackie and Peter from the town of Ost came along, with their children – all striking blonds. The new proprietors had given the *auberge* a good makeover, but when I arrived there was just the one elderly customer with his glass of wine propping up the bar.

Jackie is a bundle of nerves; thin, short spiked hair; never without a cigarette. "We've been through all our savings," she told me. "Now we have no more money, and we are not making enough. I don't know what is going to happen."

Bravely, if inopportunely for me, they had organised a rock concert that evening. A large truck was drawn up in the car park, the side of its container opened to form a stage. The group, designer torn jeans or tartan trousers barely over their bums, faces pierced with silver rings and baubles, were tuning up what threatened to be an extremely loud sound-system. I never discovered their name, but they had CHICKEN FUCKERS lettered onto the bass drum. Electric guitars, grating voices and drum-kit would reverberate across the River Marne until well into the night.

But the auguries weren't good. By eight p.m. it was unseasonably cold, with clouds gathering in the west to obscure the last rays of the sun. With them came a light drizzle. Peter started grilling sausages for hot dogs; Jackie prepared to serve wine and beer, and on cue the rock group fired up, but for the first hour no one came; and after that only a trickle of customers, some stopping a while, others just looking around curiously and going. One of the stayers was the *adjoint* of Donjeux, a busty blonde lady with buck teeth, wearing a black leather jacket zipped up to her neck to keep her warm. Of her constituency – 501 souls – the majority were middle-aged or elderly, she told me.

"It's hard for anyone to make a living out of commerce here," the deputy mayor confided. "That's why I feel I must be at this rock concert."

At breakfast the following morning, June 20th, I asked Jackie how the night had gone.

"*Pas grand chose*," she said. "No great shakes."

It was Sunday, and I had set myself another long day, so as to get to the comparative metropolis of Chaumont, the capital of the Haute-Marne, 41 kilometres along the canal. All morning, I was accompanied by a chorus of church bells which rang out from distant villages as I passed. The churches in rural France may be empty but their bells still chime. Canals can be straightish – you expect them to be – but after Donjeux mine meandered in huge loops, following the contours of the Marne Valley as the river carves its course through the hillsides. The wall of trees on the banks seemed to rise higher in sympathy; all the while the river grew smaller as I approached its source. In England it was Father's Day, and I had received SMS greetings from Sophia in Spain, Marina in London and Julius in Dubai. Resting on a bench in the pretty village of Froncles, I called Jon Harris to report on progress. I told him that I was now getting into my stride, managing 40 kilometres a day on the good surfaces of the canal towpath. He wasn't impressed.

"I was with a friend in Sussex this week, and she told me about the Gurkhas," said Jon. "They use the South Downs Way for training and do 100 kilometres in a day. Apparently they break into a trot at lunchtime just to relax a bit."

Jon was teasing, but I knew what he was talking about. I have seen Nepali mountain guides virtually run up the buttress walls below the North Col of Everest.

"How's St Luke coming along?"

"He's doing well. I read a chunk of him every morning before setting out."

"What have you learned?"

"That Jesus was a tough nut. I was reading about Martha this morning – poor thing, left to work in the kitchen while her sister Mary gets a one-to-one seminar with the Master. Then a few days ago, Jesus was talking about bringing fire on earth."

"Not bad for a man tramping through the Marne. Now, wait until you get to the bit about the camel passing through the eye of the needle," said Jon.

The Angelus pealed from the church at Vouécourt, and a while later the canal cut through a long tunnel at Condes before the final three kilometres into Chaumont. On that last stretch, I overtook an elderly local couple out for their Sunday afternoon walk, but they did not return my greetings. At high speed, especially coming from behind, I must have looked, and indeed sounded threatening. I climbed out of the valley to the plateau at Chaumont to seek out the hotel I had booked. It turned out to be in the suburbs, way off my course, so I cancelled. One of the great advantages of walking is that you can stay in the very centre of town, close to all the attractions, without having to worry about where to park or how to drive there, avoiding the now increasingly prevalent pedestrian zones. Motorists are being forced to migrate to out-of-town hotels. I headed for the *Fleur de Lys*. It, too, was Best Western, in the heart of the old city, a stone's throw from the 13th century Basilica and the elegant 18th century Hôtel de Ville; no need to walk far for my dinner, which tonight was duck *paté* and *penne all' arrabiata*.

On the Monday morning, I rejoined the canal at Chamarandes, a huddle of stone houses in the valley bottom. Here canal and river are squeezed into a tight gully. Even on the flat towpath, I had a sense of gaining height, of entering a new landscape; the canal was now bordered by high terraces of mountain ash and firs. On a hillside meadow a noisy tractor was out raking the mown hay into ridges, a sign that summer was advancing. No boats plied the water all day, and the only machine I encountered along the canal was a tractor mowing the bank at Rolampont. The sun did in fact shine for this, the last of my six days of towpath walking; the tree-lined canal was somehow at its best, and the River Marne, now little more than an energetic stream, became a playful companion at its side.

Perhaps it was the lack of complication in the path – in the latter stages, anyway; perhaps it was the constant sight and sound of water at my side; perhaps the rhythmic pace of travelling in time with the slow beat of my heart, the sense of moving across the land at the same speed with which our distant ancestors first explored the forests and mountains, but my six canal-side days opened up my mind and gave me space and time to contemplate. The long days, the long hours of walking had begun to act like a soothing drug; no longer attached to my legs and feet, I was on a walker's high.

Hilaire Belloc, too, seems to have achieved a similar tranquillity in recollection and silence. He talks of "unprisoning the soul", and he sees his soul as a separate department, removed from the normal sensory world and capable of great joy, though he does not dare to define it.

> ... Yet the wisest people assure us that our souls are as superior to our minds as are our minds to our inert and merely material bodies. I cannot understand it at all.

I took leave of river and canal at Lock No 6 and walked steeply up to Langres, the home of an orangey wash-rind cow's milk cheese with a distinguishing dimpled top, and the birthplace of someone I would have loved to have heard Belloc in conversation with, Denis Diderot. The town sits on a 400-metre spur between the Rivers Marne and Bonnelle, surrounded by impressive ramparts. Getting up to it involved crossing busy arterial roads and circling the city's cemetery – unfamiliar terrain after the Arcadian peace of the canal.

I entered by one of the City gates, passed the Cathedral of St Mammès, with its strikingly patterned tiled roofs, and walked into the Place Diderot where the wily old Enlightenment *philosophe* was waiting for me. Book in hand, coat drawn back to display a partly unbuttoned jacket, Diderot looked down from his high plinth and smiled on his birthplace; and on the approaching pilgrim, for whom, at Oxford, his were among the first French texts to be studied. I would be hard pressed now to remember much of what he wrote, but I am left with enduring admiration for his daring and originality; in a conventional age, he was a courageous iconoclast. His father was an established cutler in Langres; they fell out over his decision to become a writer, not considered a suitable aspiration; better to be a cheese maker.

As it happens, in many instances Belloc may well have seen eye to eye with him. Although opposites in the matter of religion, Belloc and Diderot had one thing in common as writers: they both churned out books. Too late to ask Diderot whether he enjoyed putting pen to paper? Belloc apparently did not. "I hate writing," Belloc was quoted as saying in his old age (he died in 1953, aged 82). "I wouldn't have written a word if I could have helped it. I only wrote for money. *The Path to Rome* is the only book I ever wrote for love." I wonder if he gave his name to a street or eating-place, or real-ale pub. Diderot does well here: a statue, a square, a *Rue,* and a *boulangerie.*

A festival was in full swing in Langres, drummers in red cloaks marching down the street, but they had nothing to do with Diderot. I was to stay in a blue room at the *Grand Hôtel de l'Europe,* overlooking the central street and the drummers, and I enjoyed an excellent meal in the restaurant below – *paté* and *coquilles St Jacques.* Unlike poor old Donjeux, they know how to party in Langres, and the songs of the festival reverberated through the shutters until early morning when the singing gave way to the persistent whine of a mechanised street cleaner.

In my rucksack, I was carrying the three heavy volumes of Chinn's ironically named Lightfoot Guide to the Via Francigena. Until now I had made my own way through France, consulting the guide only occasionally for help with my night's hotel. Volume One would take me as far as Besançon, where I would mail it home along with some used maps; I would need Volumes Two and Three to get across the Alps and down Italy. It had been a lot of dead weight to carry, but now, three weeks into my journey, I deployed it for the first time to follow its recommended route – the official Via Francigena – over the 40 kilometres from Langres to Champlitte.

On Tuesday morning, I left Langres through the city's south gate, heading out past the abandoned barracks. The near empty D122 whisked me into open country. I passed a farm shop, which carried the philosopher's imprimatur way beyond Langres' walls and sold every conceivable kind of local produce, including wine and cheese: the *Domaine Diderot*. Further on, a sign pointed to the source of the River Marne. It flows, from a rock outcrop, through a metal grille; perhaps they are afraid that someone will steal it if not kept safely behind bars. I spent much of the day on long winding roads, edging into and down the valley of the River Salon; and the woodlands and fields between offered their fair share of delights – an owl sweeping low from an overhanging branch, a fox that idled into my sights, deer leaping through standing barley, cut hay soaking up the sun. It was hot: I put on my inelegant white hat for the first time.

Local sandstone gave the farmhouses and village churches a soft hue. A stone barn at Grosse-Sauve told me that I was back in pilgrim footsteps – it stood out to the roadside from the courtyard of St Nicolas farm, and on closer inspection it revealed itself to be an old chapel, the openings of its western wall filled in with rubble sandstone which left a finely worked pointed gothic arch exposed. Like the similar farm-yard chapel in Coggeshall, it is all that remains of a former abbey which would once have sheltered and victualled pilgrims on their journeys to and from Rome. Did Archbishop Sigeric stop here for a warm mead?

An 1838 stone marker at the side of the D17 between Seuchey and La Voisine announced that I was leaving the Marne and entering the Saône, a welcome earnest of my southward progress. Stone waymarks are now rare on French roads, having all been at great cost replaced – for reasons of safety – with their plastic lookalikes; crazy because stone still remains the most certain way of passing information from one generation to another. Images and letters carved into stone will be around long after floppy disks, CDs, memory sticks, hard-drives, paper and papyrus have vanished and these plastic waymarks have become split and indistinct. In fact, I am so convinced of the lasting value of rock carvings that I am thinking of having this book chipped into stone.

The afternoon's stretch brought me to my destination, the walled town of Champlitte. It is in the heart of a wine-growing area which never quite recovered its prosperity after phylloxera got the vines, but it seems to take its Francigena credentials most seriously. To be sure, the church with its multi-layered 15th century belfry, shut since the *curé* died, was only open to visitors by appointment, and that Tuesday the château was also closed, but the *Office du Tourisme* wasn't. It has its own Francigena stamp and keeps scrupulous records of pilgrims passing through. I was the first pilgrim walker in the last three weeks and only the seventh so far in the year. The six preceding, all Italians, had started in Canterbury. I stayed at the *Hôtel Donjon* on the main road. I should have been warned by the name. The *Henri IV*, opposite the fountain on the narrow market square with a view plunging to the fields and vineyards beyond the river, looked far more inviting, but I discovered it too late, after checking in. I noted in my diary that dinner of tomato salad and *crevettes* followed by *tagliatelle* was 'okayish'. It must have been dreadful.

On Wednesday 23rd, I covered two of Chinn's suggested stages, leapfrogging through Dampierre-sur-Salon to get all the way to Gy in one go, starting at 6.45a.m. and arriving at the *Hôtel Pinocchio* at 4.45p.m. Ten hours seemed to be comfortable for the 42 kilometres along surfaced roads and over slightly hilly ground; and that became my benchmark for the distance. The Salon is an unknown and very pretty river, and I wove through a succession of handsomely set villages along its banks, each announcing itself with its church spire spotted from a far-off rise. The country was opening up, the outline of hills ahead beginning to shape the route and draw me on.

Walking out of the village of Delain I heard the distinct bark of an Englishwoman. "Sit! Sit!" she said in a voice so imperious, so insistent that for an instant I nearly obeyed her. But her erring subject was a frisky young spaniel, clearly with no respect for her English commands. I caught up with her, and I tried to soothe her obvious embarrassment over both her own raised tones and the patent lack of obedient response to her orders which rang out over the Saône countryside.

"I always tell people that dogs don't speak English," I said, "and I don't think they manage much better in French, either." She was startled to be addressed in her native tongue and she was not that amused; as the distance between us grew, I continued to hear fragments of her unheeded instructions to her new pet.

Dogs may be man's best friend, but they are often the lone walker's worst foe. In Italy I would have to contend with unchained farm dogs – the real thing. In France, more often, dogs would come lunging at me, teeth bared and claws at the ready, kamikaze-ing into a railing or fence, centimetres from my arm or jugular; the attack, springing apparently from nowhere, always left me feeling shaken and angry. I had done nothing to provoke it, except walk by somebody's house. But these are guard dogs, and Europe's middle classes are arming their redoubts.

But some encounters can be a joyful surprise, like mine with a farmer. He was turning hay; and as I walked past the field he was working he stopped his bright blue tractor, dismounted and came over to join me on the roadside. He was dressed in a blue check shirt, pre-sumably to match the livery of his Ford tractor; a peak cap with the logo of a rival agricultural machinery company, Yacco, shielded the sun from his finely cut face and trimmed grey sideburns.

"I want to shake your hand," he said. "I do so admire you pilgrims. You must have real purpose, real resolve."

"Yes, but so do you. Making hay is just as important."

"Not this year," he replied. "It's been far too wet."

"Well, it's sunny now."

"Yes indeed, but it's too late for this year."

So under bright midday sun, I pressed on to Dampierre-sur-Salon, where I recorded a new word in my diary. I 'intermarchéd', that's to say bought water and a fresh supply of dried fruits and nuts at the local *Intermarché*. Crossing the bridge at Seveux – it was the Saône now, here broad, slow flowing, and verged with swathes of water meadow – I then began the long trek through forests on the far bank that would take me to Gy.

Any hotel with the sense of humour to call itself *Pinocchio* has to be worth staying in; in the courtyard it even had a painting of the long-nosed wooden lad. It was luxurious, but, being Wednesday, its restaurant was closed for the evening. I wandered up and down the main street in Gy, admiring the six Doric columns of the Hôtel de Ville, and after extracting a pilgrim stamp from the lady at the *Office du Tourisme*, a stand-in for the usual attendant who seemed utterly perplexed at anyone needing so strange a memento, I went prospecting for my dinner. In the event, there was little choice; but the *Restaurant Charlemagne* produced a magnificent plate of *volailles* and a chocolate mousse, which only a pilgrim who had covered two of Chinn's stages could eat without guilt.

The highlands of Eastern France urged me on, and the following morning, the 24th, I climbed steadily through the Monts de Gy, modest hills rising to 450 metres but nevertheless forming an outer bastion of the Jura Mountains. The hills were blanketed in forest, oak and tall beech, and at several points along the wooded roadside I watched people scouring the sunlit ground beneath the green boughs for the flash of colour that betrays a unique species of orchid that grows here. Towards the top, a hillside valley, guarded by a bulky square farmhouse and its walled court and large stone barn, opened unexpectedly into a bowl of summer pasture: Fontenelay, fortress-like, as if it had been there for centuries, watching over the road to Rome.

A wide expanse of empty country opened up as I descended towards the valley of the River l'Ognon, and in the far distance, well over 80 kilometres away, over two pronounced ridges which receded into the horizon, I could make out a faint trace of the Jura and the Swiss skyline. No longer in the forest's shade, I now felt the full blast of the summer sun and pulled down the rim of my hat to protect myself against it. From now to Besançon it was all hot work, uphill; I would gain 732 metres over the next 35 kilometres, most of it in exposed country.

After all that early summer rain, the farms were a frenzy of hay-making; every tractor in the district seemed to be working the fields turning the hay. At one village, I stopped to drink water at the fountain which trickled into an ancient wooden trough. A notice declared its *eau* to be *non-potable,* but an elderly man told me to ignore the sign.

"We drank from this fountain when we were children, and it never did us any harm. These modern sanitation laws are crazy."

Approaching Besançon, I began to pick up more Via Francigena signs; their reassuring yellow arrows and VF initials encouraged a real sense of progress. A short cut over an old farm track led to Etuz, and soon I was across the river at Cussey-sur-l'Ognon. After the village of Geneuille, I picked my way through a large building site to clamber over the cutting for a new TGV rail track; France is building high-speed lines with the same energy that she put into creating her motorway network in the 1970s and 1980s. A pedestrian crossing assured me safe passage over the busy *Route Nationale 57* and I then turned south at Chatillon-le-Duc to embark on a final climb up the D108 to Besançon. The last stretch, passing the out-of-town shopping malls and light industrial factories, was mercifully all downhill, but I entered the city a worried pilgrim.

EIGHT
JURA

I ARRIVED IN BESANÇON WITH ONE THING ALONE on my mind – my boots. I had walked some 950 kilometres from Coggeshall and, thanks to a regular application to my feet of the magic lotion which the pharmacist had given me in Châlons-en-Champagne, everything was in good working order. Everything, that is, except my boots. Over recent days I had been looking at them with growing anxiety; the heels were wearing perilously thin, shorn almost to the core on both the outside ridges. My legs were starting to bow outwards.

This was serious. Walkers set great store by their boots, their single most important piece of kit. Nobody gets far without a well-heeled pair, which neither leak nor blister, and over many years of long-distance walking I have grown attached to one particular make. They are the only ones with sufficient last, or breadth, not to pinch my feet. I have often guessed that this was something to do with their place of origin – a small community in southern Bavaria, Kirchanschöring, close to the Austrian border: many Germans have big feet. Petrus Meindl began the family business of making boots in Kirchanschöring in 1683, and the company which bears his name has been helping people walk, trek and climb ever since.

Mind you, the state mine were in had nothing on Hilaire Belloc's as he measured himself against the Alps:

My boots in which I had sworn to walk to Rome were ruinous. Already since the Weissenstein they had gaped, and now the Brienzer Grat had made the sole of one of them quite free at the toe. It flapped as I walked. Very soon I should be walking on my uppers ...

And so, he had his boots cobbled before crossing the Alps, thereby breaking another of his vows.

Besançon was my best hope of a replacement pair; I had mentioned the problem, somewhere along the canals, to my brother Neil, based in the west of Ireland, and he had done some research and got back to me. There was indeed a Meindl outlet in the city, so I called the store to ask about repairs or replacements. No need to replace them, they said: go and see Monsieur Moisson. In those last few hundred metres, dropping down past the *Bastide* to Besançon's city centre, I mouthed the name Moisson as a sort of mantra to keep my Meindls from flying into bits before I could reach the shop. And there his name was on the *Cordonnier* sign outside No 91 Rue Battant! I entered in some trepidation. It's increasingly hard to find real cobblers in England; would France be the same? Monsieur Moisson reassured me that there was life left in my old pair and that there would be no problem in getting them done by tomorrow morning. There and then I unpicked the laces and changed into the light shoes I carried with me, and walked on down the street and over the Pont Battant in a cheerful mood. There was only one thing left niggling at me – my socks, but they could wait.

For the moment, I simply delighted in being in Besançon, a city celebrated by another of my favourite French authors, Marie-Henri Beyle, who is universally known by his pen name Stendhal. Walking from the riverside into the Place de la Revolution was like entering a bustling drawing room. The square teemed with the commerce of an outdoor market – stalls of gorgeous fresh foods, tables with antiques and *bric à brac*. It was still early afternoon – I had arrived in Besançon at two o'clock – and I wandered through the narrow streets of the old town, an excursion into one of the finest surviving medieval *quartiers* of any French city, merging the street patterns and roof-lines of the Middle

Ages with the grace of its numerous classic stone buildings. I was staying in the southern end of the old town, just below the Citadelle, in the *Hôtel Granvelle*, itself, as it turned out, a rather grand stone townhouse, set in its own courtyard.

But with what novelties and eccentricities! As if every guest was an Edward Whymper, the notice above the *Granvelle's* entrance informs you of the latitude and longitude and the elevation above sea level. Inside is a giant world map, and in a staircase niche is displayed a section of the Eiffel Tower's steelwork. On the other side of the street is a traditional Hammam, where I enjoyed a steam bath, and close by a launderette where I used my best graces to induce the lady in charge to take my washing, and to stitch up the holes in my 1,000-Mile socks and repair my torn trousers. I had used the same brand combining inner and outer sock for many walks, and they had never before sprung leaks.

In the early evening, I strolled back through the old town to the Pont de la République in order to find the tourist office. There they provide a stamp which touches all pilgrim bases – issued by the Associations of Pilgrims of Compostela and of Rome. Besançon is on a pilgrim fault-line. I was invited to sign the pilgrim book, and blow me if Carlo Carapacchi's signature wasn't there just above my row. I had last sighted him shivering under a plastic poncho in Northern France. The fact that he had passed this way two days previously was no surprise; I had taken time off to meander through the battlefields with Peter. This, though, is what he had written, and I felt for him.

"How difficult it is to walk through France – there is nothing. All the villages are empty."

Trying to balance Carlo's negative experience of walking through France with my own, I returned to the hotel. There was a message from Brigid Joyce, my French aunt who lives bang in the centre of France in a remote hamlet between Aubusson and Montluçon; this was the nearest I had been for years. She is from my mother's side of the family, the daughter of my other grandfather. While Thomas Mooney was spitting, polishing and blancoing, and being shot and gassed in the trenches, Raoul Joyce, fresh down from Cambridge, was a spy in Scandinavia: first in an assistant capacity and then as Military Control Officer Oslo and Copenhagen. No doubt the mixture of danger and the useful intelligence garnered contributed to the military MBE he earned, but his domestic life was less clear-cut. He married three times. My mother was a daughter of his first and unhappiest marriage – to an Englishwoman; Brigid, the daughter of his third and happiest – to a French Algerian. I had tentatively suggested that she might like to join me for a few days.

"Cher Brian," her message read, "forty kilometres a day is too much for me!"

Disappointed, I fell into temptation. At the *Brasserie 1802* in the Place du Théâtre, I ordered the most expensive dinner of my entire journey. I sat outside thoroughly enjoying the balmy summer evening, but the meat and wine were not worth half the 63 euros I found myself paying. I could hear Peter saying, I told you so.

My day off, June 25th, began at the *Musée des Beaux Arts*. It is a spaciously laid out former corn exchange. A giant canvas by the French Realist painter Gustave Courbet, a snowbound winter scene of a stag brought down by a pack of hounds, watched by the master of the hunt and a single follower, immediately caught my eye; not only that – it fired my imagination. To be fair, *L'hallali du Cerf* (Death of a Stag) won't really do, it's a curate's omelette of a painting. I myself register the vulgarity and sentimental edge, but I can't resist the bravura – and bravado – of a snowscape more than five metres wide and three and a half metres high. But imagine encountering it, as I did, in midsummer light, its snow and grey pink sky dominating one whole wall of the gallery. It put me in mind of the regional grit and innovation of his first paintings, like the sombre *Enterrement à Ornans* (Burial at Ornans) or the breezy cheek of *Bonjour Monsieur Courbet* (Good Day, Mr Courbet). Back in the Somme battle sites, Peter had warmly recommended the town of Ornans in what he called its very special limestone valley.

Meeting this vast canvas for the first time, I could clearly imagine the kind of landscape that would enfold me for the next couple of walking days in Courbet's native Franche-Comté; it would be an altogether necessary deviation from the official Via Francigena.

Monsieur Moisson, dressed in blue working overalls, was waiting for me at Rue Battant. He had done such a job on my boots that in my hands they felt, and even smelt, like new. I heaped praise on him, and asked about his career; he wasn't far off my own age. He had started out as an apprentice in 1964, aged 15, which means he has spent nearly half a century stitching leather and repairing shoes. That's a lot of contented feet.

"I am the oldest and longest serving *cordonnier* in Besançon, and I am proud of that," he said. What a career. My only regret was that I never asked him how he came by such a marvellous name: Mister Harvest.

My next call was the post office where I despatched Chinn's Volume One, packed up with my journals to date and all the used maps, to Gail in Coggeshall. I would be heading into the hills just a fraction lighter.

What does a long-distance walker do on a day off in Besançon? Take to the water. At the Pont de la République, together with a party of young women on an office jolly, I boarded a pleasure boat. From the viewing deck, the slow horseshoe of the River Doubs allowed me to see Besançon from all sides, even from underneath; we completed our loop by way of a tunnel hewn by convict labour under the rocky isthmus that carries the Citadelle. The chatter of my companions, suddenly shrill under the tunnel, added a piquant backdrop to the excursion.

One of the joys of somebody else's city is commemorative plaques, and on a house on my way back to the hotel I found a beauty. Here in 1839 was born Comte Hilaire de Chardonnet, the inventor of artificial silk. He found a successful process for turning mulberry leaves, the food of silkworms, into liquid cellulose.

My scenic tour over, I resumed that parallel journey through France's former colonies and overseas possessions, surrendering myself to a deep massage by a girl with a mother from Madagascar and father from the Indian Ocean dependency of La Réunion. I thought it would be impossible to find anything as exotic in the heart of Besançon. Boots repaired, limbs rested, clothes stitched and laundered, bones and joints cunningly detached and reassembled, I was as ready as I ever would be for the climbs ahead.

Paul Chinn's Lightfoot guide proposes a four-day journey to Switzerland, but I reckoned I could do it in three; in any case, my heart was set on seeing Ornans, Courbet's home town, and the surrounding gorges, the scene of so much of his painting, and that special valley Peter had promised me, even if it meant once again veering off a little from the Via Francigena.

Besançon's Porte de Rivotte leads onto the river next to a marvel of architectural intricacy, a stone *palais* of the early Renassaisance, and here soon after dawn on June 26th and with a symbolic wave to Rue Battant, my walk resumed. I kept alongside the Doubs before turning up the hill to the Citadelle, perched above the city and allowing me to count most of the landmarks and features of my route in two days previously. I was soon above that too, looking down on the star-shape of Vauban's bastions and on Besançon's modern suburbs, colonising the distant slopes beyond the old town. My days of walking on the flat were over; each day now would entail a stiff climb, and sometimes several demanding ascents and descents. Later on today, I would go over 500 metres for the first time.

Climbing through woods towards the Chapelle de Buis, I emerged at the summit, telling myself that it was for sights like this that I had embarked on my walk to Rome; a thought keenly shared with Hilaire Belloc:

> My pilgrimage is to Rome, my business is with lonely places, hills, and the recollection of the spirit.

It was still early. Sweet organ music and chant drifted through the chapel walls; I entered by the side door, the clank of the handle giving me away. White-robed Franciscan friars ringed a simple central altar, the morning sunlight filtering through the blue glass eastern window giving them a translucent, almost spirit-like appearance. No one looked up. One smile, one gesture, and I would have stayed. But the pilgrim felt like an intruder; I was on my way.

Though this part of my itinerary was still on the Via Francigena, and its waymarks had seen me to the top of the hill, they now gave out as I walked along the ridge towards the World War II memorial. This was to be a recurring problem all the way to Rome – now you see them, now you don't. Keeping track of my route was often more a problem than walking it. From the wood's edge I guessed where to aim, and taking a series of tracks which seemed to be descending towards the south I came out, disconcertingly, above a huge construction site – a new bypass for Besançon, not even a dotted line on any of my maps – but at last I found the lane which led to La Vèze aerodrome.

Following the virtually straight and almost deserted D67 to Ornans for most of a wonderful summer Saturday I had the French countryside to myself. It was noticeably hotter; the hay here had already been gathered and rolled up into big round bales. A weekending accountant pushing his garden wheelbarrow along the grass verge outside his house stopped me for a chat, talking as if in a whisper, and the director of the company for which I work in London telephoned to give me some news about a project in India. Otherwise nothing stirred. I was sitting under the shade on a war memorial at Tarcenay drinking water when the call came through. A little later, in the hamlet of Baraquet, I passed the first cows grazing with bells on their necks, a sure sign of upland progress, and a pleasurable token of how simple my life had become over the course of a month. The afternoon, when even the farmers had stopped working, was totally still, and in the heat I felt as if I was merging with the road, airily tip-toeing across a shimmering land in which I had become a transient, ghostly spectre. My steps fell lightly,

I was making good progress and I was content: I had reached my 500 metres without exhaustion or mishap.

The first shadows that wrapped coolly round me were at the end of the day when I dropped down into the *Ravine du Puits Noirs* – the Ravine of Black Wells – the narrow forested gorge of River Brème, flanked by dramatic outcrops of bare limestone cliff. In this valley alone, Gustave Courbet painted no less than 50 scenes. He described the ravine as a landscape of deep solitude. I was grateful to Peter, but I was still a valley away from Ornans: the town is built around the next of these limestone rivers, the Loue.

"You really need to know a country if you want to paint it," Courbet had written. "I know every twist and turn of my country, I paint it." The Courbets had a farm near Ornans. Gustave was very much the country boy; even long after he had moved to Paris and become famous, his heart remained here. In total he painted some 300 scenes in and around his native *terroir*.

An abandoned railway, now a *Voie Verte*, took me into Ornans, so ending a relatively gentle 25-kilometre day. I landed up at a *chambre d'hôte* on the outskirts of town. The hotel in the town centre was full, which was a pity, because of all the places that demand your presence in the middle, Ornans vies with Venice in setting its best buildings and finest views on the water's edge and clustered around the bridges. But never mind: with my pack safely parked, I had the freedom of the place, and there was something rather agreeable about my lodgings.

It didn't matter so much that the museum to the great artist was undergoing a major makeover and was closed: I knew where to find Courbet's tomb up in the town cemetery. He may have raised eyebrows here and in Paris during his lifetime, and he may only have been reinterred 42 years after his death in 1919 in Switzerland; but his townsmen found him a location he would have loved, and surely knew, facing across the valley to a promontory of white cliffs. The tombstone itself is a great wedge of granite with a marble inset inscribed: *G Courbet peintre – Ornans 1819, La Tour de Peilz 1877*. There were fresh flowers.

Courbet had died in exile. A strong republican, he had been prominent in Paris's revolutionary Commune in 1870, following the Second
Empire's defeat by the Prussians; he had overseen the destruction of
Napoleon Bonaparte's triumphal column in Place Vendôme and its
replacement with a bronze monument cast from French and German
guns. He was prosecuted, and sent the bill for wilful damage. Unable
to pay, he took refuge in Switzerland where, within a few years, he
was dead from exhaustion compounded with the effects of the lethal
drink of his own region, absinthe.

If I couldn't get to his museum, I could sup at his table: I had dinner
on a terrace above the river at the *Restaurant Courbet*, sharing a table
with a German couple, inveterate long-distance cyclists, Gerd and Bar-
bara. With a holiday home near Nice, they have made the bike trip
there and back more times than they can count. Gerd runs a successful
business manufacturing dentures, and that wouldn't have furnished a
conversation, but it was his close relationship with Israel, a former
workbase of my own, that really got us going under the Ornans evening
sky. He had been a frequent visitor to Israel and had become a passionate
Zionist; German guilt for the holocaust or his own possible Jewish roots
seemed the reason. When I suggested that the Israelis would one day
have to return land to the Palestinians, Gerd was quick on the draw.

"So the Americans should hand their land back to the Red Indians?"
he asked.

I knew I was on the wrong side; I didn't want to tell him about
the Palestinian families I had met who were rooted in the soil around
Bethlehem at about the time they invented bows and arrows, long
before anyone had a Zionist dream. I steered our conversation back
to cycling.

On Sunday June 27th, after breakfasting with my landlady, who
insisted on brewing me tea with proper tea leaves, I marched out of
Ornans shortly after seven; the town and its château were bathed in
early morning mist. Branching off the Loue into one of its tributaries,
I climbed steadily southwards up the D492 over my first recognisable

pass at 720 metres to the small town of Chantrans, where Courbet's father is buried. Here I found something most unusual for 21st century rural France – a shop that was open. "A double first," I recorded in my diary, noting that it was a Sunday. Having stripped itself bare of almost all its economic life, is the French countryside struggling to rebuild itself, or is this just a one off? As I stocked up with water against the increasing heat, I congratulated the shopkeeper on his enterprise.

"We're doing surprisingly well," he said. "We French still have to eat!"

You could see and hear the work going on all day, too, in the wayside fields; farmers were driving their tractors and machines, turning hay into bales. Otherwise, as the day before, nothing stirred; for much of the time I was a solitary figure on the near-deserted D6 which led me through Sombacour all the way to my night's destination, Pontarlier. I passed an early 18th century round chapel at the entrance to the old town where, as a token that I was back in step with the Via Francigena, suddenly you could no longer avoid the tug of St Peter. The gate I walked through was Porte St Pierre; the place I checked into, opposite, for my pilgrim palliasse, was the *Hôtel St Pierre*.

It was Sunday evening and Pontarlier was shuttered up and asleep. The only place to eat was the *Brasserie de la Poste*. The town seemed to be lost in a collective hang-over. It had, after all, been the capital of absinthe. It was here in 1805 that Henri-Louis Pernod established France's first industrial absinthe distillery, and by the beginning of the 20th century, Pontarlier had 20 distilleries employing 3,000 people – almost half the total population – and there were 111 bars in town – one for every 26 adults.

Undiluted, the spirit (originating in Neuchâtel across the Swiss border, and made with the mountain plant wormwood, aniseed and herbs) has an alcohol content varying from 47 to 74 degrees. From the 1830s it caught on with literary men such as Gérard de Nerval and Gustave Flaubert, and was favoured for the lucid drunkenness it induced, a claim later made for LSD. But it was also attacked as a dangerously addictive hallucinatory and even psychotic drug. Visual artists from Edouard Manet to Henri de Toulouse-Lautrec contributed to the black legend by portraying its devotees or victims as part of their attempts to show modern life in all its aspects. Oscar Wilde in all probability never became a true devotee, but as ever can be relied on for a sound-bite. He felt, he is supposed to have said after drinking absinthe, as if there were tulip flowers on his legs.

In time, country after country would ban absinthe, Switzerland even hard-wiring the ban into its constitution. In 1914, it was outlawed in France, leaving Pernod to modify the mix to produce an anise-flavoured *pastis* which did not contain wormwood. A century later, watered-down absinthe is back on the supermarket shelves in many European countries, but its heyday when consumption spread around the world, and when it was so established that it was served to French soldiers as an anti-malarial medicine, is long over.

On a hot summer's evening in Pontarlier in June 2010 sitting on the terrace overlooking Rue de La République, I made a point of drinking red wine with my supper and celebrated a major milestone – in just over a month I had walked more than 1,000 kilometres from Coggeshall.

On Monday morning, June 28th, I left Pontarlier with Chinn's Light-foot guide in hand; it would be my companion now most of the way to Rome, and, together with the Via Francigena waymarks, I would develop a love-hate relationship with it. Finding the route and sticking to it was never that straight-forward: at best it entailed leafing through several pages of route directions, glasses on, glasses off, then cross-checking with a waymark or by fixing on some prominent feature: at worst, if the waymark was missing or hidden in foliage, I would have to ask a local – not always easy in empty countryside, and by now you know my rule – or guess the way, and hope for the best. There were anxious moments most days.

My way out of Pontarlier was unambiguous, but tough. I was now entering the Jura proper. It was uphill on steep woodland paths, and soon I was above 1,000 metres. Three kilometres on, the climb offered its rewards. The path broke out of the woods, and from the edge of the precipitous cliff over the valley of my old friend the Doubs, the outlines of a castle emerged below me from the early morning mist. The Château de Joux sits on a promontory at the head of a narrow gorge, doing all the things a hilltop castle fortress should do. The upper keep is protected by sheer drops and high turreted walls. The place looks at once romantic and forbidding, and, long after the age of castles, its remoteness made it an ideal repository for prisoners of state. François Toussaint L'Ouverture, a black colonial slave turned heroic father of Haiti, was imprisoned and died here. Toussaint had been an inescapable choice for me when I was asked to write a book on great leaders: a self-educated, brilliant and intuitive military commander, he led the rebellion which would, in 1804, make Haiti the first independent nation of the Caribbean. But he missed the party, though, and was outwitted by Bonaparte, and defeated and captured in 1802. Brought back to France in chains, he was confined here in the Château de Joux where he died the following year of starvation, cold and neglect.

This landscape makes a natural home for strongholds: I came on another, though less grand, as I followed the steep path down to the valley-bottom, and it was nearly my last. The only route here is the N57, busy, narrow and with blind-spots. A four wheel drive BMW took the dust off my trousers overtaking another vehicle from behind me on the offside. I know that if I am to die walking on a road, it's the overtaking car (coming from the rear) – the one that I cannot hear nor look in the eyes – which will deliver the fatal blow.

Thank heaven, that short stretch of *Route Nationale* was my last bit of exposed walking in France. I soon turned off up the D6, and regained the 1,000 metre contour. I was now in the heart of the Jura. Les Fourgs, the highest town in the Doubs, is in its winter plumage a sought-after ski resort; but in high summer, without snow, it looked bare. I celebrated my arrival at the top of the pass with a cooling lemonade at the only bar which was open, and I sat on the bench outside in warm sunshine and gave my feet a ritual application of the magic lotion; even after more than a month on the road they could still grumble.

Hilaire Belloc had a far tougher journey over the Jura, which he described as "somewhat awful, or naked and rocky". The old dog, the route he had drawn with his ruler had taken him into German-speaking Switzerland; so when he entered the range at Porrentruy he found he had five supplementary ridges to traverse. At one stage he was so tired that he hitched a ride on a cart; well, not on it; by hanging on, and letting his feet move passively under him, he avoided breaking, for the time being at least, his vow "to ride upon no wheeled thing".

Belloc undoubtedly made his journey over the Jura more difficult by attempting to stick to his plan to walk to Rome in a straight line. By his own admission, this confronted him with a terrifying crossing of the Doubs Gorge on the sleepers of a railway bridge; and with a vertiginous descent from the Weissenstein to the valley floor to cross the River Aare at Solothurn.

> I was an hour or more going down the enormous face of the Jura, which is here an escarpment, a cliff of great height, and contains but few breaks by which men can pick their way. It was when I was half-way down the mountain side that its vastness most impressed me.

I walked into Switzerland through the deserted customs post at L'Auberson: nobody was there, and my only witnesses were the cows grazing the hill on the Swiss side. My pilgrim's arrival in Switzerland was clearly not a noteworthy event. Apart from a little sign telling me that I was in the Canton of Vaud, the only indication that I had crossed a frontier came a little later on the hill leading up to the town of L'Auberson where I noticed anti-tank concrete defences. Not much has changed since Steve McQueen on his motorbike failed to scramble across the border in the film *The Great Escape*.

Beyond L'Auberson, the road climbed more gently through forests of monotonous pine, before steering its way between the rounded summits of the Jura range. By the time I reached Sainte-Croix, my night's goal, I had topped out at 1,114 metres above sea level. I was early; it had been a short day, just 24 kilometres; that gave me time to be a good citizen. On entering Sainte-Croix I had seen documents scattered along the roadside, and out of curiosity I picked one up. They were the immigration papers of a Lebanese woman; and I wondered what mishap had swept them out of her hand. I gathered up all that I could find, and sought out the local police station. Here at last my presence in Switzerland was duly noted; the policewoman at the reception desk, to whom I handed the stray papers, asked to see my passport!

For my pilgrim stamp, I also called on the town's tourist office where Michel Ruchet, *chef d'office*, greeted me with unbounded enthusiasm. Monsieur Ruchet has high hopes for developing Sainte-Croix's role as a staging post on the way to Rome.

"In a few years time we will have thousands of people walking the Via Francigena," he told me. "It will be just like the way to Compostela."

This was a horrible thought. Had he ever seen the shuffling crocodiles of pilgrims who now clog up the *Camino Francés*?

"How many come through here now on their way to Rome?" I asked.

"About one a day, but there is going to be a boom. You'll see," he said.

I am not so sure. Walking to Santiago has become a sort of secular sport, one of the great adventure walks of the West. My guess is that few people on the *Camino Francés* care much for the Apostle James, and fewer have given much thought to his subsequent role as 'slayer of Moors'; in all likelihood he is probably not buried in Santiago at all. The Compostela story is a fudge of myth and legend. Rome – the engine room of the Catholic Church – is quite another matter, precisely because it is the See of St Peter, and maybe walking to Rome has, on that account, less secular appeal. I put this consideration to Monsieur Ruchet.

"Ah, but you underestimate the sheer beauty and the challenge of what lies ahead," he retorted. "A lot of effort has gone into waymarking the route, and when the word gets about it we will have to start preparing for an invasion. It will become one of the great European cultural walks."

The *Hôtel de France* served a late breakfast. You cannot beat the clock in Switzerland, so I started from Sainte-Croix later than usual – just after eight – and, then, for the first time since leaving Coggeshall, I had to retrace my steps. The hotel keys were lumped in my pocket, and I went back to return them.

I descended into the valley below the Montagne de Baulmes on an ancient path down steep zigzags to the village of Vuitbœuf: for much of the way the track was paved with stone slabs, rutted and scoured over parts by the passage of wheels. I had the footfall of centuries beneath me. Now and again I would catch a glimpse of the country far below, its squared fields and trimmed vineyards laid out on the valley floor like a chess board. I replenished my water from a fountain at Vuitbœuf – the start of a new experience, which made the pilgrim way that much more agreeable. In France today, often the only public tap you will find is in the community cemetery, but in Switzerland, and, as I was to discover, in Italy too, every hamlet and village has fresh running water. Switzerland also has a network of pedestrian ways, and down them, through small villages and across sloping vineyards in gently rolling country, I walked into Orbe getting there just in time to see its extraordinary Roman mosaics: the *piano nobile* of what is said to be the largest Roman villa north of the Alps. Several of the wonderfully preserved mosaic floors depict chariots, but chariots of peace, one of them laden with corn-stocks, and I thought of the ancient rutted road down which I had descended into the valley. In Orbe, Rome was beckoning me on.

Pretty as this little town is, it just wasn't far enough along the way: the tourist office helpfully found me a hotel room in the next town, Chavornay. But Orbe wasn't quite ready to let me go. Walking out through a side street, just below the main square, I saw a South Asian girl, Thai I guessed, sitting in the doorway of a shop, enjoying the hot afternoon sun. I looked up above her head – the shop sign said: Massage. Of course, it is well known that you cannot go ten paces in Thailand without being offered a massage. The beaches ring out with that strident and elongated nasal Thai pronunciation of the word – *Maasssaaage*! Female caddies offer you a massage at the end of a game of golf. What goes on in Thai massage parlours is not a subject for this book. But here I was in Orbe, a small landlocked community in Protestant Switzerland at the foot of the mighty Jura. The girl smiled at me, and I stopped.

"Do you do feet?" I asked her.

She looked puzzled. I pointed to my boots. Ah, she understood. Within a few minutes, I was comfortably seated in her salon; my feet dipped in soft warm water, washed first and dried, and then rubbed tenderly with aromatic cream. I fell fast asleep, and that would have been the moment for her brothers to steal my rucksack and make off with my money and passport. But this was Switzerland, and I woke refreshed and renewed with nothing missing. It was a well spent 30 Swiss francs, and in high spirits I hit the road for Chavornay.

I was soon aware of another pungent scent – a chocolate-like flavour in the air. I was passing a giant Nestlé plant which advertised itself with the purposeful title of Product Technology Centre.

Chavornay was nowhere near as beguiling as Orbe, but it was 32 kilometres from Sainte-Croix: a decent day's hike. Besides, it threw up the day's second unexpected Oriental delight – the *Rangoli,* an Indian-run hotel, where under the watchful gaze of nine golden elephants I dined on *Curry al Gambas* and began the last day of June with a breakfast of yoghurt and raisins.

In writing up his ideal pilgrim's approach to Lausanne for the Lightfoot Guide, Paul Chinn set himself an unenviable task. This leg of the Via Francigena cost him four tightly-packed pages of instructions and warnings. He was up against the arterial motor routes converging on the city, and he did well in his choice of forest path and farm tracks, bringing the pilgrim safely into Lausanne through a succession of rewarding villages and hamlets, and past some of those not quite rural surprises that presage a major city. My diary records two such: a zoo, and a golf course – in Switzerland? Good heavens.

But there came a moment when pavement appeared. Whatever Chinn had in store, I abandoned him and plunged down the main road towards the city centre, led on by the spires of the cathedral. It probably gained me half an hour; in any case I was in Lausanne just after two o'clock; it left me time to explore the city, stamp the pilgrim passport, and draw breath before the Alps that I must soon cross, and which on this hot, clear afternoon were already visible above the far reaches of the lake.

NINE
ALPS

FROM THE TERRACE AT THE WEST FRONT OF Lausanne's Cathedral of Notre-Dame, above the covered steps leading down to Place de la Palud, there is an expansive view across Lac Léman to the Alps which I would shortly have to cross. At a distance of 60 kilometres, their high mountain passes shimmered in the afternoon haze – it was after all mid-summer. But turning aside from their visceral pull on me, and exchanging the hot dome of the sky for the cathedral's airy gothic interior, I made my way to the sacristy where I spread out my pilgrim passport for stamping.

"Santiago or Rome?" asked the young woman on the desk, as if checking me in for a flight.

"Both." I replied somewhat clumsily; I meant to say that I had been to the one and was on my way to the other.

Outside once again, I stopped two women by the south portal and asked if they would take my photograph, explaining that I had walked here from London. Being Swiss, they were not overly impressed but they still took an interest in my journey and we engaged in a conversation about the city and the nearby *Musée Historique* where they worked. Should I visit it, or perhaps the *Musée des Beaux Arts*? Neither, they replied in unison, there is only one must-see museum in Lausanne – *La Collection de l'Art Brut*. Mystified, I asked for a definition.

"It's hard to explain, but you will find out as soon as you get there."

I owe these two middle-aged photographers a great debt. I will admit, however, that at first ignoring their advice, I set off down the steps and narrow cobbled streets to Place de la Riponne, intent on visiting the *Beaux Arts* in its palatial home, but it was closed for renovation, so I decided to give *La Collection de l'Art Brut* a try after all. It is housed in a modern building on the Avenue des Bergières, only a short step away.

It turns out to be a collection uniquely devoted to 'outsider art', the output of ordinary people with no artistic training, and often loners, marginalised people, psychotics or the criminally insane, who were suddenly spurred to make their own art, often in middle or old age. What results is an art free of any conceptions of formal artistic rules or conventions, which challenges both our view of 'outsiders', and our expectations of what art should be about.

The collection was made over a lifetime by the celebrated and subversive painter Jean Dubuffet. He gave it to Lausanne in 1971, though he kept adding to it, and it was inaugurated as a museum five years later. Dubuffet, himself, coined the title *Art Brut* and he had this to say about what drew all the pieces together:

"Art does not come to lie down in the beds that have been made for it. It runs away as soon as anyone utters its name: it likes being incognito. Its best moments are when it forgets what it's called.

"One is witnessing the completely pure, raw artistic operation, reinvented in the entirety of all its phases by its creator, acting solely on his own impulses."

Even though the mini-biographies accompanying each artist's pieces, paintings, drawing, sculptures or strange objects, often have a heart-rending or disturbing story, I felt oddly at home, at ease, here surrounded by the output of deranged souls. Maybe it was because, in walking to Rome, I had opted out of everyone else's – and my own customary – space, and was thus out on a limb, enwrapped in my own perhaps mad project, that I could feel so attuned to the worlds of these strangers. In any case, my hour at *La Collection de l'Art Brut* was the high point of Lausanne, if not of my whole journey through Switzerland.

The rest of the day was downhill. A damsel from Geneva made a spirited attempt to dig deep into my taut muscles. Peter would not have chosen this establishment – far too upmarket – but Rue des Alpes seemed the appropriate address to prepare for my ascent of the Col du Grand St Bernard.

"Your legs are as tough as dried meat," she said.

"That's why I'm here," I moaned.

I had dinner on a terrace restaurant – my favourite *penne all'arrabiata*, which from here on became my staple; the garlic thinned my blood and the pasta was fuel for the next day's march. I was sitting all too near an Australian woman who told her companion that she was large because she was starved as a child. I caught her peeking as, to complement my pasta, I ordered a chocolate mousse: a look of pure jealousy. I was losing weight fast; in fact I had reached the point when I could eat and drink pretty much anything I wanted. It just burnt off.

The first day of July dawned with an irritation which developed into an altercation. I came down to breakfast in my hotel, the *Fassbind City* by the bridge on Rue Caroline, and I was instantly assailed by the waitress demanding my room number. A lot of hotels do that, but I prefer it when they first ask if you want tea or coffee, and this was after all a smart central hotel where they should know how to treat guests, even pilgrims dressed in walking gear. A small thing, I know; but for the second time in a few hours the spirit of Peter flew to my side when, having helped myself to a continental breakfast, cereal and bread, I was handed a bill for a full breakfast. I argued the toss. My small success probably made scarcely a dent in the outrageous 215 Swiss francs I was charged for staying, but the principle mattered.

Later, at the Post Office in Place de la Riponne, a clerk demanded to see my passport before he felt he could authorise the parcel I was trying to send home.

"What is in this package?" he asked.

"Maps," I replied.

He looked earnestly. "What would you be doing sending maps

through the mail?"

"Because I don't need them anymore," I insisted.

My good humour with Lausanne was restored by the lovely Calabrian seamstress at the *Blanchisserie* on the other side the square. She was so impressed that I was walking all the way to her country – well, almost – that she insisted on darning my socks for free.

As for the rest of the day, one brief entry in my diary: "Oh that all pilgrim days could be thus." I lay in the sunshine on the deck of *La Suisse*, an elegant steamer built in 1910, its slender elongated hull propelled by its original pistons and paddles, and glided across Lac Léman to Villeneuve. So often during my Reuters years, and on summer and winter trips to the Alps, I had careered along the shores of the lake by train and car, often glancing at its inviting waters and wondering what was out there. I now had the opportunity to find out; crossing the lake, rather than walking around it, was in the rules. Sigeric had made his journey this way, so for once I put myself under the wings of the Archbishop. I walked from the city centre alongside the rack line metro that descends the lower slopes of Mont Jorat to the lakeshore at Ouchy, and got there in time to laze in hot sunshine at the water's edge before my two o'clock ferry arrived.

The boat was virtually empty; just a few upper deck passengers taking lunch in the dining room. I found a comfortable bench seat near the bow and removed boots and socks and lay with my head propped on my rucksack. The drowsy heat brought back the notes of Claude Debussy's *Prélude à l'après-midi d'un Faune* – the flutes, oboes, bassoons and horns of the music rhyming in my head with the throb of the engines and the gentle wash at the bows. With the occasional polite · blast of the ship's one-note horn we meandered in and out of lakeside ports, but by the middle of the lake the shores had disappeared into the haze and I was fast asleep.

Thanks to his 'beeline' approach to the pilgrimage, which took him to my east, Hilaire Belloc had a more challenging experience by another Swiss lake, the *Brienzersee*. His straight line had set him on a perilous scrambled descent to the lake from the tops of the *Brienzer Grat* in which he nearly came to grief in a thick mountain mist.

> I suppose the general slope, down, down, to where the green began was not sixty degrees, but have you ever tried looking down five thousand feet at sixty degrees? It drags the mind after it, and I could not bear to begin the descent.

After this gentle 25-kilometre cruise, it was a shock to step ashore at Villeneuve and saddle up, ready to resume my march; I had quickly adjusted to travel on lake steamers, a luxury Belloc was denied. When he had finally descended to the shore of the far smaller *Brienzersee*, he walked around it.

Villeneuve had an Alpine feel about it, its narrow medieval streets with shuttered windows and sloping slate roofs looking inwards, away from the lakeside quays towards the Rhône Valley up which I would shortly be walking. I checked into the *Hôtel du Soleil* on the Grand Rue, and went down to the lakeside to dine on spiced pasta and local white wine at the *Gondola di Venezia*. Already there was a palpably southern tinge to the evening and to the landscape.

I set off early on Friday July 2nd, Gail's and my 33rd wedding anniversary, and I was soon swapping the gentle lapping of lake water for the roar of the River Rhône, and for the first time I had in my sights, not hills, but serious mountains. The jagged peaks of the Dents du Midi were still speckled in snow. Early in the day a smartly kitted rider came cantering by, and he reined in his grey to ask where I was walking.

"I am so curious. I ride along here most days and I sometimes pass people like you and often wonder where they are all going."

When I told him that I was on my way to Rome, he expressed mild surprise.

"Ah, so you are not tramps." And he resumed his morning canter.

I was walking against the flood of the river; it flowed rapidly and was a powerful sight, but more ugly than welcoming. The churned water was stony grey; I had left behind me the translucent and reflective surfaces of lake and canal. Now and then the banks were usurped by unsightly industrial complexes, causing me at one point to make an awkward and time-consuming diversion; but after St Maurice, with its ancient covered bridge over the Rhône, the valley opened up with terraces of sun-drenched vineyards replacing the bleak verticals of factory chimneys. It had been a tough day, more than 40 kilometres from the lakeside at Villeneuve to Martigny, and at the *Hôtel de la Poste* I collapsed into a shower at five thirty, far later than I intended. It is hard these days to find a hotel with a bath, and so by now I had worked out a substitute, and perfected the art of sitting, or rather lying in the shower basin with my head against one wall and legs stretched upwards against the other. The posture is a little gesture of anarchy, and I like to feel that bathing in this contorted shape required the same agility as 'doing it' on the backseat of a Fiat 500. The soothing effects of being showered from all the wrong angles were not dissimilar.

I arrived in Martigny too late to see its Roman treasures; the amphitheatre would have to wait. Instead, I enjoyed another outrageously expensive Swiss meal of pasta with anchovies, olives and garlic sitting on a covered terrace in the Place Centrale as the town was engulfed in monsoon rain and tornado-strength winds. Seat cushions, menus, even chairs were swept into the air, and for a few minutes the square was a kaleidoscope of flying objects. It wasn't reassuring: watching this violent break in the hot weather from the comfort of a sheltered terrace was one thing; the thought that I would soon be on a high mountain pass crossing the Alps was quite another.

I would love to have had Gail with me, but she doesn't do hills, let alone mountains. I had done my best to persuade several doughty walkers from among my friends to join me over the Alps, but none had taken the bait. I was now a day's march away, and all too aware that I would have to tackle those high mountain passes on my own.

Leaving Martigny on Saturday, I swapped the Rhône Valley for that of the Dranse, following it up to Sembrancher. It should have been a straight-forward day, of some 20 kilometres, rising steadily from 475 metres to just below 900. But I struggled most of the way, and my confidences as a navigator were put to the test. Paul Chinn's guide threw up its fair share of surprises; soon after joining the mountain trail it advised about crossing a railway line, but then failed to point out that the way re-crosses the same line a little later! This led me off-track for some distance. In addition, the diamond-shaped waymarks had tricks to play, disappearing at intervals and at other times only being visible from the uphill side. Sections of the path climb steeply up the side of the valley on narrow exposed ledges, with a chain on the inner side and a sharp drop on the other. Although below 1,000 metres – the height at which the terraces of vines give out – I could sense the approach of high mountains. The path started to track up an old moraine – the rocky remnant of the tongue of a glacier which would once have snaked down as far as the Rhône Valley. Oh, if only I could have shown that to a prophet or two of global warming! This is one glacier that retreated long before we had even heard of man-made CO_2, and the evidence could teach them to reflect on the far more tangible powers of nature.

After Sembrancher I followed the left-hand side of the valley along roads and forest paths into Orsières, a pretty stone village huddled in the crook of two valleys. I asked two elderly gentlemen standing against the churchyard wall for directions to the *Hôtel Terminus;* that was where I had booked for the night. No such place, they told me. The hotel didn't exist. So I ended up by mistake in the *Hôtel de l'Union.*

The hotel was out of shampoo, but that was my only complaint. Monsieur Facture, the *patron*, was friendly and helpful in a way that I really appreciated. He advised me to climb to the Grand St Bernard in two stages, stopping for the night at Bourg St Pierre.

"Two Dutch women left here the other day trying to reach the col in a single day, and they got themselves lost and didn't arrive till after midnight. They were half dead."

Spreading out my map and pointing his finger with obvious knowledge, he told just where I should take extra care; his best bit of advice was the simplest to retain and follow: stick close to the mountain river. I absorbed this with due attention, rolling it round in my mind to make it mesh with my determination to be over the pass in a day.

I just succeeded in getting my foot inside the door of the village food store before it closed so that I could buy bread and chocolate for the climb, and then returned to the *Union* for an early meal. The bar was in uproar; a group of German cyclists were following their country's 4-0 win over Argentina in the World Cup. Fuelled with home-made mushroom tart, linguine and apricot pie, I retired to bed early with Monsieur Facture promising to leave some breakfast, and my flask filled with freshly boiled water, outside my room so that I could get off at dawn. Sleep came fitfully: I had visions of joining those Dutch ladies on some stray mountain track.

I was on my way by 6.30 a.m. It was July 4th, and a bright sunny day – not a cloud – and needless to say, the first thing I saw as I struck out up the hill was the *Hôtel Terminus*; it was situated at the top end of the town, and so it did exist after all. I marvelled once again at the lack of knowledge of locals, and then asked myself: terminus to what? It was a stiff, steady climb, but none of my fears proved justified; the only casualty of the day was my last silk handkerchief. Silk is light and doesn't jam up the pocket, but it is slithery and must have slipped out as I reached for my compass. That was a check I made frequently as I switched from mountain track to the narrow forest paths that would serve me for the duration of the morning, never far from the roar of the mountain river, and for once following a series of consistent way-marks which showed up just when they were most needed. But it was solitary work. I didn't encounter a soul until I passed the large reservoir on the approach to the col itself.

Here the path threads past a lonely stone house. At first sight it could have been an abandoned shepherd's hut. But a Swiss flag fluttered by the doorway and the chimney had smoke rising from it. I peered behind the door; inside stood a man brewing up on a camping gaz stove. He invited me in; the interior was set up like a snug winter cabin, with a raised sleeping platform over what must have once been a byre for animals. There was a log fire in the stone hearth next to the stove. I turned down his offer of coffee but asked if I could replenish my flask with water. He filled it from the tap whose tank is fed by the nearby stream; what could be simpler? Having walked for several hours through deserted forest paths, it was strange to come across this mountain retreat, this little domestic oasis.

"Isn't it weird to be living on top of a mountain path?" I asked its contented looking proprietor.

"Not many people pass this way," he said, "and if I don't like the look of them I discreetly close the door."

Above the reservoir the upper valley opened out, with on the one side a spectacular view of the road far below snaking in and out of its avalanche tunnels, and on the other a panorama of summer pastures on the high valley slopes; ahead were the snowy flanks of the col. High above, my waymarked path would merge with the mountain road, before crossing to the opposite side of the valley. At the point where they met I had another welcome encounter – a Frenchman from Quimper, picnicking with his wife. He had taken part in the previous day's 110 kilometre Alpine ultra marathon – an annual long-distance mountain run that might even challenge the Gurkhas – but more than half the competitors in this year's event, including the sturdy Breton, had given up because of the extreme heat. They offered me a bottle of chilled *San Pellegrino* mineral water from their picnic cooler – the brand was fitting – and took my photograph. It shows me leaning, strained and tired, into the camera. But I was content; I had heeded Monsieur Facture's instructions and would get to the col on schedule.

The final few hundred metres to the col, often the hardest, were snowbound; I could have usefully employed crampons to negotiate the compacted ice, instead of having to scrabble my way up the rock and loose scree on the edge of the snow-filled gullies. As the ground levelled out the path broadened, revealing the old paved Roman road, ancient and well trodden stones; they brought my halting paces into step with the footfall of centuries. At last, the grey outlines of the *Hospice du Grand St Bernard* loomed out of the thin mountain fog which by early afternoon had enveloped the col. In the swirling mist, when I got there, the only glimmers of colour were from the parked tourist buses.

Just below the hospice, a group of young Swiss girls were exercising their giant St Bernard dogs, their sturdy charges tugging energetically from their harness leads – a friendly welcome, it seemed. The famous dogs are still kept here, now under a franchise. The Hospice has provided shelter and hospitality to travellers and pilgrims for almost ten centuries, but the canons and brothers who run it today have given up looking after these huge creatures, partly because there are not enough of them to do the work, and partly because the dogs – in one story a cross between Pyrenean sheepdog and Newfoundland, in another originating in Syria – are no longer used for mountain rescue. They traditionally carried a cask of brandy round their necks – probably of more use to the rescuers than to the stranded travellers – and they have been superseded by technology. Heat seeking sensors and echo sounding equipment are far more effective in winkling out travellers trapped in snow, and don't need feeding. Cleverly, though, the brothers decided to keep their dogs for breeding, and for the tourists. Since 2005, they have been looked after and bred by a charitable organisation, *La Fondation Barry,* named after a heroic Saint Bernard who saved many lives during the first decade of the 19th century. They would be greatly missed if no longer here; brought in to save travellers, they remain to prolong the Hospice's existence and work.

It wasn't my first time at the Hospice. Years before I had arrived in mid-winter when the col is utterly cut off by road from the valleys. I had skied up on skins. This time, I felt more authentic, certainly more like a pilgrim to Rome. I had arrived at the 2,477 metre pass on foot. It had taken me just under eight hours to make it up from Orsières. I was 1,162 kilometres and 39 days from Coggeshall and I was over the Alps. I was elated.

Before climbing the outside stairway to enter the Hospice, I joined a knot of cyclists who were preparing to descend the col. On two wheels they would be back down in the Rhône Valley in just three hours, compared to the two days it had taken me to haul myself up on foot. Among them was a young Englishman working in Switzerland for a multinational company. Impressed that I had walked all the way from England, he willingly stopped his preparations to take another photo of me standing on the col.

"Well, at least it will be downhill from here," he said.

"Yes," I agreed, little knowing, or little thinking about what lay ahead. For the moment I was just content that I had reached the high point of my journey; the hills of Italy could wait.

Saint Bernard of Menthon founded his order here in 1049, setting up a safe haven for weary travellers. After nearly 1,000 years, this ministry remains the Hospice's remit, though over the last hundred years the self-sufficiency of the men and women who run it has diminished – just four when I was there, three brothers and a sister, aided by summer volunteers. And of course its guest list has entirely changed: fewer pilgrims, merchants and invading armies, thousands more leisure visitors, including the highly vocal group of students from Germany that I coincided with. They were accommodated in one of the dormitories, which mercifully I didn't have to share. The guest-master, Brother Frédéric, sensitively booked me into one of the Hospice's individual rooms, on the upper floor next to the glazed doors to the monastic quarters, spacious, with shuttered windows onto the bustling tourist shops below. It had two wooden beds implausibly covered in bright yellow duvets, and a small table and chair, and that was it. For the showers, it was like being back at school; you had to walk the length of the corridors on cold flagstones. As a walking pilgrim I was invited to dine with the volunteers: they included a thoughtful young Vietnamese theology student who was thinking of taking holy orders. What had brought him all the way from Southeast Asia to this Alpine pass, one of Europe's highest inhabited spots, and cut off from the outside world for six months a year?

"When I know that," he answered, "it will be time to return home."

I dined at one end of the table, generally shunned by the volunteers who had been together since early June, and who, perhaps without meaning to, made me feel somewhat unwelcome; they all but ignored me. I, the pilgrim, once more felt like an intruder.

But, then, apart from the white-robed canons and brothers, perhaps everyone is an intruder here. The guidebook catalogues a long line of kings and generals who have passed through – Hannibal, Caesar and Charlemagne – but it's Napoleon who has captured the brand. The plaque at the top of the col, recording his crossing in May 1800 at the head of an army of 46,000 is crowned with an outsize replica of the tricorne hat he wore, as in Jacques Louis David's commemorative painting. One of his generals, Desaix, who would fall in that Italian campaign, is buried here in the ornate upper chapel. From the start, spin attended Napoleon and his expedition. He was First Consul at the time, and he rode through the col modestly and sensibly on a leading-rein, seated on a mule. David's painting is fully imperial, and has him rising from the saddle on a prancing white charger. But, more seriously, he was a cheat – both to the 40 men that he stationed here for months without any funds, and to the Hospice, which he never paid. It took a much later French President, François Mitterrand, to discharge Napoleon's debts. It must be the cheapest war reparations ever. Mitterrand paid the local commune one single, symbolic franc.

For me, the best part of the Hospice is below ground, the vaulted and whitewashed lower chapel, hewn out of living rock. Here the brothers assemble to pray at regular intervals day and night. Its eastern apse is furnished simply, a stone altar and cross flanked by niches, one for St Bernard, and one for the Virgin. I sat through evening Office, lulled into prayerful trance by a rhythmic, slightly watery tick-tock sound; and there it was again accompanying the morning's devotions. What was it, I asked one of the brothers after the service; had they installed some sort of water instrument or fountain to accompany their prayers?

"Good heavens, no," he said. "It's the ice melting and dripping through the rock surrounding us. It's our summer delight: in winter it all freezes over and we don't hear it."

In my long walk to Rome this unelaborated, chaste space was the one church, apart from Evensong at St Paul's, where I attended a service, in contrast to Hilaire Belloc, who punctuated his journey with regular attendances at Mass. As an imperturbable High Catholic, he revelled in both the Church's innate arrogance and in the ornateness of its ritual. Indeed, *The Path to Rome* reads not so much as a journey of discovery, as a triumphal procession. More than that – I am thinking of his description of parishioners flocking to Mass in the village of Undervelier in the Jura – Belloc saw the Catholic Church as the lifeblood of European civilisation.

> My whole mind was taken up and transfigured by this collective act, and I saw for a moment the Catholic Church quite plain, and I remembered Europe, and the centuries.

Belloc met both God and his match in the Alps. He was in awe of mountains and also afraid of them. When he first viewed the Alps from the distant Jura, he became ecstatic, and he underwent a deeply religious experience.

> Here were these magnificent creatures of God, I mean the Alps, which now for the first time I saw from the height of the Jura ...

> These, the great Alps, seen thus, link one in some way to one's immortality ... Let me put it thus: that from the height of the Weissenstein I saw, as it were, my religion. I mean humility, the fear of death, the terror of height and distance, the glory of God, the infinite potentiality of reception whence springs that divine thirst of the soul; my aspiration also towards completion, and my confidence in the dual destiny. For I know that we laughers have a gross cousinship with the most high, and it is this contrast and perpetual quarrel which feeds a spring of merriment in the soul of a sane man.

Since I could not see such wonder and it could work such things in my mind, therefore some day I should be part of it. That is what I felt.

This is also what leads some men to climb mountain-tops, but not for me, for I am afraid of slipping down.

Bent on walking to Rome in a straight line, Hilaire Belloc first attempted to cross the Alps by way of the Gries Pass, between the Swiss Valais and Formazza in Italy. He hired a guide and together they neared the summit of the col, 2,469 metres above the sea, in a raging blizzard which forced them to turn back not 300 metres short of the Italian border. His description of the attempted ascent and the no less dangerous descent is powerful and authentic.

The surface snow was whirring furiously like dust before it: past our faces and against them drove the snow-flakes, cutting the air: not falling, but making straight darts and streaks. They seemed like the form of the whistling wind; they blinded us ... the guide shouted to me that nothing further could be done.

This was a major setback, and Belloc was forced to take the more roundabout, and, to him, desperately commonplace Furka and Gothard Passes, further to the east – a deviation from his straight line which cost him precious time, and which he regarded as a bitter defeat.

Indeed it is a bitter thing to have to give up one's sword ... My heart was like a dully-heated mass of coal or iron because I was acknowledging defeat. You who have never taken a straight line and held it, nor seen strange men and remote places, you do not know what it is to have to go round by the common way.

TEN
VAL D'AOSTA

BECAUSE OF THE BROTHERS' MORNING OFFICE AND MASS, breakfast was not served until eight o'clock, and so on July 5th I left the Hospice later than I had intended. But I still had the crisp early morning to myself when I stepped outside into the full grandeur of the Alps, an amphitheatre of high peaks dominated by the Grand Golliaz. The road descends gently from the Hospice in its col, curling round a lake towards the Italian frontier, where the granite walls of Mt Fouchon and the Pain de Sucre seemed to be ablaze with the sun's eastern light. The border post was deserted, and I walked unchallenged into Italy, little imagining how Italian state bureaucracy would duly make up for this omission, and that showing my passport at hotel reception desks would become a nightly and torturous ritual all the way to Rome itself. Hilaire Belloc had made a similarly uneventful passage into Italy at Chiasso, and he, also, clearly had little respect for frontiers.

> I crossed the frontier, which is here an imaginary line. Two slovenly customs-house men asked me if I had anything dutiable on me. I said No, and it was evident enough, for in my little sack or pocket was nothing but a piece of bread. If they had applied the American test, and searched me for money, then indeed they could have turned me back, and I should have been forced to go into the fields a quarter of a mile or so and come into their country by a path instead of a highroad. This necessity was spared me.

The Val d'Aosta has good claims to be the prettiest corner of the European Alps. Ringed by a majestic arc of south-facing granite and gneiss walls, crowned with jagged, snow-covered peaks, this great natural bowl is a richly layered country of meadow, forest, and vineyard, with its own micro-climate and particular atmosphere – pleasantly hot in summer, cool and dry in winter. The path from the col scrolls down from the sparse, rocky landscape of the high Alps into green upland pastures and flowering hedgerows, and through a succession of hamlets and villages, at first just single streets of stone and timber houses with big overhanging slate roofs, until at last it enters the tree line.

Mountain streams cascade down the slopes from the glaciers, eventually forming their own river and then also feeding the many man-made irrigation channels, or *ruas*; one bordered the first woodland path I came to. These channels were conscientiously cut six centuries ago to bring water to the fields and vineyards, and they give off the same freshwater scent and sun-dappled sparkle as a stream in a desert oasis. One stretch was so inviting that I found a little bank where the sun filtered through the canopy of pine branches and I sat there for a while bathing my feet: just as I had them both dunked in my *rua*, washed and cooled in its flow, along came a mountain jogger. I remembered his disdainful glance as he ran past: call yourself a pilgrim? What a wimp!

The Via Francigena waymarks are perfectly placed throughout the descent – the image of the cowled pilgrim with staff and satchel, paid occasional lip service to north of the Alps, is here even cast in metal on the street lights in the pretty little village of Saint-Rhémy-En-Bosses. The Val d'Aosta is a self-governing region of Italy, which takes pride in itself and its unique environment and culture – French remains widely spoken – and it does things well.

It was a long descent and it wasn't until early afternoon that the valley floor could be fully distinguished in the distance, with the city of Aosta spread below me, forming a narrow linear sprawl with the *campanili* of the medieval Cathedral of Santa Maria and collegiate church of San Orso rising over the city centre. Several dusty hours later

I entered the main square and made my way to the tourist office. The appropriate choice would be the *Hotel Roma*, three stars, but it was full, and so I settled for the four-star *Hotel Europe* – a decision I didn't ultimately regret. A fine modern building, with a handsome mansard roof, it was just off the Piazza Chanoux: bang in the centre, precisely where I like to be in big towns and cities.

But I got off to a bad start with the young girl at reception; or rather, she did with me. Sweat-streaked and grimy, with a bulky rucksack and dressed in heavy walking boots, I cannot have had quite the cut of the hotel's normal clientele. As I approached, she asked to see my passport; it was like being challenged to draw in a Spaghetti Western.

"It's right at the bottom of my rucksack," I explained. "I keep it there when I am walking. Do you mind if I bring it down once I have unpacked and sorted myself out?"

"No, it is law that we see it first *before* you go up to your room!" she insisted.

I gave in and dug deep for the document which I stored in a plastic folder tucked into the bag's inner pocket, and as I handed it to her an old tale came back to haunt me. It was a tale from Aosta, and a tale about passports – the national kind, not the pilgrim.

Gail and I stayed here in the summer of 1971. I had just left Oxford and was due to join Reuters in September; Gail still had another year before taking her degree. We were hitch-hiking to Sicily and had just spent a few days walking in the Alps above Chamonix – the experience which put her off hills for life. Aosta was a staging post on the way to Rome. Hitching was all the rage in the 1960s – everybody did it. There were no cheap flights, and railways were expensive; besides, cadging rides from the sides of Europe's then tranquil roads was an adventure, almost a game in which you sometimes got lucky. Gail and I did in Aosta: we managed to pick up a lift in a red Maserati outside the city walls that took us all the way to Rome. This was the hitch-hiker's dream, a journey of 1,000 kilometres which normally would have taken several days and relays of lifts. Our driver dropped us within a whisker of Rome's *Stazione Termini* just under eight hours later.

"I think we can celebrate that amazing hop with a grand plate of pasta," I said to Gail. "I'll go and change some money."

Nothing has changed in Italy and then, as now, passports are required for just about any transaction. This hangover from Benito Mussolini's Fascist paradise intrudes into virtually every area of daily life. You cannot, for example, access the internet at an internet café today without proof of who you are. On that evening in Rome, 40 years ago, we needed to show our passports to cash our travellers' cheques; of course, we didn't have them. They were still in the hotel in Aosta where we had stayed the previous night. Oh yes: the *Hotel Monte Bianco*. We took an overnight train back to Aosta to recover the mislaid documents and never did get to Sicily; well, not that summer; in fact we ended up in Ireland. It was a lesson about passports neither of us ever forgot.

I hovered over the receptionist while she laboriously transferred the details – passport number, date of birth, country of origin, home address – before returning the precious document to me. I would judge each subsequent night's lodging on how gracefully it handled this irritating procedure. My hackles would immediately rise, on entering the lobby, if reception's first words, almost without looking up, were: "*Mi lascia il suo documento per piacere.*" It meant that they hadn't thought that, after walking 30 or more kilometres, often under a blazing hot sun, it might be quite a process to un-harness my rucksack and rummage for it.

Pragmatic and sympathetic receptionists, and occasionally the proprietors themselves, would give me a break, saying that they would be happy to let me bring my passport in due course. The really sensible ones – just occasionally – were anarchists like me, and they did not ask for passport details at all. In any case, at each hotel, whenever I was asked to sign the supporting scrap of paper which was supposed to be delivered to or picked up by the local police, I would invariably scrawl in the signature box: Mickey Mouse. It was my way of dealing with mindless Italian bureaucracy.

In Aosta, state passport attended to and free of my boots and bag, I strolled into the cathedral to get my pilgrim passport stamped, and settled, in the warmth of the setting sun, in a terrace café on the Piazza Chanoux to admire the chain of snow-tinged mountains above the city. That's where I've come from today, I told the cold beer in my hand. Then I lowered my eyes to scan the other end of the square, and there to my amazement were the sculpted head and shoulders of an old friend from my years as a correspondent in Rome, Giorgio Forattini – or, to be more precise, Forattini's upper half, big nose and flowing hair. His hands, drawing a bow with pointed pencil for arrow, and his trunk emerged from the front shoulders of a horse, and the horse stood on a plinth. Forattini as an armed centaur: he is a brilliant cartoonist whose remit is to mock Italian politicians and anyone else he thinks needs bringing down a peg or two.

I interviewed Forattini in Rome in 1979 and wrote a story about his work. I still have the original of a cartoon, apposite then, and unpublishable these days, of Ayatollah Khomeini, the Iranian religious leader who toppled the Shah, cutting off his own head: the ultimate act of fundamentalism. There is no caption: Forattini's best work doesn't need words. So what was he doing as a centaur in the Piazza Chanoux? Advertising a major retrospective of forty years of his barbs at the Castello de Ussel in Châtillon. I might just pop in: Châtillon was on my way. My centaur was setting a pattern. This wasn't the last time that the middle-aged pilgrim would find his path intersected by shadows of his earlier existence in Italy.

It was time for dinner: I wanted my first meal back in Italy to be special, otherwise why walk all that way! I settled for the *Brasserie du Commerce*, and installed myself in the inner courtyard where, even after nightfall, it was still baking hot; I didn't know it, but Italy was steeling itself for a mid-summer heat wave. I soaked up a carafe of local red, and devoured a plate of pasta and garlic, and in the lull before ordering my dessert I found myself falling asleep. I took urgent stock. Dropping 1,800 metres in 30 kilometres had taken it out of me; the descent had proved more exhausting than climbing up from the Rhône Valley. I needed time to recover. My state passport had somehow put me in the good graces with the *Hotel Europe*; now reassured that I owned a valid document, when asked, they were happy for me to stay a second night.

I had washed my clothes, socks as well, and dried them overnight; my first call in the morning was to the tailor's shop which I had spotted in the old town. Signor Bertey, more used to cutting suits and jackets, kindly agreed to repair my socks. They were still springing large holes in the toe area; I was increasingly dismayed that this make of sock, which had never let me down, had suddenly turned out to be flawed. I reckoned I would be lucky to cover half the distance promised by their name; in other words, well short of Rome. Replacing double-skinned socks would not be that easy, and the last thing I wanted was to experiment with a new brand.

The culprit turned out to be not the sock, but me. As soon as I got back to the hotel, I sat in my sunlit bay window and sorted them into pairs. Only then did I understand why they were causing me grief. I saw that they were marked with red and green blazes, for port and starboard. This was advanced sock technology which, as a typical male, I had not noticed before. Little wonder that, prodded with a big toe where only a little toe should go, they had developed holes.

There was a fancy hair salon next door to the hotel. I thought I would treat myself to a proper *Valdotan* haircut. I might as well have taken a disposable razor to my own head: each pleading cry of "*non troppo*" the girl took as an invitation to chop off more. Only "Stop!" worked; but by then I was all but scalped on one side.

"But the spiky look is all the rage here," the girl said.

"Not where I come from!" murmured the pilgrim.

In truth, I didn't mind that much, and whether shorn for battle, or tonsured for execution, maybe after all, in view of the *Bollettino Meteorologico* forecasting a prolonged spell of extreme heat, the convict crop would stand me in good stead.

Valdotan Roman and Romanesque architecture filled the remainder of the morning – first the Arch of Augustus, built to mark the city's foundation (Aosta = Augustus), and the impressive remains of a massive Roman theatre and arena, then the collegial church of San Orso where the marble stairs to the crypt had been whittled down by centuries of footfall: there I felt the energy of my long journey stamped onto a single flight of stone steps. The cloister boasts a display of carved biblical scenes on a succession of ebonised stone bosses; the one that caught my eye was of saddled camels, but with no riders, (Hannibal wasn't the only person to bring exotic animals to the Alps) as if waiting for someone to mount them. At the thought of walking another torrid 1,000 kilometres to Rome, I was sorely tempted.

Not far from San Orso, I spotted a plaque commemorating Canon Maxime Durand (1885-1966), a distinguished academic and defender of the French language and of local customs and rights in the Val d'Aosta. Italy is a patchwork of kingdoms, regions and fiefdoms and this frontier valley, though conquered and occupied by the Romans, has kept its independence. French, for example, is still spoken here as much, if not more than, Italian. Even the girl from faraway San Sebastian, who plied her massage oils over my legs that afternoon, agreed with the Canon when she assured me: "You need to speak French to work here."

It was evening. I left the hotel, and – refreshed and ready to walk halfway down Italy – I returned to the *Brasserie du Commerce*. Aosta was a strange, deserted city: Holland was playing Uruguay in the World Cup, and all *Valdotan* eyes were fixed on the small screen.

The way the pilgrim leaves Aosta is pure Roman: first the cobbled Via Praetoria to the parallel arches of the Praetorian gate, then through the Augustan arch, and finally up and over the perfectly preserved first century Roman footbridge across the River Buthier. It's a shock, but a brief one, to then exchange a street of such modest scale for the 21st century ring road and its noisy pedestrian bridge, but with the village of St Christophe the way soon peels off into quiet hills on the northern slopes of the Val d'Aosta, where I spent the day, gradually tracking eastwards.

My walk on July 7th proved to be tough going, steep up and steep down, but entirely redeemed by the breathtaking landscape. I walked beside vineyards, through hamlets of rough stone houses with over-hanging wooden balconies, and past frescoed churches and wayside shrines. Throughout, the Francigena waymarks were unambiguous and in every village I could help myself to cool, clear mountain water. On the valley's southern side, I made out a succession of castles, perched on strategic bluffs overlooking the main road and River Dora Baltea, and towering above them, all day, was the giant granite pyramid of Monte Emilius, whose northern crags, brooding over the valley, served as a gauge by which to measure my progress; though the best way I had of sensing the ground that I was covering came from turning round from time to time and seeing the upper end of the valley receding further into a narrowing V, while the snow-capped Mont Blanc massif above Aosta faded little by little into the blur of the day's heat.

I was still on the north side of the valley as I entered Châtillon; I therefore missed seeing Forattini's work which was down on the other side in the Castello di Ussel – the last castle before the river and valley bend to the south towards Montjovet. The town is at an important crossroads: from here the Marmore Valley winds up to Cervinia to an ancient route through a pass to Zermatt which I had skied through many times. Somewhere up there, invisible, was the Matterhorn, on whose summit I had stood; it thrilled me that I was walking through vineyards and orchards fed by her glaciers.

As you follow it down, the Val d'Aosta steadily yields more from its rich soil, first grapes for the local wine presses – there is even a village called Champagne – and then olives, and soon an orange tree. Now I was brushing the leaves of ilex oaks as I descended paths criss-crossed by my enchanting *ruas*, and it was through this ever more fertile land that I walked on to the town of Saint Vincent, 36 kilometres from Aosta, and a good day's march.

Even here I could sense that I wasn't yet truly in Italy: many street and shop signs were in French, and my chosen hotel, the *Lion d'Or*, and the architecture were still uncompromisingly Alpine. But my evening meal was joyfully Italian – *pasta ai porcini* with fried *zucchini* washed down with a tart, full-bodied Muscat from Chambave, the *commune* through which I had walked just hours before.

Up early on the morning of July 8th, I had problems finding the Via Francigena – nobody seemed to know where it came through Saint Vincent, and they actually hadn't heard of it: the idea of being connected, here in Northern Italy, to a path which led to Rome doubtless seemed alien. Back on course, at last, I spent the morning strolling pleasantly by farmsteads, up and down small country lanes and tracks, and through orchards, vineyards and meadows, until I came to the hilltop town of Montjovet. By now the day was heating up rapidly, and on the approach to each hamlet and village my eyes and ears strained for that spigot in the wall or the grander, more decorated fountain from which gushed fresh drinking water.

At Montjovet the path changed bank for a while, and gave me a few level kilometres. I followed the west bank of the Dora Baltea on a small country road before recrossing it at Hône. As the valley narrowed, I grew increasingly aware of the *autostrada* following the same way of least resistance along the riverbed from Aosta. And it was here that difficulties with the waymarking set in; the clear signage of the upper Val d'Aosta became more erratic, signalling a new phase of my walk. From now on, most days, I would have frustrating moments wrestling with guidebook, map and compass to find the authentic route. Waymarking in Italy turned out to be like a child's writing – good in parts, but not joined up.

As the Dora Baltea turns east at Bard, the valley presses into a tight neck. Here a formidable multi-layered fortress, like a lopsided wedding cake clinging to its rocky escarpment, guards the approach to Pont Saint Martin at the mouth of the Val d'Aosta, my resting place for the night after 28 kilometres. Just out of Bard, I found myself on the old Roman road, rutted with centuries of wheel marks, as it passed under the Roman arch at Donnas. Cutting through the cliff that stood in its way, it exemplified the Roman engineers' pragmatic, no-nonsense, approach to road building; and doubtless Hilaire Belloc would have much approved of this uncompromisingly straight line. Here, too, by the roadside was a link to home and Coggeshall, a church dedicated to San Pietro in Vincoli. The day's other trophy was altogether different – the biggest viper that I ever saw in Italy, coiled and sunning itself on the hot tarmac road – presumably waiting to be run over by the next car.

The south-facing side of the valley had been appropriated by the Romans for vineyards. Here they still cling to the steep hillsides, a concentrated cascade of man-made terraces: I counted more than 40 on one hill. Access to what was to become known as the Val d'Aosta was difficult before the Romans threw a single arch of 36 metres span across the steep gorge of the River Lys which joins the Dora Baltea at Pont Saint Martin, where the valley comes to its narrow neck. Here they would control all traffic in and out, and their bridge remained, until well into the 19th century, the only way to get up to Aosta, and I stayed at the *Hotel Ponte Romano* which overlooked it. I crossed it later that evening for a meal at the *Pizzeria* on the other side, the tourist menu, cooked and served by the owner who was from Messina, and had spent 20 years firing and selling pizzas in New York. How strange where we all end up. It was the best value *pasta all' arrabiata* that I had anywhere in Italy; accompanied by a good jug of local wine, the entire meal cost 15 euros.

It was by the same bridge that I left Saint Martin and the Val d'Aosta the following morning, July 9th, and entered the Provincia di Torino, but the country felt the same; I was still in old Piedmont. The familiar yellow fingerpost waymarks, which had guided me from the Alps, now gave way to more provisional signs – sometimes just a pilgrim's silhouette daubed on a rock with a blob of white paint and an arrow pointing ahead, left or right, or just the letters VF. The same steep hillsides were still peppered with vines, but now trellised and supported by rows of stone pillars; they gave the vine terraces the appearance of stepped temples. I could see the ripening fruit suspended in succulent bunches in the scorching sun.

The western bank of the River Dora Baltea offered flatter ground and so I walked that side for most of the day, sharing the country with the A5 *autostrada*. I also shared the road after the village of Quincinetto with an elderly man who was walking home, a small plastic shopping bag in one hand, a stick in the other. I sailed past him and then, using Paul Chinn's Lightfoot guide, followed a farm track with a ford over a dry stream. A few kilometres later, the path brought me back onto the road; there was the old man, ahead of me. He had simply carried on, while I had been lured off on a scenic detour. He was extremely pleased with himself; having outpaced a 'youthful' walker, and I took a photograph of him, grinning from ear to ear.

I started passing, or at least noticing, many more wayside shrines – little alcoves with statues of the Virgin, or primitive wall paintings of local saints. France and Switzerland also have wayside markers of religious devotion, but usually in the form of simple crosses. In Northern Italy the shrines become more theatrical, varied and demonstrative.

It was a short day to Ivrea, just 23 kilometres, and I arrived soon after one o'clock, leaving plenty of time to take in the city. I probably would have done better to walk on. Ivrea straddles the Dora Baltea and its old streets around the castle and cathedral have some charm. The best sight in town is underground – the cathedral's frescoed Romanesque crypt. In any case I used my time off profitably. At an old fashioned stationery shop, I bought maps and a new notebook, and from the resplendent neo-classical post office, I mailed home my empties, maps no longer needed, and some notes. Such routine office work seemed appropriate in a city that till recently was the headquarters of Olivetti; the typewriter and office equipment company no longer exists.

The biggest happening in Ivrea today is the annual carnival street fight with oranges as weapons, and in keeping with this important tradition the city victualled me well. My hotel, the *Eden*, was conveniently located next door to the local tourist office – two steps to get my pilgrim passport stamped – and the old city boasted a fine ice cream parlour – *Gelato Rosso* – and a rather exciting restaurant, with a name almost as long as its menu – *Antica Trattoria-Cafè La Mugnaia Di Marra Felice* – where I dinned on *gamberetti, zucchini and tagliatelli*. It was too hot to sit outside.

The following morning, July 10th, I had to phone the hotel on my mobile to rouse the night porter; the boy who was meant to prepare early breakfast for me had overslept. It was, of course, Saturday. I had a long day ahead, so for the first few kilometres I dispensed with Chinn's advice and the official Via Francigena route and set off down the main *statale* road which being a weekend was still quiet. I passed the local prison, where the guards gave me a more than curious look. At Bollengo, having put on the necessary kilometres, I reverted to the Via Francigena on small roads and farm tracks.

The country was flattening out; for the first time since I had left the high mountains affording expansive views ahead. Already in the distance I could see my first big lake – Lago Viverone – with white sails drifting across its calm bluey surface under a cloudless sky. But perfection, at the very side of the Via Francigena, came in the form of the Gesiun, a tiny ruined chapel from the 9th century, surrounded by fields, dedicated to Saint Peter. The roof has long gone, but apse and belfry still stand, along with part of the nave, and in the spandrels of the three surviving arches and round the apse are traces of frescoes; one fragment showing the hand of Saint Peter, holding a book. It is a quite magical place.

Rounding the lake and arriving at its far end by the village of Ropollo gave me a real sense of progress. Iced tea seemed a good idea. The narrow central street had a café sign. I went in, to find myself confronted with a welcoming party – not for me but for a new baby girl, the daughter of the proprietor and, of course, the sole centre of attention. I felt sorry about breaking into the baby worship to give my order – but it wasn't long before I, too, had joined in. In Italy this is mandatory. The grandparents were there as well; the grandfather suitably bearded, with wispy threads of thinning grey hair that was overdue a visit to my sporting hairdresser in Aosta. He was a former pop star, and he looked the part. Bryan – that was his name – had played in a rock group called Horoscope of Love. He showed me a programme from the San Remo song festival in which his group had performed. Like him, it was very faded.

A few minutes later, Bryan and his wife drove past me. They were in an appropriately battered car. He offered me a lift: "It's far too hot to be walking."

"No thanks," I replied. "I haven't come this far to give up."

"Yea," said Bryan. "I guess we all have to keep on rocking."

The day grew hotter and that afternoon, somewhere after Carvaglià, I banged on the metal gates of a farmhouse to ask for some more fresh water. The courtyard was a chaos of barking dogs. I counted eight; and some of them looked most ferocious. The farmer gave me water, perhaps rather reluctantly; besides, it was tepid.

"Eight dogs!" I said. "Surely one is enough?"

"You never know," he said. "Round here we can never have enough of them."

With that warning ringing in my ears, and after another bout with missing waymarks, I entered the first rice-fields of Lombardy, their deep green plants glistening in the sunlit water, and walked on into Santhià. It had been a hot 36 kilometres, or so I thought.

At this stage of his own journey Hilaire Belloc was sitting on a train, fast asleep, as it pulled him from Como to Milan. His decision to 'cheat' and hop a ride stemmed from all the customary pressures of walking; he was hungry, and short of money, and running out of time.

More specifically, he had lost time. Belloc cited his abortive attempt to cross the Alps by the Gries Pass as the beginning of his undoing. The retreat from the Gries and the abandoning of the straight line he had sought to walk cost him several days and he began to run out of money, or at least out of cash. Today he would have carried a credit or debit card, as I did; but things were not that simple in 1901.

It seemed on the map perhaps twenty-five, perhaps twenty-six miles to Milan. It was now nearly noon, and as hot as could be. I might, if I held out, cover the distance in eight or nine hours, but I did not see myself walking in the middle heat on the plain of Lombardy, and even if I had been able I should only have got into Milan at dark or later when the post office (with my money in it) would be shut; and where could I sleep because my one franc eighty would be gone?

Belloc enters the cool of Como's Cathedral of Santa Maria Assunta and sits at a shrine where candles are burning. He sees two where the flames are nearly extinct and makes a pact, submitting himself to "heavenly judgement". If the right-hand candle goes out first, he will continue walking; the left-hand will mean taking the train. The left-hand candle is the first to gutter and die.

None may protest against the voice of the Gods. I went straight to the nearest railway station (for there are two), and putting down one franc eighty, asked in French for a ticket to whatever station that sum would reach down the line. The ticket came out marked Milan, and I admitted the miracle and confessed the finger of Providence. There was no change, and as I got into the train I had become that rarest and ultimate kind of traveller, the man without any money whatsoever – without passport, without letters, without food or wine ...

Thus did I break – but by direct command – the last and dearest of my vows, and as the train rumbled off, I took luxury in the rolling wheels.

ELEVEN
LOMBARDY

SANTHIÀ IS A SORT OF CREWE IN THE middle of rice-fields. Nine rail routes converge here. The name itself is Sant'Agata, Chinese-whispered over many generations. I wouldn't be going sight-seeing. I booked in near the station and sat down to supper served with raw garlic; the waitress misunderstood, or over-interpreted, my request for "molto aglio".

I left Santhià for Vercelli on a pedestrian bridge that crossed those nine lines and entered a land eerily flat and unremittingly hot. Where rice grows there is no shade. It was Sunday, July 11th, so I decided to walk some of the way on the *statale* as there would be no heavy trucks to contend with. There was a reasonable shoulder to separate me from the oncoming traffic; I settled into a comfortable pace, entertained by the thought that here I was at least on the Via Francigena, the route which pilgrims actually walked before the arrival of the motor car. The re-born Francigena meanders by way of lanes and farm tracks through rice-fields; deliberately chosen to take walkers off the authentic Via Francigena, which for much of Italy is now just a busy traffic artery. I thus evolved my own compromise between history, convenience and safety. While walking down a motorway or dual carriageway was out of the question, I would give a *statale* a go, provided there was a decent hard shoulder, and when the Paul Chinn alternative entailed a long and tedious deviation. On the whole, this worked well for me in Italy: only once, just as in France, did I feel threatened by the traffic – but that was still days ahead.

On a whim, I pulled off the *statale* to walk through San Germano Vercellese. It looked inviting; and as I neared the central square my white hat and yellow rucksack caught the interest of a stranger. He was wearing shorts and sandals and had a Baltic sailor's cap to shield his head from the sun, and he was visibly excited at meeting a pilgrim. He introduced himself: Antonio Corona, working journalist, aged 78.

"Have you time to stop a moment? I'd love to interview you."

"Of course," I replied, and agreed to wait at the café on the square while he beetled home. He came back with his notebook and thrust a bottle of fresh water upon me. We sat on the steps by the church while he grilled me. When I think about it, his questions were pretty routine: where I had come from, what did I think of his country? That sort of thing – all easily answered. He was, after all, just the local stringer of a provincial daily. But that wasn't the point: he was a lovely man and his conversation plunged me into the history of rice cultivation in Lombardy. I was walking through an area, he said, that began as marshland. Rice came here in the late 15th century, brought from the Orient by Venetian merchants, and with its cultivation and the extra irrigation required came mosquitoes and malaria. The latter – as in our Fens – has long gone, but the mosquitoes, as I would discover, are still thriving along the water courses and in the paddy-fields. Lombardy rice is the best in Italy and arguably the finest in Europe. Having myself seen rice grown, harvested and milled in Bangladesh, I was amazed that such labour intensive farming could survive in Italy's high-wage economy. Easy, said Antonio, rice production in Italy today is almost fully automated. It was time to move on; I made my farewells with a sense of indebtedness. In the end, I had learned more from him than, with all his charm, he had extracted from me.

And so when I finally forsook the *statale* for gentler tacks between the rice-fields, I did so with a much greater appreciation of what I was looking at. Before, around and behind me lay a sea of greening shoots, the flat unending expanse broken here and there by the raised bank of an irrigation channel or the sluice of a water course. The stony paths led from one isolated farm to another; their barrack-like outbuildings, once the seasonal lodging of hundreds of labourers, standing empty and abandoned. From noon onwards that day the only two souls out in the rice-fields were two Chinese, whom I took to be agricultural technicians; sensibly, they wore hats with large brims, and scarves to shield neck and shoulders. The day grew ever hotter, and by the time I reached Montonero my sports wristwatch told me that I was 130 metres above sea level and that the temperature was 40 degrees. My little sunhat began to feel very inadequate; I found myself making frequent stops for water, and several times gave in to the temptation to sit and rest. It was my first serious encounter in 40 days of summer walking with dehydration. My diary for the day notes that I 'crawled' into Vercelli. I had only walked 27 kilometres, but it felt like 54.

The air conditioning in the *Hotel Giardino* was like a soothing balm, and a session in the shower put me back in the mood for a little exploration – and, of course, there was my pilgrim stamp to get. Friends had alerted me to the Basilica San Andrea, one of the finest late Romanesque churches in Northern Italy, and I had read about its curious connection, over two and a half centuries, with East Anglia. There it was; its triple arched western facade, with blind arcading above, perfectly balanced between two slender square towers. It was built in the early 1200s by Cardinal Guala Bicchieri on his return from serving as Papal Legate to the English crown, and it was funded by a gift King Henry III had made him on his departure – the perpetual rights to the income of Saint Andrew's church in Chesterton, just outside Cambridge. The house where the representative from Vercelli lived from 1350 still stands in the village. There is another English connection, too: the library houses the original manuscript of the Old English visionary epic, *The Dream of the Rood*. But I didn't have the strength to inspect it; after visiting the Basilica and the adjoining Cistercian monastery, all I could manage was to sit in Piazza Cavour and down two cool beers.

Not that I cut an entirely debonair figure as I sat there. I like to have a pocket comb to straighten out my hair which, even with the emergency trim I'd had just six days before in Aosta, tends to coagulate with sweat during a day's march. To add to the trail of silk handkerchiefs I had left as I marched, on one of my enforced rests that day, that comb had fallen from my pocket. Finding a replacement in a city centre on a Sunday afternoon became an acid test of modern Italy – just how deregulated was its retail economy? It failed the test; I remained combless for the next few days.

Vercelli marked the end of Volume Two of Paul Chinn's Lightfoot guide. Volume Three would be my companion from now on. I dipped in. It told me what I needed: only 836 kilometres to Rome! A quick calculation: three-fifths of the journey completed.

For dinner, I stayed close to the hotel, a restaurant on the Corso Garibaldi, and with what seemed a lifetime of paddy-fields behind me, I eschewed the local product and gladly tucked into my staple of *pasta* with fried vegetables, this time washed down with a *frizzante* wine, and I was in bed, fast asleep by the half-time whistle of the World Cup final.

There is something quite definitive about leaving Vercelli; it has virtually no urban sprawl. I crossed the long bridge over the River Sesia, one of the Po's larger tributaries, and walked straight into rice-fields again. Turning down a country lane, I crossed paths with a woman exercising her dog. She surprised me by stopping to talk.

"I know you," she said. "I saw you yesterday. You were walking into Vercelli on the *statale*."

"Yes," I said, relieved that she had simply spotted me walking on the roadside. "I hope today will be a lot quieter."

"It certainly won't be as hot. Yesterday was truly an *inferno*. How did you manage to walk in such heat?"

The questions that Antonio Corona had put to me were so much easier to find an answer to. I could only shrug my shoulders, but I was intensely grateful for this stranger being concerned enough to think, and ask. A pilgrim needs people like that.

The way followed the embankment set back from the river, leaving a wide floodplain for spring snow-melt and the autumn rainy season. From this eminence, I looked out once again over an infinity of young green and golden rice shoots. I've been here before, but in Bangladesh. At least today brought a cooling breeze; and I bent to the path and walked on briskly.

My way was often accompanied by a watercourse, with here and there a sluice-gate that provided a crossing-place. The plain south of Vercelli was no longer entirely treeless, and it was a relief from the full sun when the Francigena path found its way into one of the plantations; but apart from the shrill birds and loud crickets and grasshoppers I had the country to myself. The only sign of human presence were footprints in the sandy soil; I knew I was closing in on another walker. I caught up with her on the outskirts of the village of Palestro. She was a young woman from Lausanne walking with two ski poles, and she had a *bandera* round her head. She looked whacked. I told her that she was the first pilgrim I had met since Northern France.

"I'm not surprised," she said. "It's just too darned hot."

She was walking the Via Francigena in small bites, and had re-started this year at Pont Saint Martin in the Val d'Aosta.

"I don't know how much further I'll go," she said. "I just take it a day at a time."

We were on the same route, but on different journeys. I wouldn't know how to walk a day at a time. That doesn't mean that I am a better or a worse pilgrim; each way is the right way. The Swiss girl was journeying with time; I was travelling against it. I never asked her name, nor did I see her again.

I changed to the *statale* for the remaining few kilometres into the miniature city of Robbio, sharing the road for a time with red-overalled workmen laying a fibre optic cable in a trench.

"The new Italy," I said to one of them. He was feeding out the cable over his shoulder, as if handling a giant anaconda.

"No. The same old *porcheria*; it will just move around a lot faster."

That got me thinking about the Italy of Silvio Berlusconi. Was it the same old rubbish? Had Italy changed, for the better or worse, since I had been a keen and impressionable young foreign correspondent here more than 30 years before in the late 1970s? Walking is the only activity I know which allows me extended thoughts on such questions, time for the distillation of ideas; now, a reel of fibre optic cable had set the process in motion. I began to reflect on how Italy was different; perhaps, above all, it had become harsher, the edges less soft.

Robbio proudly proclaims that it is on the Via Francigena, and everywhere I went I got the impression that the townsfolk value their pilgrims. The *Poste* delighted in helping me parcel up Chinn Volume Two for England; freed of that weight and recharged with two bottles of iced tea, I sat in the shade of the lovely red brick Romanesque church of San Pietro and enjoyed my lunch break with fresh fruit and dried nuts. A welcoming place, it felt – the *Commune* of Robbio – even though I left with one niggle. The *farmacia* had not been able to come up with a replacement pocket comb for me.

At the tiny chapel in Nicorvo, the next village, the open door invited pilgrims to enter and stamp their own passports, the only time that I encountered such a self-service facility. The plaque above the desk with the stamp and inkpad called on pilgrims to stop here a while and pray for the 'true way'.

Such prayers were not altogether misplaced. On a wall at the far end at Nicorvo were two conflicting Via Francigena signs – one pointing left, the other right. Paul Chinn told me to bear left; but it wasn't long before I was lost amid the rice-fields, with a marker failing to show up at a critical junction. I wandered various tracks until I found myself back on course at the hamlet of Madonna del Campo where a lady with watermelon-sized breasts cascading out of her dress, was sitting on her ground floor Juliet balcony overlooking the roadside. It was as if she were there to patrol the street, or to lure pilgrims from their path; at any rate, she made an irresistible sight.

1. At the oak tree – leaving Coggeshall on the Essex Way.

2. Crossing the Millennium Bridge – St Paul's Cathedral.

3. Jon Harris at South Darenth after walking from London.

4. Peter Jenkins in the French war cemetery at Rancourt.

5. Approaching Reims near Cauroy-les-Hermonville.

6. Ornans, birthplace of the artist Gustave Courbet.

7. Château de Joux, where the father of Haiti died in chains.

8. The old Roman road ascending the Col Grand St Bernard.

9. Descending to the Val d' Aosta beside one of the ruas.

10. The old Roman road cutting through the cliff at Donnas.

11. A drinking fountain – there is one in almost every village in Italy.

12. Danilo Parisi, ferryman of the Po, with his pilgrim stamp.

13. Carved medieval pilgrims on Fidenza's Cathedral.

14. Looking back to the towers of San Gimignano.

15. A room with a rooftop view in Siena.

16. Kees Venema, a Dutchman walking to Rome.

17. View through an archway at Vignoni in the Val d' Orcia.

18. A hilltop farmhouse in the Val d' Orcia.

19. A Via Francigena waymark.

20. First sight of Rome from Monte Mario.

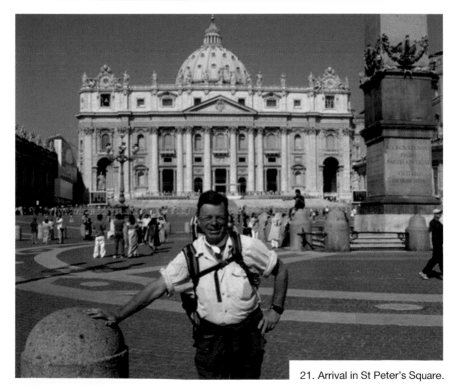

21. Arrival in St Peter's Square.

22. Journey's end – San Pietro in Vincoli.

"Could you please fill my water bottle?" I asked her.

"Of course," she replied. "Wait a moment."

She came back from her kitchen with a bottle of chilled sparkling water, and quite deliberately she leaned over the rail until her bosom was right in my face.

"In Italy," she said, "we deny water to no-one."

My destination was Mortara, just far enough on to let me simmer down, and close enough for a bell to be striking three o'clock as I entered the city through a tunnel under the railway tracks. It had taken just over eight hours to walk the 32 kilometres from Vercelli. There was plenty of time to rest, and even finally to locate a replacement comb. I booked a room at a hotel in the heart of the old town, where the owner charged me a modest 45 euros for bed and shower and a really good dinner – on condition that I paid him in cash and that I did not ask for a *scontrino*, or receipt. The request took me by surprise. In my time with Reuters, the Black Economy was endemic; modern Italy, by contrast, seems obsessed to the point of irritation with receipts and so-called fiscal proof of payment. It is impossible to purchase even a single piece of fruit without being handed a receipt; and by law customers are supposed to keep the printed chit with them until they have left the stall or premises. Failure to take one and failure to give one are held equally punishable.

Perhaps it was a whimsical gesture to a pilgrim: anyway my host was not keen on waking early to serve me breakfast, so he left out two succulent peaches for my journey. Mortara in this way contributed greatly to my regime; every day thereafter I sought out and bought a ripe *pesca* that I would eat on arrival at my night's resting place, often together with or after an ice cream.

I awoke on the 13th to the distant rumble of aeroplanes: Milan's *Linate* Airport is only 40 kilometres away – a day's walk, though I wouldn't be going that way. I would skirt Milan, leaving the city well to the south as I tracked eastwards to Pavia and Piacenza.

Paul Chinn's guide has an ominous warning for the stage from

Mortara to Garlasco: "The route continues through rice-fields. Care should be taken with navigation as the countryside has few clear landmarks and it is easy to get lost if you divert from the route." I consulted his map; the official Via Francigena meanders drunkenly across country. There were about 30 twists and turns to the day's route. That's a lot of waymarks to count on. I decided to brave the No 596 *statale,* which went straight as an arrow all the way to Garlasco.

It was the wrong decision. The 596 runs along a narrow causeway with no hard shoulder; and up and down it sped a succession of huge trucks. On several occasions, like a matador swivelling to avoid a charging bull, I had to stop and spin round side-on to let them pass. This was no fun; and it was in fact near-suicide. Provoked and unnerved, at Casini di Sant' Albino, I turned south off the road into the rice-fields and submitted myself once more to Chinn's rule and to capricious Italian signage. Initially the way was well marked as it took me alongside irrigation channels and down deserted tracks, passing the occasional ghostly farm, far to the south, and a long way from the *statale.* So far, so good; then, in the middle of nowhere and as if by appointment with providence, the waymarks gave way; and suddenly there were unmarked paths leading off in all directions. There was no grange or barn nearby, no sign of life, no one to ask; I was lost in a maze of rice-fields, a swamp drained by multiple water courses – exactly as Chinn had warned – and the parable in St Luke, which I had read a few mornings back, presented itself to me in its full bleakness. "Can a blind man lead a blind man? Will they not both fall into a pit?"

The map I carried did not have all the paths and tracks, and to make things more complicated the paths did not appear to follow logical routes. They went down one side of a water course, then inexplicably ended, or turned abruptly to the left or right. The best I could do was to construct a rough compass course to the northeast out of the available zigzag of paths until I intersected the *statale.*

What happened next was that I walked bang into a military camp, an area sealed off with barbed wire and guarded with gun emplacements.

Notices on the fence told me that I was under 'armed surveillance'. The track was taking me round an enormous closed military zone; I had visions of walking round it for the rest of my days. Yet though the camp seemed deserted, I had company. Just as I stopped to drink what was almost my last drop of water, something slithered by my dusty boots. It was a large snake.

The *statale*, when eventually I got back to it, seemed like a good idea after all. I dodged the trucks for a few more kilometres and then turned off into the small town of Tremello to revictual at the bar with water and iced tea. My spirits a little revived, I took once again to the rice-paddies, still ill-served with waymarks; but from here on the path to Garlasco was shorter and mercifully straighter. I tumbled gratefully into a shower at the *Hotel Il Pino*, but I wasn't pleased with the day. I had made a hash of walking a mere 23 kilometres, and for the first time since leaving Coggeshall I had got myself seriously lost. I wondered how the girl from Lausanne was managing.

Hilaire Belloc had a similarly uncomfortable passage through Lombardy; he also got lost, but he had to contend with the rain, not the burning sun.

Lombardy is an alluvial plain.

That is the pretty way of putting it. The truth is more vivid if you say that Lombardy is as flat as a marsh, and that it is made up of mud. Of course this mud dries when the sun shines on it, but mud it is and mud it will remain ...

Lombardy has no forests, but any amount of groups of trees; moreover (what is very remarkable), it is all cultivated in fields more or less square. These fields have ditches round them, full of mud and water running slowly, and some of them are themselves under water in order to cultivate rice. All these fields have a few trees bordering them, apart from the standing clumps; but these trees are not very high. There are no open views in Lombardy, and Lombardy is all the same.

Somewhere between Lodi and Piacenza, a bit to the east of my route, Belloc lost his way in a comparable maze of featureless fields and farm tracks. It was all too familiar, and I begin to sympathise with him, even like him.

These "by-roads" of the map turned out in real life to be all manner of abominable tracks. Some few were metalled, some were cart-ruts merely, some were open lanes of rank grass, and along most there went a horrible ditch, and in many fields the standing water proclaimed desolation. In so far as I can be said to have had a way at all, I lost it.

Garlasco is one of those towns that do not appear in guidebooks. There is nothing particularly venerable, let alone scenic about it, but, sitting in the central piazza on the terrace of the *Caffè Gobbi*, I found lots to interest me. This was an upmarket terrace, cooled with a chilled spray which gave the place an agreeably misty atmosphere. I watched Garlasco's fashionable singles and divorcées parading for their evening cocktail. Dolled up and in dangerously high heels, several of them eyed me with what, under brave layers of panstick, might pass for a twinkle or knowing wink. Their conversation turned to death: a local man had just died, aged only 40, and the ladies were interested in why he had "departed" at so young an age. They finished their drinks and walked across the piazza in a showy, elegant procession. There, much to my astonishment, they mounted bicycles and cycled off into the night, leaving me to stroll across the square to inspect the death notice of Enrico Sampietro on the portals of the town's baroque church. It was still open and I peeked inside – dark and empty, like so many I visited in Italy.

Il Pino is run by a friendly brother and sister team, Emiliano and Ana Galli. They wouldn't rate a line in my story but for the assurance with which they informed me that Italy was in the grip of an African heat wave, and that it would be cauldron-like for at least another ten days. It was now July 13th – that meant walking in near unbearable conditions until almost the end of the month.

With this warning in mind, I took out my map and for July 14th devised a route avoiding the rice-fields. In the morning, I picked my way towards Pavia down country lanes which took me through the towns of Sant Biágio and Zerbolò. As I went, I passed substantial old farmsteads, most crumbling and in a state of such disrepair that in England would presage total loss; yet every so often the entrance to one such *cascina* or grange had been newly gated and restored – signalling that it had become the country retreat of a wealthy Milanese. Two worlds resided here side by side. But the biggest divide came in Zerbolò, a town cut in half by a motorway: the Milan-Genova A7 *autostrada* slices through the middle of the town over a viaduct, glassed in and shielded by high walls. Astonishingly, the town doesn't seem to notice its high-speed intruder. I walked through it, along the main street and under the bridge, and life was going on as normal. On one side there is a café and the other a small park. It takes more than a motorway to kill an Italian town.

Leaving Zerbolò down another lane, I fell in with a workman riding on the footplate of a three-wheeled tractor from which he was repainting the lines along the roadside. As befitted a charioteer, he was naked except for a striking pair of red shorts – it was that hot. I noticed that he was leaving a generous verge; by diligent steering with the handlebars he contrived to produce a line that was nigh-on perfectly straight. In this land of painters, here was a true craftsman drawing a white line along the roadside.

"You're keeping me alive with that protective line," I told him as we passed each other.

Shortly afterwards I dropped down from the road to the sandy bank of the River Ticino, walking into Pavia by riverside thickets where cuckoos and warblers chattered in spirited chorus and grasshoppers and crickets pierced the air with their screeching. I approached the city by the side of its country club, a gated community from where people lazing by the poolside could observe the riverside path and keep an eye on this pilgrim and others who came this way. I climbed the steps to the covered bridge – *il ponte coperto* – and crossed it into Pavia, my first major city since Aosta.

Once known as the 'the city of a hundred towers', Pavia has lost some of its former splendour – there are only three of the medieval towers left, though one of them is a prize specimen with a topknot of trees – and the heritage is not all that it seems. The original bridge built on Roman foundations, and covered in 1583, suffered from bomb-damage in World War II and collapsed in 1947. What I entered the city by is a splendid replica built a few metres up river. But the old city retains its Roman pattern and medieval feel, and I ambled jauntily down its bustling cobbled streets to Piazzale Stazione and my hotel, the *Excelsior*, situated just outside the city walls.

With due respect to Emiliano and Ana, the day had made for idyllic walking; the African heat wave would return the next day, Thursday 15th, which I had set aside for exploring Pavia, a city I barely knew. My first call was to the tourist office, just off the arcaded Piazza della Vittoria. Here they take Pavia's role as a stage on the Via Francigena most seriously; in an impressive leather-bound book, pilgrims are invited to inscribe their names. Its front endpaper is an attractive collage of Pavia's pilgrim stamp, the familiar hooded pilgrim with satchel on his shoulder and staff in hand. Nine pages had been filled by pilgrims since April 2007 – not a lot. One was from England – Edward Condry, Canon of Canterbury Cathedral; he had led a group of pilgrims from the Via Francigena's starting point, but on bicycles, not foot. The most memorable inscription, however, was not a name at all. "*Lunga è la via,*" it said in local Pavian dialect – the way is long.

There was plenty to see in Pavia, but I favoured the Lombard Romanesque church of San Michele, its light sandstone facade a delicately harmonious creation; the balance of decorated portals, arched windows, roundels and blind arcades represented to me some sort of perfection, against which I would measure all subsequent Romanesque sightings. Next, I sought out the shrine of Lanfranc, the son of Pavia who became William the Conqueror's first Archbishop of Canterbury, brought home for burial in a church dedicated to him. Lanfranc consolidated the Church's power in England under the new Norman rule, and saw off the challenge from York to make Canterbury the primary see. That act alone makes him, in an important way, a father figure of the Via Francigena: without his ascendancy at Canterbury, English pilgrims to Rome might well have had to set out from York.

I also inspected the statue of Alessandro Volta, the 18th century scientist and pioneer of electricity, a professor here, and found a plaque commemorating Albert Einstein, the 20th century physicist, who wrote his first scientific paper in Pavia. I strolled around the university, impressed with its antiquity, and with the city's remaining medieval tower-houses which overlook its campus. Pavia's University was founded in 1361, a good few centuries after my old University, Oxford, where, although there is no formal date of foundation, teaching began as early as the 11th century.

A day in a hot city makes for fidgety feet and it was a relief to be on my way again on the 16th. As I walked east, the land began to hint at a slope or an incline offering the promise of some natural feature to break the monotony of flat marshland fields. The way followed country roads and white farm tracks; at San Giacomo, on the roadside, I encountered an exquisite red-brick Lombard Romanesque chapel. Nearby, on the wall of the bridge over a small stream, somebody had scrawled an encouraging sign: an arrow and the single galvanising word: *Roma*. Once at Beligioso, I resumed the *statale* to the village of Santa Christina, where in a house behind his church the *parroco* had set up a pilgrim hostel and youth centre. Don Antonio showered this pilgrim with a warm welcome, insisting on giving me water and stamping my pilgrim passport – even though I wasn't staying – and refusing to take my offering of money. That's another way of showing a pilgrim charity – even if he goes on his way feeling a fraud.

"Just pray for me in Rome," said Don Antonio. His request made me guilty: after all he was making an assumption about my intentions, and I was the last person to understand precisely what they were.

If there is any divine providence for pilgrims, I got my comeuppance within minutes of leaving Santa Christina, lost in a sea of pampas grass. I ended up taking the wrong white road towards Miradolo, my destination for the night, and when I finally worked my way out and arrived after 36 kilometres and enquired in the village bar about the location of my hotel, I was informed that it was four kilometres out, up the hill. That would make the day 40 kilometres and add an extra four to the next day.

For the first and only time in my journey, I let fly with a loud "Fuck", and ordered an iced tea. The *Albergo Castello*, when I had booked there on my mobile, had assured me that it was just outside the town – perfectly correct, if you are in a car. My English expletive had an unexpected result. A young man drinking an afternoon coffee offered to drive me to the hotel. The heat and the distance up a hill from the Francigena made acceptance easy. I would, in any case, have to come back down here in the morning to resume my walk. I wonder, though, how Hilaire Belloc would have worked that one out.

Set on the emphatic slopes of a hill overlooking the Ticino Valley amid vineyards and hazelnut groves, the *Albergo Castello* is the principal hotel of the Terme di Miradolo, a spa dating back to Roman times. The hotel is a sprawling family-owned complex, begun in 1913, and bits of it haven't changed much in the intervening century. I was installed, however, in the modern wing, in a vast room with a jacuzzi which was bigger than the double-elephant, floor-level bed; it seemed more suited to footballers and their girlfriends than pilgrims. In fact, lying in the jacuzzi I felt distinctly guilty and out of place. Shouldn't I have accepted Don Antonio's hospitality and stayed at the hostel in Santa Christina? From my luxurious vantage point in the jacuzzi I also had a chance to contemplate my boots, and suddenly noticed the heels, once again worn down to the uppers. They would need repairing, and soon. I was furious with myself; I could so easily have had them re-heeled in Pavia on my footloose day off. I was embarking on ten unbroken days of walking when it would be almost impossible to find a wayside cobbler.

I now had a challenge.

Nevertheless, I spent the rest of the afternoon lazing by the thermal baths in the *Centro Benessere* of the newly refurbished Spa; here I underwent a bruising massage, before returning to the cavernous and almost deserted dining room at the hotel for an indifferent meal of *Tagliatelle ai porcini freschi* – pasta with mushrooms that were far from fresh. I was back in the main square at Miradolo at seven o'clock the following morning, still missing the intelligence of Don Antonio and keen to put the entire thermal experience behind me.

Happily the day brought me back into the pilgrim fold.

For the first few kilometres of July 17ᵗʰ I walked contentedly down country lanes as far as Campo Rinaldo, delighting in the gentle vine-clad slopes that rose to my left – the low hills from where I had come that morning. For a while I paced a rather pretty early morning jogger, marching to the neat swing of her lycra-cupped bum, and it was a moment of disappointment when she turned off the road onto a white track climbing up through a vineyard. I then dropped down onto a *statale* as far as the bridge over the Lambro, one of the 141 tributaries that feed the mighty River Po.

Here, following the border between the provinces of Milan and Lodi, I turned due south; the turn renewed my sense of being a pilgrim. With the pretty town of Orio Litta on my left, and a distant line of hills on the far horizon, I set off on a track along the man-made embankment which snakes in and out of fields of rice and maize and alongside wooded groves, following the Lambro to its outfall into the River Po. There I had an appointment with Danilo Parisi, the ex-rugby player who forms a vital link with the myriads of pilgrims who passed this way over the centuries. Danilo ferries modern pilgrims across the River Po, taking them on the same water-borne route by which pilgrims walking to Rome originally approached the city of Piacenza.

The assignations are made – as on the East Anglian estuary and creek crossings – by mobile phone, and so, reaching the little riverside jetty about 30 minutes before Danilo had arranged to pick me up, I had time to visit the farming hamlet of Corte San Andrea before returning to the white sandy shore, where a brick plinth marks the point from which pilgrims embarked on the sailing craft that once ferried them down and across the river. Here there is also a small shrine and statue of the Virgin; represented as the Madonna of fishermen, with the prayer: "Protect us" – a reminder that even the seemingly tranquil inland waters of the River Po could turn stormy, and claim lives.

In a country where Dante's imagery still holds, Danilo has been likened to Charon transporting his cargo of souls across the Styx, but it's far better to see him as a 21st century Saint Christopher. I had my boots and socks off, and was airing my weary feet on the warm stone plinth when Danilo arrived early – typical of the man. He relishes his role as the Via Francigena's modern ferryman, and takes great pride in it.

He operates the white open launch *Sigerico* – as Sigeric is known in Italian – and has been ferrying pilgrims across the River Po from the moment when the European Union first invested serious money in its endeavour to revive the Via Francigena as a cross-border 'cultural itinerary'; ever since 1998 Danilo has been keeper of the gates, the route-master, record keeper and guide to this section of the Via Francigena.

Bulky, as befitting a former front-row forward, he showed up in a blue tee-shirt, shorts and flip-flops, together with his dog, Nilo. I hurriedly rebooted and stepped down the gangway to board his craft. The journey was like none other on a river. The 200 horse power Evinrude outboard propelled us over the water like a rocket; as sole passenger I sat in the bows letting the cool air and spray waft over me. Danilo steered his craft with the intent and concentration of a Formula One racing driver; but with his grey stubble glinting in the sun on his weatherbeaten face, and hair flowing from a bald crown, he looked more like the jolly friar than skipper of a river taxi. The tree-lined banks, bordered by large stretches of white sandy foreshore laid bare by the hot summer drought, rushed by as we descended the river for five kilometres in a wide sweeping arc towards Calandasco. Enthroned in this air-cooled craft, I wanted the journey to go on, to progress all the way to Rome; a common feeling, surely, among all who enjoy the ride with Danilo.

We moored on the far shore, and dropped down the raised embankment to his riverside home, an old brick farmhouse whose lovely shaded patio, on hot days such as this, becomes his pilgrim reception room. Danilo returned from inside the house holding a large leather-bound book – his *Liber Peregrinorum*, Book of Pilgrims, in which he records every foot passenger he ferries across the Po: a marvellous record of one man's passion for the passions of others.

And yet, at first glance, what is surprising is how few pilgrims have passed this way since the ferry service was reinstated – many fewer than the 3,000 odd who have climbed Everest. Numbers started at a mere trickle, and didn't reach more than 100 a year until 2008. They now hover at just under 300 a year, virtually nothing compared to the thousands who trek to Santiago. Besides, most of those who cross the Po on Danilo's launch have started in Lausanne or at the Grand St Bernard; very few have come all the way from Canterbury, and only a handful more from Holland and Germany. There was no record in the book of anyone before me walking from London. After I had inscribed it, he took hold of a large wooden shaft the size and shape of a pepper grinder, and with due ceremony fixed a most decorative stamp onto a page of my pilgrim passport.

Danilo is a harsh critic of the hands that feed him. His ferry is subsidised, but he relies on contributions to keep it going. The ten euro fare paid by most single passengers is insufficient to cover his costs. Danilo is convinced that the Via Francigena could one day rival the *Camino Francés* to Santiago, but he is also painfully aware that the infrastructure is nowhere near ready.

"The sad reality is that too much of the European Union funding has gone into roadside signs which show off the Francigena, but not into hostels and better waymarks, which actually help the pilgrim," he told me. "In 2008 they spent some two million euros of European Community money on fancy Via Francigena road signs, but they are not much help if you are trying to find your way on foot.

"The *Camino Francés* in Spain has added affordable accommodation every year, but here in Italy we simply haven't done enough, and too often pilgrims are offered a room in a parish house with a cold shower, and given a key and told the nearest pizzeria is two kilometres away – that is not my idea of providing pilgrim hospitality."

I agreed with Danilo about the waymarks, but kept quiet about the hostels. I didn't want to tell him that last night I had bathed in a jacuzzi rather than washed under a cold tap in a parish hall.

True to his reputation for kindness to pilgrims, a short while after I had left his hospitable patio, Danilo spotted me on the road and pulled up. He was on his way back from picking up fuel for his boat. He had done a bit of reconnaissance for me, establishing that I could cross the bed of the Trébbia, another tributary of the Po. That short-cut would save me six further kilometres in the extreme heat of the afternoon, making the day 36, rather than 42, kilometres. Indeed, at Puglia, the riverbed was almost dry, and so after slithering down its steep sandy bank, I walked across the Trébbia to enter the city of Piacenza. On a day crowned by a ferry ride down the River Po, it seemed the right way to arrive.

Piacenza is the first city where Hilaire Belloc's and my separate journeys actually intersect. Belloc had approached from Milan, via Lodi – further to the north – but his crossing of the River Po was also water borne, by way of a pontoon bridge, and in the rain.

> It is a very large stream. Half-way across, it is even a trifle uncomfortable to be so near the rush of the water on the trembling pontoons. And on that day its speed and turbulence were emphasised by the falling rain ...

> Once across, it is a step into Piacenza – a step through mud and rain.

> Neither of us was to stay there long.

TWELVE
APENNINES

PIACENZA IS THE ROMAN PLACENTIA, THE NAME RUBBED a bit by two thousand years of saying it through pasta in the hot sunshine. There is much to see, but the five kilometres in Signor Parisi's *Sigerico* down the Po had brought home to me that there was more to attend to than just my boots. I checked into the luxurious *Grande Albergo Roma*, and instantly lowered the historic surroundings by hanging out my washing – done as usual in the shower – above the street that leads to Piazza dei Cavalli. I took another look at the boots; they would just survive a few more stages, whereas my back now needed instant attention. It had grown increasingly sore, and my hot shower had been excruciating. I stepped out of the hotel in search of the nearest *farmacia* where I stripped for one of the pharmacists. He was proud that he spoke good English, and after giving the raw, red circle on the centre of my back a professional inspection, he declared that it had to be sun burn.

"That's impossible," I said. "I wear two shirts and cover it with a rucksack."

"The Italian sun penetrates everything," he assured me. "And it will get down that gap in your neck."

So I spent 30 euros on a powerful sun cream and on a tube of after-sun, which I applied in lashings under his eye. Uncomfortable as it had been till then, my back instantly erupted in violent convulsions, as if rubbed with burning coals.

"Wow! That hurts," I said.

"It's meant to, but don't worry it will soon feel better."

I left the *farmacia* poorer and in more pain than when I had entered. The hot coals gave way to crawling ants, but still disagreeable enough to forestall any pleasurable sightseeing. I struggled round the Duomo, admiring its sturdy Romanesque columns, but I didn't have the energy or inclination to visit the museums. Even my appetite lost its sense of adventure, although an early evening beer, and the carafe of white wine which I drank with my pasta and fried vegetables out on the terrace at the *Trattoria Pasquale* facing the Duomo, seemed to calm my raging skin, and, after retrieving my washing to restore propriety to the beautiful city of Piacenza, I retired to bed determined to apply plenty of sun cream the following morning and to try sleeping on my stomach to avoid further chafing.

There were no Saturday night high spirits, or, if there were, I slept through them. Paul Chinn's guide gives Firenzuola d'Arda and Fidenza as the next two stages, and the official Via Francigena approaches the two by a rustic and roundabout route – more farms and villages, more rice-fields. I gambled on getting to Fidenza, 40 kilometres, in one go by the Roman road, the Via Emilia. Sunday meant none of the truck traffic which had made Tuesday's walk so disastrous. And indeed, though the sun beat down on me all day, the Via Emilia provided a quick and relatively safe passage: for much of the distance it is accompanied by an irrigation canal, culverted over and raised above the road and fields, and I made good use of this. I had time to reflect on Italian road signs, and made two observations. One was that Italian towns tell you what is in them only after you have left. Firenzuola d'Arda was still advertising its monuments and restaurants when I had left it long behind me and was back on the Via Emilia. My second says much about the state of the Italian economy – then, and even more now. Unlike Britain, Italy has always gone in for roadside hoardings. Many that I passed were empty, and were advertising '*Spazio Libero*'. Hills gradually converged from the south, the first traces of the Apennines ahead, and by the time I entered Fidenza I had happily seen the last of the flat irrigated fields.

Hilaire Belloc made a similarly swift passage down Via Emilia, but in pouring rain. His visit to Piacenza had been even more cursory than mine, and far briefer. He broke his journey for a meal with Malaga wine, and noted that he also "bought a bottle of a new kind of sweet wine called *Vino Dolce*".

> It rained all along the broad and splendid Emilian Way. I had promised myself great visions of the Roman soldiery passing up that eternal road; it still was stamped with the imperial mark, but the rain washed out its interest, and left me cold. The Apennines also, rising abruptly from the plain, were to have given me revelations at sunset; they gave me none. Their foothills appeared continually on my right, they themselves were veiled. And all these miles of road fade into the confused memory of that intolerable plain.

If the Via Francigena were an ocean liner, Fidenza would be its bridge. This charming small city on the first finger of the Apennines stands watch over the way to Rome. At the western portal of the Duomo, a statue of Simon Peter portrays the Apostle holding a scroll which reads in Latin shorthand: "*Simon Apostolus eundi Romam demonstrat hanc viam.*" The Apostle Simon shows forth this way of going to Rome, it says. With his free hand pointing in the direction of the See of St Peter, this is surely one of the world's first fingerposts.

A milestone in Roman numerals is engraved under the capital on the other side of the portal, but the well preserved Romanesque cathedral has something even more special to show the footsore pilgrim. Inset well up on the southern tower is a stone frieze: a procession of medieval pilgrims. Ever since leaving Coggeshall, I had been searching for any small window my journey might give me into the mindset, and faith, of the pilgrim. These sculpted travellers, halted in their tracks at Fidenza, had the power to draw me instantly in, back into their world, and I spent many minutes gazing at them.

The central group is a quartet of pilgrims. Two, their heads hooded or cowled, keep their left arms snug within their cloaks: the other two, one bearded and with bared head, keep hold of their shoulder bags, one hitched over a stick for balance. Each man grasps a staff. Nameless, like the mason who carved them, their story is plain to see. The hooded pair huddle inside their cloaks against the cold, while the other two are carrying the supplies for their simple needs: their staffs are for their long journey on foot. They are set high on the wall, making it hard to read their expressions, but they are looking up, and they seem both determined and contented.

These timeless figures have re-entered time, brought back to life by the revived Via Francigena. The pilgrim in front with the heaviest bag, which he has suspended on a stick for better support, has been re-drawn with touches from the other three to stand as the official logo of the modern pilgrimage route. In different guises and in a rainbow of colours, he appears on Via Francigena signs all the way from Canterbury to Rome. In many regards, Hilaire Belloc was close to him. The revolution in walking clothes postdates World War I, and Belloc remained a great cloak wearer all his life. To walk to Rome, he carried a staff, which he used to good effect in the storm in the Alps, and he also slung what he called a sack or 'pocket' over his shoulders, just like the two bag carriers and the pilgrim of the logo.

The four Fidenza foot-pilgrims are not alone. They are bunched in between knights on horseback, the two immediately behind them leading a horse on which sits a leopard. This animal would have been brought along by a wealthy knight to hunt him his supper – pity the poor peasant farmer who objected. Maybe they are crusaders, but wherever these knights are going, they are on an earthly pilgrimage, and far from poor. And not being poor, stripped down to the minimum, became relevant to my own status as a pilgrim the very next day.

In sympathy with its medieval pilgrims, Fidenza, and not *Urbs Roma*, has become 'mission control' of the modern Via Francigena, the official seat and headquarters of the *Associazione Europea delle*

Vie Francigene. It was Sunday afternoon, of course, when I first popped into its office, close by the cathedral. An attractive face welcomed me, Elisa Rizzardi, working there alone; as well as giving me a lot of useful information – including the name of a local *calzoleria* where they could repair my boots – she stamped my passport with the logo based on the cathedral pilgrim, and asked me to write some comments in a book the office was compiling on, and for the benefit of, modern pilgrims. I noted my infuriation at the inconsistency of the waymarks – particularly their absence at crucial turning points – before coming to a section which invited pilgrims to record their daily expenditure. Most people had written around 30 euros, some much less. I decided to be honest, and gave my daily expenses as 100 euros. This wasn't meant boastfully, nor as a confession of un-pilgrim-like indulgence, but it was to catch up with me the following day.

Fidenza's main street, the Via Berenini, offered a choice of chemists; I chose the one where there were no customers so I could strip off my shirt without shocking old ladies. The pharmacist examined my sore back intently: his verdict rang a whole lot truer to the back's tenant than the Piacenza pharmacist's theory of the sun finding its way down there from my collar. He said it was simply rubbed raw by the straps and frame of my rucksack. A cortisone cream would rapidly repair the damaged skin. I applied it, with familiar results – my back flamed up like a brazier.

But I had a day off in which to recover, or let my back simmer down. I was in a comfortable hotel, the *Astoria*; it was in the heart of the city, in the square facing the Palazzo del Comune, or Guildhall. Many northern Italian cities have grander government palaces, but Fidenza's, neither too big nor overly ornate, has a charm of its own. Built in the 13th and 14th centuries, the palace was badly damaged in a Nazi air raid during World War II but sensitively restored afterwards: a plaque inside the main gates commemorates the attack on Fidenza on 13th May 1944 and its subsequent twinning with Guernica, the Basque political capital, similarly bombed by the Germans in 1937 during the Spanish Civil War. Many people believed that Fidenza fell prey to German bombs because the city fathers had changed its name in 1927, abandoning Borgo San Donnino for the modernised version of its Roman name, *Fidentia*. Only Fidenza's cathedral is still named after San Donnino, who was martyred here by the Romans. He is buried in the crypt.

When I returned to the Francigena office on Monday morning, there was no welcome from the lovely Elisa; in her place was Flora, and when I asked her for a list of hotels going forwards into the Apennines, I received a frosty reply.

"We only have lists of hostels, parish houses and convents. We cannot tell you about hotels. We don't cater for rich pilgrims."

"Excuse me, but why not? Because I stay in hotels, does that make me less of a pilgrim?"

Flora did not answer, but while she was attending to another visitor I took the book I had filled in the previous evening and added (+/–) in brackets to the 100 euros I spent each day. Flora had made me feel guilty; and I also remembered Luke: blessed are the poor, and woe to the rich.

My boots were re-heeled by a swarthy Italian with an English forename – Thomas Ghilani. Later, in the *Centro di Benessere*, a Romanian masseuse gave me a thorough going over; and she would not merit a mention in my account were it not for her gloss on the 1,500 kilometres I told her I had walked since leaving Coggeshall.

"About the same distance to my home in Romania," she said. "It's a flight of one and a half hours." That cuts the long-distance walker's world down to size.

The early morning sun of Tuesday July 20th shone directly on the clock face of the Palazzo del Commune as I walked by. It was 6.45 and I was heading into the Apennines, to cross their hilly spurs which sprawl in defensive tentacles down to the Mediterranean, guarding the route to Tuscany. After days of walking on the flat, I registered the renewed sensation of pressure on feet and calves as they took the unaccustomed strain of rising ground. All day, I tracked south under bright blue skies and a hot sun, ascending slowly from Fidenza into rolling farmland 200 metres above sea level, then zig-zagging through wooded groves and vineyards to the banks of the River Taro. Suddenly the countryside was opening out to provide spectacular vistas; in the first hour or so I was able to look back towards the Po from the hilltop chapel and shrine at Siccomonte, and, soon, the high ridge of Castello di Costamezzana unveiled the horizon to the south, and the broad view of the mountainous valleys ahead.

At first the waymarks held good; in the fields outside Fidenza I passed an elderly couple who told me with great pride that they had helped in installing Via Francigena signs on posts and gates throughout the neighbourhood – but before long I was in trouble. Near the village of Cella, a track across a harvested cornfield suddenly forked, leaving a broken waymark hanging limp from its post. My guess led me straight into a farmyard, and two unleashed Alsatian dogs, teeth bared and growling. Running away is the instinctive reaction, but probably the least sensible and last resort. In these situations I try instead to slow down, talking reasonably to my assailants in their own language. I recalled the expat English woman in France trying to instruct her pooch in the art of sitting and, putting up a splendid barrage of canine Italian for the benefit of this pair of would-be killers, I walked gingerly between them. I had been bitten by a dog a few summers before in France, not an agreeable experience. The teeth went in deep, the scar took a long time to heal, and the wound was painful. In Italy, of course, there is the additional 'attraction' of rabies. Quite unexpectedly, just as we came broadsides like enemy battleships closing with one another, a small, infinitely fiercer, terrier bounded across the patio – and, to my astonishment, this later intruder set upon the two dreadnoughts, chasing them away. At this signal, I broke into a gentle trot, so I would never discover if this was an act of canine friendliness or whether the terrier wanted my calves for himself. Looking back, all I could see was the notice on the farm gate: '*Attenti ai Cani feroci*'. The warning about fierce dogs hadn't helped me; I had come into the farmyard the wrong way. There you are: the Italians really do plant their placards and hoardings on the downstream side.

It was an arduous and hot day. Passing a mobile food shop, I was offered a *pesca* and apple juice for free: "*un omaggio*," said the owner, "it's far too hot to be walking to Rome." I sat by a farmhouse dousing myself in the cool water of an outside tap. The last six kilometres to Fornovo di Taro went by in a daze. I followed the riverbank, a stony track which led through brushwood, in and out of dried beds of subsidiary streams. The one thing I can remember quite clearly is the incessant drill of crickets filling the dense afternoon air with unbearable insistence. The pain in my ears was compounded by the sensation of being flogged on my back. I had applied a cocktail of creams to the sore area in the morning – one to alleviate sunburn, the other to calm the irritated skin. As I was about to discover, I might as well have poured olive oil onto my bare back and let it sizzle in the sun.

I straggled across the bridge into Fornovo and fell into the chair at the tourist office, which was similarly geared to the Via Francigena. Here I submitted myself to the usual polite questions, and gave my standard reply about the awful waymarks – "*i segni sono atroci e cattivi.*" The kind girl assistant nodded in agreement and duly noted my comments, but I sensed a perverse delight in her voice when she told me that the hotel where I was to stay was a further two kilometres on. That would make the day's total 36 kilometres; in such extreme heat I felt 34 was already quite sufficient.

Fornovo di Taro guards its river crossing jealously; a largely medieval town constructed in a bubble around the spine road leading to the bridge over the Taro, in April 1945 it had the unusual distinction of being liberated from its Italian and German Fascist occupiers by the Brazilian army that had entered World War II on the Allies' side. Knowing that my night's bivouac was half an hour out of town, I called into the *farmacia* on the main square, where I was sold an even more powerful anti-burn cream. But I was still not satisfied: passing yet another *farmacia* on my way out of town, on a whim I threw myself on the mercy of one more pharmacist. I removed my rucksack and peeled off both shirts ready for inspection. However, instead of examining my back, this woman pharmacist held up my two stinking, dripping shirts.

"This," she said, "is your problem." She was now holding the sweat absorbing undershirt which I had worn since leaving home. "The artificial material here is combusting with the heat. I recommend you buy a cotton shirt, and that you stop walking for a few days to let your back recover."

So that was it. I had a combustible material on my back which I had been fuelling with lotions and a cortisone cream that simply fanned the flames. No pilgrimage, is seems, is complete without some degree of hardship; I had been prepared for blisters, which I never got, and I had marched with painful feet, but I had never expected to scald my back. I walked on to the *Hotel Cavalieri* chastened, and bent on finding a cotton shirt.

The *Cavalieri* is a fine three-storey ochre palazzo, clad in creeper and set in its own grounds with spectacular views over the Taro Valley. Round its splendid marble fountain sweep the arriving and departing cars. My own approach was at a bare hobble, but I was well received: the staff treated me as a special guest, solely because I had walked so far.

Reading between the lines, you may have guessed: I was on the point of calling it a day. Perhaps it was this kind reception at the *Cavalieri* that turned it for me. Cooling down in the swimming pool, I decided that, come what may, I would press on. I called an old friend in Tuscany, Jonathan Mennell, and asked him about the heat. If I got that far, I hoped to stay with him, but what he told me was not hugely encouraging.

"It will cool down," he said, "but not yet."

In the evening, I was plied with beers and served delicious *casalinga* (homemade) pasta with *zucchini* and *gamberi* – the fresh prawns giving off both a hint and promise of the sea beyond the Apennines. The waiters offered me a stiff Fernet Branca on the house after dinner, and a little later I fell into a deep sleep dreaming that Jonathan had driven all the way up from Tuscany to the Taro Valley with a fresh cotton shirt for me.

At breakfast the next day, the 21st, I had the nerve to ask one of my fellow guests whether he had a spare cotton shirt; he looked a bit surprised. In any case, I had dressed without my artificial undershirt, and I harnessed my rucksack loosely so that it hung away from my back. I also tied the cotton handkerchief, the replacement I had bought in Aosta, round my neck to block out the sun, and reminding myself that it was my feet I walked on, not my back, I descended the hotel driveway and stepped out onto the road.

The first thing I saw was an upturned bicycle. Cyclists are generally not the friendliest of people; they tend to whizz by walkers, sometimes close shaving them with their handlebars. From the humble pedestrian's vantage of the kerbside, cyclists convey an air of superiority behaving as if they own the road. Here, though, was a grounded cyclist, repairing a puncture, and I asked if I could help. It was a fortuitous encounter. He thanked me, we started talking. Where was I was going? To Berceto, I told him.

"Well, if I were you I would take the *statale*. It's quiet, I frequently cycle here."

This was heartening knowledge. From looking at Chinn, I was aware that after crossing the Taro, the Via Francigena breaks out into mountainous trails, winding its way laboriously over steep broken ground in and out of hilltop hamlets, while the SS62 offers a far more direct, albeit switchback, route through the same country. My back was still roaring, and I needed every comfort I could get. With this in mind, and with my faith in Via Francigena waymarks at a low ebb, I opted for the road.

It was to prove a good choice. All traffic heading through the Apennine foothills to the coast now takes the A15 *autostrada*, leaving my *statale* virtually deserted. There is ample shoulder space for the pedestrian and I shared the road with just the occasional large truck shunting up from the valley with tarmac to repair a broken stretch of old highway near Cassio. It was a demanding day: twice I encountered cols over 900 metres, but it was pleasant, and steady going through a mix of pine forest and hayfield, and as I climbed higher, valley floors opened up below me, and views of distant hilltops came into play. At those heights, it was also mercifully cooler; for the first time in days I felt a refreshing breeze.

Closer to the road, rock face graffiti caught my eye, proclaiming a message that partly resonates with me. "*Non a tutti gli eserciti, Non a tutte le frontiere,*" it said: No to all armies, No to all frontiers. I thought of the Africans I had encountered on my arrival in Calais and about the seemingly unstoppable shifts of populations. Although I might have my doubts about abolishing all armies, even if I have often wished that aid to developing countries be geared in inverse proportion to their military budgets, I am all for doing away with borders.

Hilaire Belloc, who had served in the French army and was of a generally conservative disposition, would not have agreed. He recorded a conversation he had with an exiled French anarchist he met shortly after arriving in Switzerland.

He was a sad, good man, who had committed some sudden crime and so had left France, and his hankering for France all those years had soured his temper, and he said he wished there were no property, no armies and no governments.

But I said that we live as parts of a nation, and that there was no fate so wretched as to be without a country of one's own – what else was exile which so many noble men have thought worse than death, and which all have feared? I also told him that armies fighting for a just cause were the happiest places for living, and that a good battle for justice was the beginning of all great songs; and that as to property, a man on his own land was the nearest to God.

Via Francigena signs began to reappear, the Fidenza pilgrim imprinted gnome-like in the milestones at the roadside. As befits an ancient route from Northern Italy to Tuscany, the verges were also peppered with wayside shrines. The best was the simplest – a statue of the Virgin pinned to an ilex tree with a fresh rose stuck in a plastic bottle, held up on a crudely knotted hank of wire.

After the morning climb, Berceto, snug in its valley a few kilometres away, came into a view, the essential elements of an ancient North Italian hill town clearly legible, but still miniature, and like a beacon growing ever more distinct it guided me down into the valley at the end of the day's walk. I checked into the central *Hotel Vitoria* where my bedroom looked onto wooded hillsides. In such a small town of narrow cobbled streets now given over almost entirely to tourism, it was surprisingly hard to find something as simple as a cotton singlet at a price my friend Peter would have appreciated. In the end I paid the tourist price for what should be one of the most basic items of clothing.

Even though it only has 2,000 inhabitants, Berceto boasts a scaled down 12th century Duomo, with a tympanum of the Crucified Christ which is carved with wonderful untutored directness. An extravagant frieze below the tympanum has a lion and mythical winged beasts dancing to the music of a harp-playing horse, accompanied by three figures performing an Oranges and Lemony dance, and a chevalier jousting with a harpy; a stimulating aperitif for my evening meal.

The *Vitoria* has a gourmet restaurant, *Da Rino*, where diners have been known to stuff themselves to the point of having to stay the night, and here I enjoyed a dinner based on the house speciality, *funghi*, a variety of local mushrooms both as a side dish and with my pasta. The menu carries a map of the Via Francigena on its back cover, but that doesn't mean the hotel has any real commitment to those who walk it. Eating may be the way here, but the hotel would not serve me breakfast until after eight o'clock.

So the morning of the 22nd began with coffee and croissant in a workmen's bar. That was sufficient fuel to get me up to the Passo della Cisa, the high point on my route over the Apennines. I had stuck with the *statale*, which remained almost devoid of traffic; and for much of the day I could see where it had all gone – onto the *autostrada* far below the old road, cutting through the mountain spurs in long tunnels and striding across the valleys on stilts.

An intriguing vision greeted me at the col – a pedal rickshaw and, peeking out of the back window of its miniature wagon tent, the black muzzle of a giant Doberman. The driver stood at the bicycle end, eating his breakfast, tall, with long, blond hair neatly pony-tailed, and dressed in Lycra shorts and shirt. His smile of greeting was unguardedly young and curiously feminine. The whole ensemble was worth more than a mere wave, so I crossed the road and we quickly struck up a rapport: that of two foreigners travelling under their own power through Italy.

Christian Spang was pedalling from his native Munich to Sicily, where he runs a children's adventure holiday charity. His rickshaw journey was part of a publicity campaign for his work. He shared his mobile tent with his dog, Phoenix, and whenever the going got tough Phoenix's 45 kilos were harnessed up to contribute to the pull. This was quite as good as leopards on horseback.

I told Christian that I had great affection for Sicily.

"My father ran part of it," I said, adding with a degree of light-heartedness, "he became CO of the occupying force after we kicked you guys out."

Christian's smile clouded over. I had offended him.

"Not us guys, but the Nazis," he corrected me. "It was the Nazis not the Germans who made the war."

I bit my tongue. Christian's firmly held revisionism was at variance with my own reading and understanding of what happened in Germany in the 1930s when Adolf Hitler rose to power. So, for some of his generation, guilt for a collective past has now been conveniently hung on the Nazis; the rest of the German soul has been cleansed. Part of me wanted to challenge him about all those good Germans who had voted and later fought for Hitler, but I backed off. Far better to steer the talk round to his own idealistic mission, and to compare notes about how the two of us had fared over our different journeys, and, in any case, I concluded that my gripe was not with him, but with those who had collectively re-written history so as to feed his generation with a new, and equally misleading German mythology.

At 1,039 metres, the summit of the Cisa Pass is a bleak place; a scatter of grey houses and two wayside hostels, where I stopped briefly for water. A little further, where steps lead up to a pretty art deco 1920s chapel, I crossed into Tuscany. Italy's finest region hardly bothers to announce itself to the arriving pilgrim; the only hint of change is the backs of road signs, now stamped with the acronym of the Italian roads authority under its regional headquarters: ANAS Firenze. There is nothing else to suggest that this is the gateway to the land of cypresses and hilltop towns, of golden expansive country and medieval towers and palaces. I felt as if I was sneaking through the back door onto the sets of the films, *The English Patient* and *A Room with a View*; indeed I didn't feel that I had arrived in Tuscany for several more days, not until I had broken out of the Ligurian Apennines and reached the Mediterranean.

Crossing the Apennines was one of Hilaire Belloc's finest achievements on his journey to Rome. He was no wimp about waymarks; nor was he scared to go off piste. After leaving the Via Emilia, he stuck to his resolution to walk in a straight line, and, in order to do so, he had to make four risky river crossings. Never entirely unaided, it should be said; in fact he was carried across two of them: a bare-legged six foot man shouldered him over the Taro, although not without tumbling with his passenger into the icy waters, and a man on stilts hefted him across the River Parma. It was still possible, a century ago, to hire a local Saint Christopher!

It is hard not to admire his passage across the Apennines; and Belloc himself is not overly humble about his achievement.

But here I must make clear by a map the mass of mountains which I was about to attempt, and in which I forded so many rivers, met so many strange men and beasts, saw such unaccountable sights, was imprisoned, starved, frozen, haunted, delighted, burnt up, and finally refreshed in Tuscany – in a word, where I had the most extraordinary and unheard-of adventures that ever diversified the life of man.

From Cisa, the road descends into the valley of the River Magra, which flows south to enter the Mediterranean at La Spezia. It takes a long time to reach the valley bottom, though. I stopped in the hilltop town of Montelungo for iced tea and an unexpectedly delicious home-made pastry with *frutti di bosci;* the blackberries took me back to my childhood. Archbishop Sigeric and his party made a point of lingering in Montelungo on their journey from Rome back to Canterbury, and in other circumstances I would have, too. But my destination that day was Pontrémoli, and I pressed on, swapping the pines for sweet chestnuts; and by mid-afternoon I was on the floor of the valley, following the still youthful Magra down towards the red Roman roof tiles and *campanile* of this small and attractive city.

I stayed just beyond the bounds of the city at an idyllic bed and breakfast. You reach it over an ancient three-arched bridge and under a stone gateway at the end of a lane. *Ai Chiosi* is a pair of former manor houses set in open farmland, with views back to the Duomo and its bell tower. My hostess Adriana Necchi, who inherited the property from a great-aunt and has restored it beautifully, greeted me with a ripe fig which she plucked from the tree in the courtyard; before long I was lying in the sun while she herself washed and dried my clothes. I crossed back into Pontrémoli for pilgrim stamp and evening meal; but how could my *pasta ai funghi* in the piazza opposite the town hall compete with my culinary experience at *Ai Chiosi* the next morning? Adriana settled me down at a table in her spacious granary dining room, and served me her own apple crumble. I would never in a thousand years have expected to eat my favourite English pudding for breakfast in Italy.

As I left on the morning of the 23rd, cloud was swirling over the castle of Piagnaro above Pontrémoli; not, as I first read it, the last of the early morning mist, but the harbinger of overcast skies – the first I had seen since before the Alps. But it was still another sweltering day, and I spent most of it happily ambling beside the Magra or through woodland paths among the slopes of the Candida hills. This part of Italy has a character and name of its own: Lunigiana. Aulla, its chief town, was my night's staging post. I covered the 24 kilometres without distraction, and arrived by one thirty. My afternoon was full of things to see. Backing on to the jagged Carrara hills and like many of the towns along the River, Aulla has an impressive castle perched high above it, the Fortezza della Brunella. For a long time it was the home of the early 20th century English landscape and flower painter Aubrey Waterfield. His daughter Kinta Beevor described the castle in her autobiography, *A Tuscan Childhood,* as the "most beautiful and magical place in the world" and, returning after a long absence following World War II, it still rekindled childhood magic for her 70 years on. Seeing it once again, far off from the Magra Valley, she wrote: "The castle stood on its spur in the distance with the wooded hills still sloping in on each side like the scenery in a toy theatre." *A Tuscan Childhood* is mostly about life inside the castle looking down onto Aulla from its bastions and the extraordinary 'garden in the sky' created inside the upper ramparts by her father, but this toy-like image is how I, too, saw it from far below.

Aulla is a communications hub, the confluence of the Magra and Aulella Rivers, a railway junction and the exit point to the sea from the Apennines – so important, in fact, that it was bombed by the Americans in 1944 in their attempt to dislodge the Germans, and accidentally flattened again in April the following year when a partisan shell hit a German ammunition train parked at the station sidings.

Aulla's principal attraction remains the Abbey of San Caprasio, and I had the good fortune to be shown round by Enrico Fregosi, who well remembers the bombing. He was aged ten when the bombs fell in the spring of 1944, killing more than 100 civilians. That, he said, was an accident of war; far worse was when, in reprisal for partisan action, German soldiers under Major Walter Reder rounded up 200 civilian hostages in the Aulella Valley and executed them.

But for Enrico other aspects of the city's history were more absorbing. He took me across to the little museum and showed me one of its prize exhibits, one that would especially appeal to me – a scallop shell worn by a pilgrim 800 years ago. Aulla was an important staging post on the way to Rome, because of its strategic position and because pilgrims stopped here to venerate the 5th century hermit Saint Caprasio whose bones are buried beneath the high altar in the abbey church. Recent restoration work has uncovered and reverently re-covered the sarcophagus where his remains still peacefully lie, despite being bombed by the Americans, and blasted by the Italian partisans.

The Apennines were to take one more bite out of me on Saturday the 24th during the final 17 kilometres to the coast. The day started with a stiff climb of 500 metres, past the hilltop village of Bibola, to a forested ridge where there was a confusion of paths and no waymarks to help. The Via Francigena was up to its customary tricks of disappearing in woods. An elderly couple picking blackberries did their best to put me right; but had to admit that they were not sure of the way. For an anxious hour I followed my instincts and compass until suddenly, *thalassa!* Like an excited child seeing the sea for the first time on his way to a seaside holiday, I glimpsed a chink of blue through the thick canopy of chestnut trees. Soon the whole Gulf of La Spezia was before me; blue sky and blue sea merged into one glorious blaze of bright light. I sat myself down on a warm rock and fell into a contented trance, embracing with all my senses the Mediterranean Sea to which I had been walking for eight hard weeks.

With lighter step, I descended towards the sea, picking my way in and out of olive groves. The path led through the village of Ponzano Superiore and from here it was but a short walk to my night's resting place of Sarzana which I entered under the arches of the Porta Parma;

still a few kilometres from the coast, but I could sense the sea air. The medieval town has the visible trappings of a seaside resort, with the tourist shops selling the usual holiday kit, from picture postcards of topless sunbathers to colourful beach *ombrelloni*. There is also a strong Tuscan accent to the old city; the Duomo is planked in the local marble and down its narrow streets are several houses banded in black and white like some of the great cathedrals and churches of the region. The city was in festive mood; young girls dressed in the shortest of skirts and in the highest heels, all with bared shoulders, were congregating in Piazza Matteotti, waiting to attend a wedding in the City Hall. Their young men, each one of them wearing dark glasses as if recruiting for the Mafia, stood in separate groups with suits of shiny material polished for parade. On the other side of the piazza, there was indeed a parade – of Vespa scooters. These little two-wheelers, with their flat running-boards, were one of the iconic images, and indeed part of the reality, of Italy's post-war prosperity, and the 1950s and 60s models have a club of dedicated enthusiasts. The turnout in Sarzana was impressive; I counted 30 with kempt paintwork and decorative chrome fittings, all lined up on the side of the piazza, their drivers ready to whisk away Sophia Loren or Audrey Hepburn on their pillion seat.

The *parocco* at the church of San Francesco jealously guards the right to stamp pilgrim passports in Sarzana in person. The tourist office told me this in a whisper. Like most of the parish priests I met in Italy, he was very old, and rather slow in his movements. He led me into the darkened office behind the sacristy, and sat at an enormous desk piled high with leaflets, letters, files and forms; he was visibly sinking beneath a sea of paper.

"*Da Inghilterra?*" he asked, and I nodded.

"Elizabeth, Charles," he said, enunciating their names in English with great care and deliberation, as if he had invoked God the Father and the Holy Ghost. The names of the British monarch and her heir appeared to be the sum total and absolute limit of his spoken English, but I warmed to his unusual selection of words; normally foreigners alight on "Manchester United".

I returned to Piazza Matteotti for dinner; I could not resist eating at a restaurant which called itself *Sorelle Gambas* – literally 'prawn sisters'. It seemed to go well with the name of my hotel – *La Stella*. I had a vegetable stew starter, a local speciality, and then *gambas* on rice, accompanied by a fresh Tuscan white. By now I could truly smell the sea.

THIRTEEN
NORTHERN TUSCANY

AFTER SATURDAY AFTERNOON'S REVELRY IN SARZANA, SUNDAY 25TH began in great tranquillity. What I had proposed was an easy day's walking – the remaining stretch of Lunigiana to the sea, and a left turn along the shore to the hotel that had intrigued me for its literary connection. High to my left, as I set out seaward, stood Sarzana's castle; beyond it the ruins of the once important Etruscan and Roman town of Luni. Wholly abandoned now, it gave its name to an entire district – some memorial, at least. And now, in the higher Apuan hills beyond, I began to make out the shining white gashes where precious Carrara marble had been carved from the mountainside. Their unseasonal illusion of snow would be the backdrop to my journey for the next two days.

Trusting that early Sunday morning traffic rules applied in coastal, as well as inland, Italy, I had ditched Chinn and stepped straight out on the hard shoulder of the main road between Sarzana and Marinella di Sarzana. My only company was a ceaseless succession of weekend cyclists, each on an expensive racing machine, each kitted in the latest Lycra shorts and shirt, high-speed helmets and designer sunglasses. They weren't great wavers-back. My sole roadside distraction was the recurring hoarding telling me that, in Sarzana, I had missed 'Sexy Shop Amsterdam'. What do the Dutch know...?

The sea's approach was proclaimed by a row of Mediterranean pines lit by early sun, and by roadside hedges of vivid bougainvillea.

The humbler weekend cabins gave way to gated villas and soon I was in the bustle of a resort, with the sea to my right as well as bars that had only just closed their doors to the last late night customer, seasonal clapboard shops, familiar from my home Essex coast, opening their shutters to unfurl their holiday gear, morning joggers pounding the palm-lined esplanade, young men sweeping the sand before setting out the sun beds and *ombrelloni* on the private beaches, and to my left an unending parade of hotels, grand and not-so-grand, ready to disgorge their holidaymakers across the road for another day of sun, sea and sand. I couldn't wait to join them.

Marinella gave way to Carrara, which proclaims itself the 'World Capital of Marble'. The next two places, Marina di Massa and Forte dei Marmi, have long found favour with wealthy Florentines; Gail was brought here by a rich young suitor when she was studying in Florence. The hotel that, when I was planning this part of my adventure, had taken my fancy was the *Regina*. What was good enough for Thomas Mann would do me fine. But when I walked in, the one room on offer was scarcely Mann-size, and so, with half a shrug of disappointment, I returned to the pleasures of the seafront, working two hours off the next stage in the agreeable company of growing throngs of happy, scantily dressed vacationers.

The beaches had an authentic feel about them, and it was only after a while that I realised why. Everyone was Italian; there were no foreigners. I was the only outsider, the sole intruder in their midst, although there was a sharp reminder on the seafront of one rather less peaceful bunch of intruders who came here two generations ago. A contemporary white marble statue stands at the water's edge to commemorate the starting point at the Tyrrhenian Sea of the Gothic Line, the defensive wall which the Germans threw across Italy in 1944 and which was broken at the cost of so many lives. I remembered from my time as a foreign correspondent in the country that Italians would rather recall their heroic struggle to free themselves from the Germans after the Allies, including my father, had invaded them from the south in 1943 than on the years before when, under Benito Mussolini, they were in close embrace with Adolf Hitler. True to form this statue, unveiled by President Carlo Ciampi in 2004, honours the civilian and partisan victims of the fighting along the Gothic Line in 1944-1945. That does at least give a place of honour to those who were bombed in friendly fire by the Americans in Aulla.

I arrived by happenstance at the *Hotel Coluccini*, a spacious 1920's 'ocean liner' set back from the seafront at Marina di Pietrasanta. A venerable old working canal for shipping marble comes out at the sea here, and the *Coluccini* stands next to it in its own miniature park at the confluence of the Via Apua and Via Roma. With a royal charter of 1923, it was one of the first hotels built in Versilia, the local name for this coastal area which caught the fancy of artists, composers and writers in the late 19th century and early decades of the 20th. Giacomo Puccini, composer of *La Bohème*, the author and journalist Carlo Collodi, creator of the long-nosed wooden puppet Pinocchio, and nationalist poet Gabriele D'Annunzio, all spent time in Versilia. Unaccustomed to receiving guests in tattered and dirty clothes who hobbled along in big boots carrying a bulging yellow pack, the hotel's youthful manager did his job magnificently: when I told him that I would take the only room on offer – the most expensive – he didn't bat an eyelid. It was ample and light, with marble floor, luxurious bathroom, and a terrace overlooking canal and sea; and whether out of duty to a pilgrim or sheer sporting decency (I like to think the latter) the manager allowed me a single occupancy discount: overall, a good welcome.

That was all but undone the moment I crossed the road. It was the afternoon of Sunday July 25th; 59 days since I had left Essex. In 53 of those I had walked just over 1,000 miles, some of that distance through an African heat wave, and crossed three mountain chains, and now there was nothing but a strip of sandy beach separating me from the refreshing cool of the sea, nothing, that is, except the seemingly outrageous sum of 30 euros for a perch – sunbed and *ombrellone* – on that beach opposite the *Coluccini*. But tomorrow was my rest day, and, having forked out for both days, I tip-toed slowly towards the sea, scalding my feet on the incandescent white sand. I wanted to plunge in, but after all that walking it seemed somehow more dignified to launch out a little more gracefully, surrendering myself to the water without a splash. As I glided in, the sea enveloped me like a healing balm more pleasurable and more effectual than all those indulgent massages, more refreshing than all the beers and iced teas, and more soothing to the body than all those salves and liniments. I let myself float away in the waves, pummelled, pulled and pushed by the currents, blissfully aware that for the first time in two months my body was moving without having to make any effort. I gazed up at the hills above, their marble quarries like glaciers glinting in the sun, and let the stress of my journey wash away to leave a core of inner calm. I sort of knew that there might never again be such a special swim. Ah, but "who of you by worrying," Luke quotes Jesus as saying, "can add a single hour to his life?"

I spent much of Monday 26th on the beach, rousing myself in the afternoon for the short walk inland to the Villa Versiliana, where D'Annunzio had lived for a time. A classic square three-storey Tuscan house surrounded by tall mushroom-shaped pines, the villa was host to a summer cultural festival; the main rooms were given over to an exhibition of modern Italian painting. I kept going back to the work of one of the artists, Concetto Pozzati, whose paintings seemed to be obsessed by boots, the subject of several still lifes with open laces in yellows, pinks and greens. To find the real D'Annunzio, I had to climb to the attic rooms. Somehow I was expecting his taste to be for Futurism. What I found was nearer to Puvis de Chavannes, murals of vestal virgins, somewhere between symbolist and *art nouveau* decadent, which D'Annunzio had commissioned.

In the garden's open theatre, a government minister enthralled his audience with talk about culture and the importance of a planned high-speed railway; I was struck by how many armed guards he had with him; but then I remembered March 1978 when the Red Brigades kidnapped the former Prime Minister, Aldo Moro, in Rome's Via Fani and shot dead his five bodyguards. After 55 days of interrogation, and pleading letters to fellow politicians, all ignored, he was bundled into the boot of a car, and told to wrap himself in a blanket. One of his captors pumped bullets into him until he was dead; and they then drove into the centre of Rome and dumped the car and its contents in Via Caetani. It was a huge international story, on which the Reuters bureau worked night and day; the country was on red-alert for almost two months. But a lot of what we wrote was speculative 'hot air' about possible sightings, rescue attempts and deals with the kidnappers. In truth, Moro was doomed the moment he was grabbed. Perhaps, therefore, in Italy you never can have too many bodyguards.

After my day-and-a-half stripped for the beach, when I finally left the friendly *Coluccini* on the Tuesday morning, July 27th, I felt, and probably looked to the few Italians around at the hour, like a galleon under full sail. I could sense them asking: what is that man doing at the seaside, in the height of summer, in mountain boots and with an alpine rucksack on his back? Well, it wasn't going to be seaside forever. I followed the palm-studded esplanade as far as the Lido di Camaiore, before turning sharp left and heading inland. I was sorry to leave the sea shore; with its liveried private beaches, its enticing restaurants and bars, and its cavalcade of imperial hotels, it had been colourful and fun to walk by. If I had stayed, as planned, at Thomas Mann's hotel, I would have passed through the town of Pietrasanta, one of Archbishop Sigeric's stages and which I regretted missing, but my route now took me directly towards Lucca. I crossed beneath the A12 *autostrada* and over the main coastal railway, swapped the scent of the sea for that brackish smell of fresh cut hay, and walked quickly towards the last low lying hills of the Apuan Alps.

At the wayside shrine on the canal that leads into the village of Camairore, the Virgin has been transformed into philosopher. Set in her alcove, surrounded by gifts of flowers, rosary beads, and a range of votive offerings, including a ceramic jug with five ducks sprouting from its sides, she delivers a message whose real challenge is to those who don't stop. The inscription at her foot reads:

"I stand serenely in this shaded corner, coloured with flowers and ornamented with offerings, watching in amazement as the world goes by."

On the farm track leaving the village, a straggling narrow street of tourist shops, I came across an old man who had clearly heeded the Madonna's message. Bare-footed and bare-backed, in a pair of light shorts held to his firm waist by a well worn leather belt, he was chopping logs. He looked immensely fit, but there was nothing boastful about his strength – no show of muscles. The only real sign of age was his swept back grey hair. We chatted and I coaxed it out of him that he was 76.

"How do you manage to stay so youthful?"

"Simple," he replied. "I have always worked, and I have always worked on the land, cultivating my plot."

So often, making my way on foot through Europe, I have encountered just such contentment – men digging vegetable gardens, tending vines, and chopping wood in their backyards invariably appear to be happy or, at least, they have the time to smile back to me. Voltaire came forcefully to the same conclusion in the strife of the Enlightenment. At the end of his hero Candide's misadventures, there is only one thing to do: "*Il faut cultiver notre jardin*". Whether or not this was really the philosopher's recipe for life, the man chopping logs in Camairore was ample proof that the formula of domestic labour works.

The final kilometres to Lucca were in the same rural spirit. Farm tracks and small roads led me across gentle hills to the River Sérchio; one stretch down a footpath in a rocky gully bordered by fens and bracken led out, as if by magic, to an abandoned 12th century chapel and hostel dedicated to the Archangel Gabriel. Later, I passed a wayside chapel of St James, before crossing the bridge over the Sérchio at San Macario Piano which is guarded by a statue of St Peter clasping the symbolic key to Heaven. The shrines and saints came on me unexpectedly; but by them I felt the tread and passage of pilgrims past.

Lucca, a city that grew rich on silk underwear, should have been better. I approached its outskirts with a hard march along the banks of the river, fighting off swarm after swarm of mosquitoes and contending with the intense heat of the early afternoon. I was 36 kilometres closer to Rome, but as I entered the city through the Porta San Donato I didn't feel a sense of progress. In fact it seemed as if I was being gobbled up inside the city's wonderfully preserved Roman brick walls. Lucca, in high summer, was like a spin dryer, tossing tourists up and down its narrow streets and whirling them round its walls. After so long in peaceful solitude, I felt uncomfortable. I loved the Duomo's richly adorned west front, with its arched loggia, and went back there several times, even fighting my way through the crowds to walk all the way round it, but otherwise Lucca was a bad experience. It didn't feel like the birthplace of Luigi Boccherini and Giacomo Puccini – they would have joined me in my execration of the evening meal; the pasta was tasteless, rubbery and expensive. Even my hotel, the *Ilaria*, an upmarket establishment named after Ilaria del Carretto, the wife of a Lucchese ruler whose serene beauty is immortalised on her tombstone in the Duomo, threw in its own sour note of embarrassment. I had stripped off and was stretching before my bath (yes, it had a bath!) when I glanced out of the window overlooking the Bottini Gardens and realised that I was in a room which also gave onto the hotel terrace. Two Canadian tourists were sitting there observing me intently.

"Everything in Lucca is good," wrote Hilaire Belloc, never slow to disagree with his later follower. He admired its "un-crowded streets" and "contented silent houses", and stopped there to eat and sleep for a few hours during the hot day, before walking on towards Siena through the cool night. By now, Belloc was in a hurry to get to Rome, and he had made huge strides to reach Lucca.

If his account is to be believed, in completing his march across the foothills of the Apennines, Belloc seems to have covered the 120 kilometres from the River Enza to Lucca in a little over 48 hours, much of it walking by night. Belloc's narrative is often a muddle of anecdotal asides and philosophical observations, so it is not always easy to follow the precise stages and timings of his route; perhaps this is intentional. At any rate, aged only 30 when he completed his walk to Rome, he was certainly capable of covering huge distances, and by now, by his own account, he was in haste. He doesn't make light of his efforts:

> I hobbled on in despair of the night, for the necessity of sleep was weighing me down after four high hills climbed that day, and after the rough ways and the heat and the continual marching ...

> But now, on this ridge, dragging myself on to the main road, I found a deeper abyss of isolation and despairing fatigue than I had ever known, and I came near to turning eastward and imploring the hastening of light, as men pray continually without reason for things that can but come in due order. I still went forward a little, because when I sat down my loneliness oppressed me like a misfortune; and because my feet, going painfully and slowly, yet gave a little balance and rhythm to the movement of my mind.

Not everything was bad, of course, and in extricating myself from the city early on July 28th, stepping briskly along the Viale Luigi Cardona, I spotted a striking porticoed villa. Someone had taste: it was the British School of Lucca. Freed from the grasp of the walled city, soon I was walking down country lanes, surrounded with birdsong again, under bright open skies. By the time I reached the town of Capannori, I was ready for my morning drink and I had just spread myself out on a bench when I was joined by an elderly man and a small boy, his grandson, whom he was walking to school.

"Are you going all the way to Rome on foot?" asked the grandfather. "It would be wonderful if you could come with me to Giovanni's school?"

I looked at the boy, thinking now if I were you, Giovanni, would I want to walk into class or playground accompanied by some dodgy middle-aged mendicant that grandpa had picked up in the street? But the grandfather insisted, and as the school was just a few metres away I accepted. The *Scuola Elementare* was a simple affair, a modern single-storey building, and I was duly marched up the steps to the reception area and introduced to the boy's teacher – no questions here about proof that I wasn't a child molester, or worse. But that is not quite the point of the story; she presented me to her pupils as if I were a visiting John the Baptist; and in a country where church attendance is now no greater than in the rest of predominantly secular Europe, the children responded with little handshakes as if I were indeed some holy man. Such is the pull and power of the Via Francigena.

The pilgrim went on his way with a certain embarrassment, but the episode wasn't finished. A few kilometres beyond, Giovanni's grandfather stepped into the road, flagging me down as if I were a racing car being pulled into the pits. He lived in a fine stone house on the Via Romana, and invited me for a drink. Having plied me with water and lemonade, he insisted that I read aloud some of Dante's *Inferno* from a large leather volume which he said he had inherited from his father. I began to question the reality of the situation; I recalled Evelyn Waugh's Tony Last, condemned forever to read Dickens to his captor in the South American jungle, and I wondered, first, whether I would ever escape and, second, why it had to be the *Inferno*!

The state of the Italian Church was all too visible on the approach to the village of Badia Pozzeveri. The track into the village was bounded by the tall rendered wall of the cemetery, and I could see from the central columbarium building that it was 'alive' and open for business. Round the corner, though, lay the abandoned shell of an 11th century abbey church and cloister, with ivy growing over its brick and stone Romanesque structure, and nesting birds occupying its belfry. This was St Peter's in Pozzeveri, the abbey church of a Camaldolese Benedictine monastery which thrived here in the middle ages as a halt for pilgrims. Until a few years ago, it was in congregational use, and its few remaining friends have nailed this notice on the front above the door arch to warn pilgrims of its plight:

"The abandonment of this historical building, which dates back to the 10th century, is a disgrace. We call upon the community of Badia Pozzeveri to save this church."

My next church, also Romanesque, was in much better care. I perched on a grass bank in the shade of the campanile of San Jacobo Maggiore in Altopascio with my back to one of the neat row of cypresses that line the churchyard. I was in trouble with my night's accommodation, making a series of increasingly fruitless calls on my mobile. My day's walk was taking me inexorably towards a hostel in which I had no wish to stay: the *Ostello Ponte dei Medici* at Ponte a Cappiano. It was awaiting me like a lobster pot. I tried option after option, noting down numbers and calling the offices of all the local *communi*. At last, I walked on in frustration, resigned to a night of communal snoring. This had been my experience on my walk to Santiago de Compostela, when smelly and noisy dormitories had been the norm. Pilgrim hostels are fine when you are aged twenty, but not much fun at sixty, when sleep, even after a 20-mile walk, is harder to come by.

I put these horrible thoughts out of mind and walked on, only to discover a few kilometres later that my little round compass was missing. I felt for it in my pocket, and it was gone. It must have fallen out when I was making those phone calls. At any other time, the loss of a 15 euro pocket compass at the side of a road would not even register; but right then it was a real blow. I had come to depend on the little thing both for direction, and as a lucky charm, or talisman. How quickly we revert to being primitive; here I was on the road to Rome, practising good old fashioned idolatry – compass worship. I seriously thought of returning to pick it up and then my rational, non-superstitious brain kicked in, as did my memory of my morning dose of St Luke: that in the end all possessions are of no worth. I decided that my friend from Reims, which had been my guide over the Jura, Alps and Apennines, had done its job and should now find a new home. I rather hoped a child would find it, and that its cardinal points and magic constancy might open a youthful imagination to far horizons. I reached down into my rucksack and retrieved my original compass; the one that had unilaterally realigned itself on the *Chemin des Dames* making north become south. Welcoming my old friend, I wiped its face and put it in the lost one's pocket, murmuring: just stay there. Little did I know that by the end of the day I would be sorely grateful that I had kept this dud compass with its strange upside-down readings, and that I had carried it as dead weight all the way from Northern France.

Not long after, I turned off the road and was transported back to the Middle Ages. The approach to Galleno preserves the ancient pilgrim route, as a hollow way between the fields. The surface is embedded stone, ground down and smoothed by centuries of footfall. Ash trees lined the banks, and through their pale canopy the sun sprinkled fingers of light for several kilometres on a path seemingly unchanged and untouched by time.

Leaving the village I was soon lost in woods. A roadside Via Francigena sign had sent me down a dusty track past two houses and an equestrian centre and within minutes, I was deep in a wood and upon a seven-went-ways choice of well trodden paths, all leading in broadly the same direction, but none with a Via Francigena waymark, or for that matter any waymark. Paul Chinn's guide was not much help and my map next to useless. The sun high in the sky and hiding in forest boughs wasn't much help either. Out came my broken compass; I would have to trust its upside-down directions; southeast, where I was heading, would be northwest. An hour later I emerged from the woodland tracks a relieved, chastened man. Even the prospect of a night in a hostel now seemed dimly agreeable. In the distance below me I could see the green Arno Valley and, for the first time, a hillside line of Tuscan cypresses.

As its name suggests, Ponte a Cappiano, is built round its bridge. When Archbishop Sigeric came back this way, he crossed the Usciana River by boat; it wasn't until the 1530s that Cosimo dei Medici commissioned this grand, brick structure, a rustic cousin of Florence's Ponte Vecchio. Its arches contain sluices and locks, regulating the river as an inland waterway; and above and beside the carriageway, the architect set an arcaded and turreted palazzo which in the last century the *Commune* restored and converted into a pilgrim hostel. When I arrived, the dormitories were filled with Albanian refugees. I was put in a private room, under firm instructions to keep the door locked.

I walked over the bridge to Ponte a Cappiano's little piazza for a beer. Daniel, the barman, wanted to know if I had had a good day.

"Yes, except for the disappearing waymarks in the *bosco.*"

"*Cosa curiosa*," he said. "Funny: you are not the first person to say that."

Sitting outside the bar, I had the company of a group of third-aged men round a table discussing football and the year's olive crop. There was no restaurant in town, so I decided to make do with whatever I could buy at the shop on the other side of the square. But it was Wednesday, early closing, and therefore the town's only food store was shut. It was going to be ice cream for supper, and there would be nowhere open for breakfast the following morning. So while the hostel in the end wasn't quite the *Inferno* or *Purgatorio* I'd feared, I started my walk on the morning of July 29th on an empty stomach.

Hilaire Belloc frequently set off without eating anything, even though, an imposing fellow, he sang the virtues of marching on a full belly, and particularly the merits of a good breakfast.

> I should very much like to know what those who have an answer to everything can say about the food requisite to breakfast? Those great men Marlowe and Jonson, Shakespeare, and Spenser before him, drank beer at rising, and tamed it with a little bread. In the regiment we used to drink black coffee without sugar, and cut off a great hunk of stale crust, and eat nothing more until the halt ... Dogs eat the first thing they come across, cats take a little milk, and gentlemen are accustomed to get up at nine and eat eggs, bacon, kidneys, ham, cold pheasant, toast, coffee, tea, scones, and honey ... But what rule governs all this? Why is breakfast different from all other things, so that the Greeks called it the best thing in the world, and so that each of us in a vague way knows that he would eat at breakfast

nothing but one special kind of food, and that he could not imagine breakfast at any other hour of the day?

The newly refurbished *Smeraldo* bar at Fucecchio, a few kilometres down the road, provided me with a delicious breakfast of fresh orange juice and hot croissants; the young girl serving me smiled. That marks a tremendous change from the Italy I had worked in. Her male equivalent 30 years ago would have felt it his manly duty to be gruff.

Fucecchio is on the banks of the Arno, the last major river before Rome. I expected something dramatic – a great rush of water, a roll of drums – but it was a bit of an anti-climax. Here the Arno slouches past, sluggish and mud brown. Tall trees line the banks either side of the bridge but the predominant impression is of an industrial wasteland. Not all Tuscans can work the vineyards or tend the land for British second-home owners. There has to be industry, and a lot of it is by the Arno. I crossed the bridge and turned sharp left along the bank, to my right was the fence of an industrial estate. Path and waymarks quickly vanished and I had to hack my way up the hill to San Miniato on the side of a busy road. Once clear of the traffic, on a small lane leading up to the town, I had a chance to look round and see for the first time the full glory of central Tuscany. Here, at the mid-point between Florence and Pisa, I had at my feet patchwork geometry of vineyards, cornfields and woodlands, bordered with natural hedges and appliquéd here and there with neat rows of cypresses. The rolling landscape receded into the far distance, to a smudge on the horizon which I knew for the Apennines, now five days behind me. Nothing spoilt the view, except for a band of dark cloud building in the west.

The hilltop town of San Miniato is one of the gems of Tuscany, its medieval skyline emboldened by a lofty castle tower and the tall Duomo. There are paintings here by Filippo Lippi and sculptures by Donatello, and a monastery reputedly founded by St Francis of Assisi. In November there is an enticing festival to celebrate the local delicacy – white truffles; but this was a hot day in late July, and I am ashamed to say that I merely doffed my cap to San Miniato, stopping for as long as it takes to despatch a tuna *panino* and cold tea, and then walking straight through the historic centre along the Street of Twelve Churches, any one of which would have merited a visit. Long-distance walking does not combine well with leisurely tourism; unless, that is, you have given yourself a rest day. But there is no doubt of it: a San Miniato day lightens your heart and refills your sails.

I left San Miniato and stepped into more intimate country; small lanes and white farm tracks, bounded by stone walls, running up and down tightly woven valleys and dales, woodland of oak and linden, and patches of olives and vines sharing the land with larger cornfields. Broad-roofed villas perched with that peculiar Tuscan confidence on the hillsides, as if they had always been there. Many hadn't, being – on closer examination – 'new-build', but they blended well enough. The landscape has not been raped.

"Following a bend on the left, turn sharp right onto a track." Till then Paul Chinn's instructions and the frequency of waymarks had built my confidence. Since San Miniato, I had picked up numerous, reassuring waymarks. But I never found that sharp right turn; and once more I cursed the haphazard waymarking in Italy, and my own poor navigation. But it didn't really matter, and apart from the frustration and humiliation of yet again losing my way I just carried on down the back-lanes. As it happened, it turned out for the better.

The clouds building to the west became ever blacker. By the time I reached Castelfiorentino day had turned to night, and once distant rumbles of thunder had become great drum beats that seemed to shake the ground beneath me. I had just turned off onto the road to Gambassi Terme when the real rain started. This was no ordinary rain, not even like those sudden deluges in Dhaka that I had grown accustomed to during the monsoon; this was as if the heavens had opened a sluice gate. The verge turned into a fast-flowing stream, sheets of cascading water reduced vision to a few metres, and cars and trucks reined in, their headlights dimmed to a blur. The huge drops, interspersed with vicious pellets of hail, began to lash me. This was hard-hat rain. I had to find shelter quickly. Stumbling to the nearest farm, I dived for cover under an open barn by an orchard of pear trees, grateful at least that this farm was not guarded by hungry Alsatian dogs. The storm was one of the fiercest I have seen, and I could imagine I was witnessing the start of the next Flood. The rain streamed down the open sides of the barn, splashing upwards from the concrete apron like a fountain, and started to find its way through the roof. I sat crouched on a stack of wooden pallets and stared out from the hood of my anorak at this hostile element enveloping my world, a world now reduced to tumbling water and a midnight sky lit up, every few minutes, by a flashing blade of lightning, followed by a tumultuous explosion. This was the mother of all summer storms, breaking the mother of all heat waves; and it was the first time I had been forced to stop walking since leaving home. But I was now glad that I had missed that turning and that I wasn't walking in open country on what would be water-logged farm tracks.

Of course, like Housman's gale on the Wrekin, the storm was too fierce to last, and gradually the rain eased; I could sense it calming, rather like a Tchaikovsky symphony struggling to end with its intermittent but diminishing bursts of life. I thanked my unknown farmer as I emerged into a wet and sodden landscape to turn up the hill towards Gambassi Terme, high on the ridge above and still covered in swirling clouds. And just as peace was restored, my mobile rang. So many days out from England, and by now thoroughly cut off from my normal social and business life, this was a rare occurrence. It was my brother Neil in Ireland. Our last talk, immensely useful, had been five weeks back as I approached Besançon; he had found me the number of the Meindl stockist there, and the shop had in turn put me in onto Monsieur Moisson. This time, though, his news shocked me: one of his Irish brothers-in-law had been killed in a bar in Malaga, gunned down at random by a drunken Brit who had opened fire on his fellow customers because he had been chucked out of the bar. The bullet got him low-down. I reflected on the bizarre fate that awaits many of us, and about a gentle Irishman with whom I had once shared a round of golf who had died from lead, not beer, in his liver.

It was mid-afternoon and merely overcast when I reached Gambassi Terme, 350 metres above sea level, and 37 kilometres from my start in Ponte a Cappiano. *Commune* workmen were mopping up; rainwater was still spilling off the gutters and down the sides of the narrow cobbled streets; the town's grey stone was dripping. I did my best to dry my things in the *Albergo Pinchiorba* but I knew I would have to set out the next day in damp clothes and wait for the Tuscan sun. My trousers, though, were torn as well as soaked: however, I was in luck. In a cellar workshop near the hotel, I found a seamstress who, when I told her my mission and showed her the rips, turned from the outfit she was working on, and in an instant had my torn garment under her sewing machine to emerge with two new matching panels. She was creating costumes for the town's *Palio*. Gambassi Terme's annual medieval pageant lacks the bareback horse racing which draws crowds to the larger festival at Siena, but there are medieval ball games, jousting and processions, and they all require theatrical costumes. While she stitched them, I visited the local *parroco*, one more elderly priest scarcely able to climb his stairs. He stamped and signed my pilgrim passport with a reverence which I knew full well I did not deserve.

There was a skim of cloud over the sky when, early on the morning of the 30th, I passed his Pisan-style parish church again; not far from it, I felt a sudden snap, and the weight on my back lurched to one side. I thought at first that this was some sort of divine retribution for nine weeks of phoney pilgrimhood, and that my back had gone. There was no pain, however. I stopped by a wall, from which there was a wondrous view of Tuscany with early morning mist from the previous day's rain steaming out of the distant valleys, and unslung my rucksack to gauge the damage. And there was the problem: my back was fine, but my rucksack had given way. The metal frame which keeps the bag stable on my back had burst out of its supporting ribbed stitching and was now threatening to capsize the whole contraption. My harness was broken. This was almost more serious than an injury; I could coax my back into shape with paracetemol and lotions, but my rucksack was another matter. I juggled it and stretched and pulled it until, by jamming the loose pole of the frame into the waist strap, I managed to hoist a jury rig, good enough to walk on with. This did indeed hold it, the downside being that the motion of walking would dig it into my side; each pace across that lovely Tuscan landscape was now punctuated by an irritating jab. I needed to find a cobbler.

The clouds burned off and the sun returned, chastened by the fresh rain, and cooler. I wound my way along farm tracks over the Tuscan hills, passing through olive groves and vineyards, and through newly harvested corn fields. Often I needed no clearer guide than the next hilltop village ahead. One lonely farmstead was guarded by two dogs, running free; they merely snarled as I passed them, cooing insistently but quietly. A middle-aged moustachioed Belgian, a holidaying Hercule Poirot armed with a powerful pair of binoculars, was coming up the footpath below the farm, out for some early bird spotting. We greeted each other, and after the usual *politesse* in Italian and English we quickly switched to French.

"Where better to look for birds than in the land of St Francis," he sighed.

"Yes, indeed, things have improved," I replied. "When I used to live here, Italians shot at anything that flew over them. The countryside was a dangerous place to walk in during the hunting season."

"No longer; Europe has muzzled the Italian hunting gun. Even the wild boars are now being protected."

"Watch out for the wild dogs just up the road," I warned him.

Minutes later, I heard a savage roar from the farm; soon I became aware of a breathless Belgian trotting up behind me. He had been chased away by the guard dogs.

"How did you get past those fierce animals?" he asked.

"Simple," I said. "I talked to them in Italian."

I halted outside the village of Pancole at the Sanctuary of the Virgin of Divine Providence. Here in 1668, the Virgin appeared to a young deaf-mute, Bartolomea Ghini, who worked as a shepherdess. She was instantly cured and proper food appeared on her poor family's table. This is one of the many sites in Europe revered for an apparition of the Virgin that did not make it onto the pilgrimage circuit – Pancole was never in the same league as Fatima, Lourdes, Częstochowa, or Walsingham. The chapel of 1670 was destroyed by the Germans in World War II, but the replica had a charm and peace about it, a simple sanctuary chapel with plain rendered walls, above the altar an elaborately framed painting of the Virgin and child by Pier Francesco Fiorentino; and it is especially striking to the eye, being constructed over an archway above the narrow road. A notice informs visitors that they can obtain a plenary indulgence here – a pardon for all sins committed to date. I thought this was cheeky, having come to believe that the Roman Catholic Church no longer openly favoured such a score-card approach to religion and the after-life; if it did still do so, then I felt distinctly put out. If visiting Pancole was worth a clean slate, then what would I get for walking to Rome? I did a quick calculation and concluded: not much. But I took comfort from the typo on the English translation: in the eyes of a Canon Lawyer, that interesting spelling of the key word in the promise of a fast-track from Pancole to Heaven – 'plenery' with a second 'e' – doubtless invalidates this particular guarantee of eternal salvation.

San Gimignano comes into view from far away. This city of towers in the midst of picture-postcard Tuscan countryside is a magnificent survivor from the Middle Ages, although its towers which we marvel at today are in fact contrivances of war. There were originally 72 of them, erected by families as a sign of their wealth and as defensive bastions against hostile or treacherous neighbours. Only 15 of them now remain, enough, though, to give San Gimignano an unmatched medieval skyline which draws tourists to its city gates by the coach load.

I was privileged; approaching San Gimignano along winding country lanes at three miles an hour, to witness the city unfolding before me in the context of its countryside, a serrated line of higher hills behind it creating a deep backdrop to the gentle curving rise on which it is built. Olive trees, vines and cypresses competed for space on the land around it and covered or camouflaged the occasional red tiled rooftop outside the city walls. As I neared the city, its contours became clearer and it appeared to sprout more towers, their seemingly mesmeric powers pulling me ever towards them.

Once inside the medieval walls, however, my thoughts turned to practicalities. My rucksack's urgent need of a cobbler made me view San Gimignano in a new light. Entering the city by the Porta San Giovanni, I made straight for the first of a row of leather and shoe shops. Was there a cobbler anywhere in the city? The answer was predictable. I was in the heart of medieval Italy, where the last cobbler shut up shop more than 20 years ago. Selling shoes is far more profitable than repairing them. I carried on; threading my way through lines of tourists up Via San Giovanni, still determined that somewhere I could get my rucksack repaired. I passed the Museum of Torture and Capital Punishment – obviously the historical centre and its scenic medieval streets needed a bit of spicing up for today's tourist – and on the far side of the Piazza dell'Erbe I spotted a shop which sold proper stuff: rustic linen, table cloths with woven patterns and lace. It was the first sign of anything for sale that someone might even want, and could actually use. I stepped in, as always aware that my appearance had an element of 'shock and awe' about it. The shop assistant listened attentively to my problems and told me she used a seamstress, called Maria, who lived in the vicolo behind. She couldn't quite recall the number.

That is how I ended up walking down a narrow residential street in the heart of San Gimignano shouting 'Maria! Maria!' As if by magic, a shutter swung open and out leant a lady dressed in black. Maria was a widow, and she stuck to the old ways, going into black when her husband died. I explained my problem but had to work hard to persuade her to open the door; I must have appeared an awful ruffian. Besides, looking down on the bag, she did not think she could possibly stitch something so thick. But I eventually persuaded her at least to inspect the job. Maria came to the street door and rose to the challenge; she took me upstairs to her apartment and set to work like a bosun repairing a torn sail. I had after all found an artisan in San Gimignano.

"This will get you to Rome," she said when she had finished. And it did.

San Gimignano looked good again from my rear mirror; as I walked away along the winding lanes that led me over the hills and on to the Val d'Elsa, I couldn't help stopping to turn back and admire its slowly receding stage set. I had a *rendez-vous* in Graciano d'Elsa; I was being picked up by a mutual friend, Stephen Roach. This was intended and proved to be an extremely pleasant interlude, but it started with certain awkwardness on my part. After 66 days on the road, what if I was no longer house trained? I had grown accustomed to checking in to hotels and going off in the evenings to do my own thing; now, for the first time since staying with the Ponds in Epping Forest, I would be the guest in someone else's home; I would have to behave, and maybe even conform.

Stephen, an Australian photographer from faraway Sydney, picked me up as arranged at Graciano's central bar opposite the church. I knew him instantly from the description: willowy with longish silver hair. His voice, though agreeable, was disconcertingly soft, and I had to strain to hear him as we set off in an ancient car, which whined and rattled up into the hills between Poggibonsi and Castellina in Chianti. This part of central Tuscany is covered in woodland and I soon lost my bearings as we turned down first a white road and then a dirt track: so far from my route, I felt instinctively uneasy; and started to wonder how I would ever get back.

After eternity of rock and rut, he braked the car, and as the dust cleared, I saw a Tuscan stone farmhouse, magnificent in its restored state. Il Poggiolo has all the traditional features, a square tower with pavilion roof and arched windows, a wing with a catslide roof of Roman tiles, and curved buttressed base, and a covered terrace. The house incorporates, as a spacious living area, the old barn, with wide plate-glass upper windows and an entrance through the original cart door. Planning permission to do anything in Italy is often a matter of endless delays and disputes with conservationists. Il Poggiolo was no exception; it took three architects and a structural engineer to push the project to completion.

While the stout timbers of the barn's roof are the architectural talking-point of this living area, the predominant vision in the house when I arrived was of naked females. An entire wall was given over to Stephen's newest photographic project, young ladies floating without clothes in the rock pool below the house, while the studio where his artist daughter works was also stacked with female nudes.

Naked flesh inside, it was raw intelligence outside: out on the terrace was Stephen's Italian wife, Fabrizia. Dark flowing hair, a wide beckoning smile, razor sharp, she is Professor of Sanskrit at Florence's University. We were soon joined by her elder daughter, Iante, studying Persian and Arabic at Oxford University, and by the younger daughter, Dione, the artist, and by a family friend, a German anthropologist. After weeks of intellectual laziness and as the sun set over Il Poggiolo and the local white wine came out with the fireflies, I was put to the test.

"Are you a real pilgrim?" they all wanted to know, coming at me from every angle, but nicely.

We drank and ate well, and stayed up late into the night; I am aware that all evening I managed to avoid answering their question. I wouldn't have known how to, and still don't. All I knew for sure was that I was a long, long way from what Luke says Jesus expected of his Apostles: "Take nothing for the journey – no staff, no bag, no bread, no money, no extra tunic." Dione took my pilgrim passport and deftly penned a 'stamp' of herself and the house, signing it: 'Il Poggiolo, nowhere'.

On the morning of the 31st, Stephen drove me from 'nowhere' back to the bar at Graciano d'Elsa and left me to track east and south towards Siena. The way took me through forest with the usual waymarking problems, and it was with considerable relief that I emerged from the dense tree cover to see the hilltop town of Monteriggioni and its turreted

13th century walls. A tractor was working one of the fields below the town, turning and mulching the harvest stubble and ploughing it back into neat rows of great reddish weals of Tuscan earth. This last day of July I had noticed dew on the grass in the morning; I had walked from late spring to late summer.

It was a stiff climb. Monteriggioni had once been a Sienese fortress; now it was a tourist honey pot. In a smart upper room overlooking the stone piazza, the tourist office was hosting a Via Francigena exhibition. I went in and found a glossy Via Francigena magazine on sale, and a pretty girl behind the desk.

"What a shame the money spent producing this magazine wasn't put towards properly waymarking the woods I've just come through," I remarked. "You are promoting something that is not finished."

"Yes, we know," she said.

Woodland paths and country lanes led me to the valley's edge at La Querce where the open hilltop finally brought Siena into view. In the valley below I could hear the *autostrada*. My own road would dip steeply down to pass under it; then it would be a stiff climb up to the city walls in the heat of the early afternoon sun. Walking through Tuscany had made me appreciate the strategic sense of building towns and cities on hilltops; and it was to the ridge opposite, 345 metres at its highest, that the wonderful city I was about to enter owed its original prosperity, as well as its latter day status as a uniquely complete medieval city.

FOURTEEN

SIENA AND VAL D'ORCIA

AFTER HIS GRAND REPAST IN LUCCA, HILAIRE BELLOC slept all day and set off for Siena at nightfall. Once across the Arno, he carried on through the night into the Val d'Elsa, where he rested at dawn and ate another meal, and then took a train to Siena.

"If one man," thought I, "may take five per cent discount on a sum of money in the exchange, may not another man take discount off a walk of over seven hundred miles? May he not cut off it, as his due, twenty-five miserable little miles in the train?"...

If the people of Milo did well to put up a statue in gold to the man that invented wheels, so should we also put one up in Portland stone or plaster to the man that invented rails, whose property it is not only to increase the speed and ease of travel, but also to bring on slumber as can no drug: not even poppies under a waning moon ...

Once only, when a number of men were shouting 'Poggi-bon-si' like a war-cry to the clank of bronze, did I open my eyes sleepily to see a hill, a castle wall, many cypresses, and a strange tower bulging out at the top (such towers I learned were the feature of Tuscany). Then in a moment, as it seemed, I awoke in the station of Siena, where the railway ends and goes no further.

Unlike Belloc, I entered the city, fully awake and on foot, through the triple-arched Porta Camollia; I walked down the long Via dei Montani and out into the Piazza del Campo, not so much a square as an open arena moulded on three sides by elegant four-storey town houses and tilted like a great saucer towards the majestic city hall, the Palazzo Publico. At its side, the Torre del Mangia, the tall square tower with single-dial clock, said one thirty. I had covered my 25 kilometres from the Elsa Valley in respectable time. As you would expect in one of Europe's finest squares, and perhaps its greatest outdoor drawing room, the piazza was brimming with smiling tourists – many basking in the sun, stretched out on the gently sloping terracotta and travertine pavement. As for just stopping and standing, who couldn't in such a place? Myself, I knew (or felt I knew) what to expect, having visited Siena on several occasions, once even at *Palio* time to watch horses being raced bareback round the Campo's perimeter. The unexpected happened to me not in the hot piazza but the moment I stepped into the cool of the city's tourist office. For the first time since I had begun travelling to Italy nearly half a century ago, I found myself being charged for a tourist city map: half a euro.

"A bit cheeky, isn't it, to make visitors pay for a map if tourism is the main attraction here?" I asked.

"New orders from the cash-strapped *Commune*," replied the sassy attendant. "And in any case, remember, we are a city of bankers."

I had forgotten that; amid its medieval splendours, Siena is the seat of the Monte dei Paschi bank, the oldest in the world, which was founded under the auspices of the Republic of Siena in 1472 and was one of the first issuers of city debt certificates or bonds. Your loan to the *Commune* was secure: it was guaranteed by the great tracts of coastal grazing land, in the Maremma. Ah, well: I paid her that half euro and asked for my pilgrim stamp in return.

I walked back across the piazza and climbed the steps to the great gothic Duomo. Here my pilgrim status – or rather, for once its outer trappings, the boots and rucksack – gave me free entry, saving me ten euros; Peter would have been delighted. It was refreshingly cool and spacious; the organ (I noted) was playing a Bach fugue. Gazing up at the high vaulted roof, and down the long line of columns, all banded in Siena's trademark black and white stone, I felt a sudden elation: I could see, as if down the ages, the pilgrims before me who had stood on this inlaid marble floor, and I realised that after me more would come this way; and it was borne in on me, standing near the west doors, that those of us who arrive here on foot – good, bad, rich or poor, healthy or ill – are bound together in an unbroken, unending procession: this was enough for me. I had my pilgrim passport stamped the second time for good measure. There was sufficient space; I could see that with ten days to go, there would be some blank compartments in my little book. Hilaire Belloc may not have had his passport stamped in Siena, but he did hear Mass; and quite right, too. The blighter had arrived by train, after all.

It was a short step across the corner of the Campo to the *Hotel Duomo* in Via di Stalloreggi – the street of the royal stables – where to my joy the window of my third-floor room framed almost the entire Duomo. I could look out over the red ochre roof tiles and see the building full on – from its western portals to the cupola; my eye ran up the piebald campanile counting the succession of window-arches per storey – one, two, three, four, five, six – before the plain summit section with its silhouette of corner pinnacles and octagonal spire. A young girl named Alba, booked over the internet, had promised me the massage of a lifetime in Siena, and it was in this room overlooking the Duomo that she tended my strained muscles; working me over she spoiled me deliciously by singing arias from *bel canto* opera. She had a wondrous voice, trained, she told me, by her mother, an opera singer from Sicily.

At seven the next morning, Sunday August 1st, the Campo was deserted except for the street cleaners. How lucky we were. Early sun made the striations of the campanile glow against a cerulean sky. It would be another hot day, and I was forewarned: in the parched lands of southern Tuscany there are few trees for shade. I left the city through the Porta Roma and stepped back into open countryside. Rome was now a mere 315 kilometres away, a distance which Belloc reckoned could be covered in three days – probably true, if you use hybrid means and sleep two hours in each twenty-four.

I followed by-ways and farm tracks into the Arbia Valley, keeping broadly abreast of the Via Cassia – the old Roman road to Rome – and with a turn of the head I could see Siena receding on its hilltop. Going south the country gradually became less green, the harvested fields turning scorched brown, the enclosures of trees and vineyards becoming sparser. The tracks were coated in fine pale dust, so that where they ran along the open ridges of the undulating hills they gave the impression of long white lines painted onto the landscape. Once, shortly after Isola d'Arabia, I saw behind me a spume of dust like a little whirlwind coming rapidly my way. A figure emerged from the cloud; another walker, the first I had encountered in days. I noticed the folded umbrella protruding from his rucksack, and, as he approached, the Meindl boots – just like mine.

We greeted each other like strangers meeting in the desert. He was a Dutchman, Kees Venema: cropped silver-blond hair crowning a chiselled, classical face which would not be out of place in a gallery of Roman busts were it not for the animation of his sharp blue eyes. He wore a red sweat shirt and long trekking trousers, and it came as no surprise when he said he was a physiotherapist in Amsterdam. He slowed to my pace and we began to share our stories.

Kees, like me, was bound for Rome; he too had set out from home, but on May 13th – two weeks before me – and sharing the first part of the walk (the Low Countries and the long haul over France and the Alps as far as Aosta) with his wife. Five years before the pair had walked all the way to Santiago de Compostela, tracking west across Spain on the far more rugged northern coastal route. Kees is a serious walker, and I could feel his professional eye on me as we marched along. I was a little miffed with his report.

"You walk well for a man in his sixties," he told me. "You have quite a good pace."

I couldn't really complain. Kees gives me five years, so it wasn't such a damning statement, and also I remembered that our Dutch cousins have a way of being direct. We fell in and walked together for half a day. Kees's expertise in fitness cast fresh light for me on the political crisis simmering in the Netherlands over the swelling ranks of Muslim immigrants. The anti-Islamic MP Geert Witters had just emerged from the elections holding the balance of power; there was widespread speculation about what bargain he would strike to support a minority government. Witters had ignited a debate which had ramifications for the whole of Europe. The flamboyant bottle-blond politician was campaigning against what he saw as the erosion of traditional Dutch society and against the rising tide, as he saw it, of radical Islam. Hilaire Belloc, who saw Europe as seeded in Catholicism and Christianity, would no doubt have espoused similar views – he was at times highly critical of Islam, which he saw as a threat to Western civilisation, although it is sad to record that in 1922 he also wrote an entire book about what he perceived to be the malign influence of Jews and Zionism.

More than half of Kees' patients are Muslim, and I sensed in him an unspoken sympathy with Witters.

"I see the women mainly," he said. "They are all overweight because they are forced to stay at home and they take no exercise. They are sedentary and fat, and are therefore prone to illness. That is an example where Islamic customs and culture costs our society money, and it is something I witness each day."

That was as far as we got with Dutch politics; the sweeping Tuscan countryside was too captivating, and the waymarks too erratic. In a matter of hours, comparing notes about walking, home, and family, we managed to take three wrong turns.

"It shows what happens when you lose concentration and stop

looking at the map," I said, taking the blame. "Walking the Via Francigena and talking don't go too well together!"

We parted company at Ponte d'Arbia. Kees was going to march on at his own pace to the next town of Buonconvento, and I calculated that with the distance he would put between us he would arrive in Rome well before me. I certainly did not expect to meet up with him again. I had completed 27 kilometres, and besides, I had a date with a friend, the same friend who had warned me when I called him from the Apennines that Italy's long summer heat wave was not going to end quickly.

Jonathan Mennell goes back to my early days in Italy. The son of a successful diplomat in the British Foreign Service – his father had been an ambassador – he was working at Sotheby's office in Rome when Gail and I first knew him. Jonathan's abundance of natural charm has gained him entry into almost every aristocratic and influential family home in Italy. These days, as an independent art dealer, he is discreetly networked to the country's corridors of power and seats of wealth. And yet he remains the most effervescent and unassuming person I have ever known.

For the second time in three days I found myself the passenger in a car driving away from Rome. Jonathan, sun-tanned and well weathered, with only the light grey hair retreating from his brow to betray the passing years, had picked me up at the bar by the bridge; we drove back up the actual Via Cassia to the small town of Monteroni d'Arbia, which I had looked down onto that morning before Kees joined me. When not at either of their homes, in Rome or the Val d'Aosta, he and his wife Elisabetta live here in one of the houses in her father's domain. In English terms, San Fabiano could seem like a miniature county, with wings spreading to the visible limits of the Arbia Valley, and with unbroken views of cornfields and of lanes winding over relays of gentle hills. The heart of the estate remains the castle of San Fabiano, a simple but imposing pele tower of brick topped by an open loggia with tiled roof. All around it stand the estate buildings and houses, some now done up for summer lets, and in one of which I was housed. After being confined for so long to single hotel rooms, being in a two-storey house gave me an unaccustomed feeling of space.

Even though I never set eyes on him, Jonathan's father-in-law was in residence; and I felt his presence. Count Giuseppe Fiorentini was one of the giants of post-war Italy. In the 1930s, his father, Filippo, had started an engineering works making earth moving equipment and he had built a factory on the Via Tiburtina in Rome. It was bombed by the Americans in 1943 with the loss of 117 lives; Filippo died shortly after, apparently of a broken heart. Giuseppe, his only son, who had trained as an engineer, managed to resurrect the business; and by the 1950s he was one of the richest men in Italy. Fiorentini & Co SPA manufactured and sold ever more powerful and efficient excavators, scoop cranes and bulldozers, prospering as Italy re-industrialised and built its impressive network of new motorways. The company also had huge international reach and started making deals with the Soviet Union: 1,000 cranes alone were exported to build the Trans-Siberian oil pipeline. At the height of his fortune, Giuseppe bought a castle from the Barberini family; San Fabiano was an afterthought, purchased with the small change. But in 1975 it all came crashing down when the company filed for bankruptcy – some said the business collapsed because Giuseppe refused to pay the Italian Communist Party a bribe to keep his contracts with the Soviet Union; certainly the all important export contracts with the USSR were suddenly and inexplicably cancelled. But after the business went under, and by any normal standards, the family still had plenty left, plus San Fabiano and properties in Rome.

La Dolce Vita continued, and twenty years on I was witnessing its final act. Jonathan and I spent the afternoon at the pool, just below the windows of the tower. They were open and Count Giuseppe, now an old and dying man, would have heard our splashes. But he wouldn't have heard Jonathan's soft, melodious voice explaining to me the sad circumstances of his father-in-law's confinement in the castle. The Count, prescribed Viagra for his general health, had been living it up in the Rome apartment with high-class prostitutes; he had, when younger, been the archetypal Italian playboy, squiring many of the beautiful and great names of the time. Viagra had breathed new life into him.

"We had to move him here for his own good," said Jonathan. "He was even making substantial payments to one girl for her daughter's schooling. We had to stop it."

And so, under extreme protest, he was brought to San Fabiano where he would rage in his castle rooms, still demanding girls be brought to him. He would die early the following year, aged 85.

I was enjoying the pool and the run of a large house so much that I decided to accept Jonathan's invitation to stay a second night; that would still leave me time to get to Rome by the 11th, the date I had arranged to meet Gail. I spent some time at Jonathan's house, tapping away on his laptop writing an article for *The Times* about my experiences on the Via Francigena. The first thing I saw on entering the house were two gorgeous Ducati motorbikes – Jonathan and Elisabetta took up motorcycling as a substitute for horse riding. Later, Jonathan drove me round the estate, far into the distant hills, from where you could see nothing but more distant hills. The estate's croplands were then still green, but I was in all probability witnessing them in that condition for the last time. The land here is artificially greened; if not tilled and tended it will swiftly return to its natural state of eroded moonscape – *calanchi* they call it, or badlands – just as it appears in landscapes in 15th and 16th century Sienese painting. The estate was being broken up, and this was the last year of estate-managed farming.

While Count Giuseppe, like a prisoner let out into the exercise yard, was being driven round the estate on his daily outing, I was allowed a sneak viewing of the castle, spacious, but not grand, and piled high with mementoes of a well-spent lifetime. There were photos of the Count as a young cavalry officer being presented to King Umberto of Italy and, as a polo player, receiving a trophy from Britain's Queen Elizabeth. A framed newspaper cutting from 1956 reported that his personal income tax return for that year was more than twice the combined income tax of the actresses Sophia Loren and Gina Lollobrigida. A press photo showed him, as a Papal Prince, attending a service alongside Generalissimo Franco. A painting of the grand Barberini castle hung above the fireplace. Jonathan pointed out the table in the dining room: the one on which Benito Mussolini hammered out his deal with the Vatican, leading to the Lateran Pacts of 1929 which ended the stand-off between the Papacy and the new Italian state, and permitted the Catholic Church to retain its sovereignty over the tiny Vatican City. A letter, handwritten and signed by Mussolini, confirmed the provenance of the table, whose thick wooden top seemed to me more suited to chopping meat or vegetables than negotiating international treaties.

Back at the poolside we talked of politics. Aldo Moro's widow, Eleonora, had just died aged 94. She had never forgiven her husband's political colleagues, particularly the Prime Minister at the time, Giulio Andreotti, for failing to do a deal that would have secured his release. Moro was kidnapped, Jonathan suggested, because he wanted the Christian Democrats to share power with the Communists – something the Americans weren't ready to accept. It was surely no accident that Via Caetani, where his body was left, lies midway between the Rome headquarters of both parties.

"So the Americans were behind the kidnapping?"

"Who knows?" my host replied. "In Italy everything is possible."

And what about the current Prime Minister, Silvio Berlusconi, and all those girls?

Jonathan murmured something about platform heels and tangas, but I was dozing off and missed the juicy details.

I felt like a mere mortal when I returned to the road the following morning, August 3rd. Jonathan and I had shared an early breakfast, and he kindly drove me back to the bar in Ponte d'Arbia just before seven o'clock. I was sorry to say goodbye. I had enjoyed my interlude at San Fabiano: it was as different from my normal world as walking to Rome.

Soon, though, walking to Rome was to become a magical, almost mystical experience. I was descending into the Val d'Orcia, and after crossing the River Ombrone at Buonconvento I entered an enchanted land of sweet undulating hills, painted yellow with ripening corn, and green with vineyards, crossed here and there with neat avenues of cypresses, and watched over by hilltop towns. This is a film-set landscape, radiating in the sun, where nature and man have come together in near perfect harmony; even the occasional square farmhouse, crowning some lonely ridge, seems to sit comfortably, its light coloured stone blending with the tawny ground. The roads, like strands of cotton reeled out over the valleys, describe the contours of the land, or leave you guessing, as they wend through olive groves and ilex woods. The vines, tended daily, are marshalled with parade-ground precision, not a leaf out of line. For most of the day I had the hilltop hamlet of Montosoli and the larger hill town of Montalcino as beacons to the west, and as crisp morning light melted into midday haze I curled round their sloping vineyards on country lanes and dusty white farm tracks to Torrenieri, and then put my last effort into the long ascent to San Quirico d'Orcia. I felt totally in step with the land; it had been a near perfect 27 kilometres.

The *Hotel Palazzo del Capitano* claimed four stars, and gouged my credit card accordingly. Set in its own vine-clad garden in the heart of the small town, its stone walls and bare brick interiors had a fine medieval atmosphere, and yet, after a day of breezes, undulations and vistas, the night's quarters felt more like a cage. I particularly took to the caryatids and lions embellishing the south portal of Santa Maria Assunta – the town's Romanesque church which Belloc somewhat sniffily said could "awake interest" – and I sat for a long time in the formal *Horti Leonini* Renaissance garden, but strolling around the town, I kept catching glimpses of the country below its walls, and I couldn't wait to get back out there.

And so it was in a mood of high expectation that I set out on August 4th. Beyond San Quirico, the Val d'Orcia opens into ever more extensive views, the hills floating at daybreak above a shroud of mist. At Vignoni, where I climbed as the strengthening sun burned off the haze, the Via Francigena confronts you with the open arch of a long abandoned church, the viewfinder for a landscape in which time has stood still: on the next hill a castle, and beyond the hill town of Castiglione d'Orcia, whose twin, Campiglia d'Orcia, would emerge on my right, rising and eventually falling away behind me as I worked my way, down valley, towards the great rocky fortress of Radicófani. All day the brooding pyramid of Monte Amiata dominated the southern skyline. To the east lay the ample farmlands of La Foce where Iris Origo wrote *An Italian War Diary*, the record of her quiet and courageous resistance to Italian Fascism and German occupation during World War II. My eyes, and feet, and nose confirmed it to me: this was the Italy I had come to walk in. It made me feel, more than elsewhere, the strangeness of that fellow Belloc who had chosen to pass through most of this exquisite country by night.

> Do not blame me that Tuscany should have passed beneath me unnoticed, as the monotonous sea passes beneath a boat in full sail. Blame all those days of marching; hundreds upon hundreds of miles that exhausted the powers of mind. Blame the fiery and angry sky of Etruria that compelled most of my way to be taken at night. Blame St Augustine who misled me in his Confessions by talking like an African of the "icy shores of Italy".

I took a short cut along the modern Via Cassia as far as Gallina before the Roman road parted company with the *statale*, shedding all its traffic. Here a young man, in the heat of the day, jogged past me, and I flagged him down with a greeting. He was from Poland, from the miraculously preserved medieval city of Kraków, a member of his country's newly enriched middle classes, whose parents had eked out a living under the Soviet-dominated Communists. He was aged only seven when martial law was imposed on his country in 1981 – the biggest news story I covered for Reuters, and the beginning of the last chapter of Poland's and Eastern Europe's long struggle for freedom from Moscow, the meltdown of the Iron Curtain. Talking to him about witnessing it – how the Generals had shut down the entire country on a biting cold night in December – I felt as ancient as the Via Cassia itself.

A welcome breeze was blowing as I turned up towards Radicófani, that gentle zephyr the poets of the Val d'Orcia have likened to the planet's breathing. Radicófani's great fortress had stood before me in the distant horizon for many hours. At first it seemed so high that I was convinced a valley would open up to provide a way round, but gradually the hill consolidated on all sides, shaping itself into an enormous and lofty wall blocking the way to Rome. I would need to climb it. A castle has crowned the crag above the town for centuries, monitoring the old road which snakes up through Radicófani. Today's N2 *statale* runs straight through the hill, leaving the town on its peaceful crow's nest high above the valley. So, for the second afternoon running, my day was ending with a stiff climb, but I was in my stride and, after a glorious 30 kilometres, I entered town by the church of San Pietro where I was greeted inside by a lovely Della Robbia Madonna and Child being crowned by angels. I spent the early evening on the terrace café opposite the church watching the sun set over Monte Amiata, the conical extinct volcano which guards the Val d'Orcia from the west.

Radicófani, 800 metres above the sea, is the last natural barrier before Rome, high enough to attract clouds. When I woke on August 5th in the *Albergo la Torre* my room, which the previous evening had given me a neatly-framed panorama of the valley, was dimmed with the mist that had seeped in through the open shutters.

The Via Francigena's long descent from Radicófani takes the original Roman road, now no more than a farm track. It follows a narrow spur for ten kilometres, and in some sections the paved stones are trodden flat and smooth by centuries of hooves and feet. As the clouds lifted I could see the flanks of the valley baring their sides of scrubland and eroded rock; the steep ground of *calanchi* here had not been cultivated or pastured for centuries. It was a lonely, barren place and from deep down in the valley below I began to hear the howling of wolves.

I descended to where the Francigena joins the bank of the River Rigo; and at the approach of the hamlet of Ponte di Rigo I was met by a woman in a striking blue and white dress running straight towards me, hair loose and obviously highly agitated. If I hadn't put my arms up at the last minute, I think she would have jumped into my lap.

"*C'è un lupo, un lupo,*" she said. She had seen a wolf and she was terrified.

"*È grande così, e mi fa paura,*" she continued, raising outstretched palms to waist-level to indicate the height of this terrifying monster.

I did my best to calm her and escorted her back to her cottage. The wolf had apparently come into her small garden and climbed up to a window. That is when she fled from her house. I advised her to get back inside and lock the doors: the wolf would not come in and get her. The fact that she was alone and presumably a widow, though not wearing traditional black, suggested to me that she was not a country girl, and that this intruder had really shaken her. Anyone brought up in the Tuscan countryside would know a bolted door was quite sufficient to deny a hungry wolf the contents of your larder.

I walked on, congratulating myself on the way I had coped with a somewhat hysterical Italian lady, and then I looked down the track ahead and saw a large animal bounding towards me. It was the wolf. I had heard wolves before in various parts of Europe, but I had never seen one. In my imagination, a wolf would be a larger model of the foxes that cross my path wherever I walk. The first thing that struck me was that the woman had not exaggerated: it was at least waist high. And then I noticed its movement – this animal bounded up and down with something of the action of a kangaroo. More to the point, I noticed it was bounding directly towards me. I instantly wished I was with that hysterical woman behind a bolted door. But at top speed, I unhitched my rucksack and grabbed my camera. If I was going to be eaten by a wolf I would at least like to leave behind a photograph of my assailant. The sudden movement of my rucksack worked a miracle; the wolf veered off the track and hurtled away from me towards the river. I managed to get two grainy shots.

I sat by a chapel at the end of the road, munching some dried fruit and drinking water. An old boy was tending his vegetable plot nearby, clearly a man of the country. Resting my hand on the wall, I told him I had just seen a wolf, and that it had terrified the lady up the road.

"Was it alone?" he asked.

"Yes," I replied.

"Nothing to worry about," he smiled. "A lone wolf is always scared. Wolves hunt in packs, and it's when you are confronted by a lot of them that you have to worry."

I thought of the howls I had heard from unseen packs of wolves that morning, and walked briskly on to rejoin the Via Cassia which I could follow for most of the way to Acquapendente, my night's stop. It was therefore another shortish day, 28 kilometres, and in the last stages I crossed from *Toscana* into *Lazio*, the northern part of Rome's home province, exchanging the serene landscapes of the Val d'Orcia for a country forged by volcanoes and grounded on basalt rock.

FIFTEEN
LAZIO AND ROME

A MERE COLLECTION OF HUMDRUM HOUSES — NOT MY summing-up of Acquapendente, but Hilaire Belloc's, in a hurry by this stage of his journey to press on to Rome. Approaching the town as evening drew in, and assailed by hunger, he was overtaken by a pair of oxen drawing a cart. He seized his opportunity, and not just of something to hold onto as he walked: "the devil tempted me, and without one struggle against temptation, nay with cynical and congratulatory feelings, I jumped up behind." Set down in Acquapendente, he filled his belly and walked on into the night.

I found the town pleasant enough, with a harmonious dignity lent by its dark-coloured building stone. As for the flowing water or cascades that gave Acquapendente its name, the closest I got was the fountain behind the *Albergo Toscana* where I was staying. Here the owner kindly rigged me up with the hotel's laptop and I continued to write my article for *The Times*. Later, I wandered around the paved streets in the centre and found myself a table at one of the terrace cafés on the main piazza. A mother and daughter struck up a conversation with me, and, in reply to their question about what brought me to these parts, I was in the course of telling them that I was nearing the end of my long journey on foot to Rome, when a swarthy sunburnt man in shorts sitting at the table opposite, whom I'd noticed scribbling furiously into his diary, suddenly looked across. "Walking to Rome?" he asked, rather dismissively. "I've just bicycled across Russia to Japan and back, starting from Barcelona."

So there. We long-distance travellers are a strange lot; I felt firmly put in my place. Without further ado, he thrust a card into my hand and got up and left. The card told me that he was Jesús San Augustín, and that he was a Catalan writer. It made for a somewhat downbeat end to my Thursday evening.

I spent the morning of August 6th walking through countryside with an altogether different feel – flowering meadows and hills that were no more than gentle hummocks; I could have been in rural Suffolk. The first hint that I was so far from home came when soon after San Lorenzo Nuovo the blue expanse of Lake Bolsena appeared – garlanded with green woods and fertile fields, and with its islands like floating lilies in the middle. Within almost a stone's throw of its shores, I rejoined the Via Cassia; and here for the first and only time walking across three countries I was hit by something coming towards me. It was a bicycle, laden with shopping on the handlebars and ridden by a young Italian camper; but he stopped to apologise, and I wasn't hurt.

The lakeside city of Bolsena is part fortress, part resort; its imposing castle and medieval quarters sit astride a basalt plug above the lake shore. Bolsena has much to answer for in Church history, and could be seen as an essential staging post on a pilgrimage to Rome because of what happened here in 1263. In that year a priest from Bohemia was saying Mass in the church of Santa Cristina and was convinced that blood had dripped from the communion bread. If it did not originate the doctrine, this miracle helped to underpin the Catholic Church's teaching that the consecrated Host is Christ's actual body. From the first murmurings of the Reformation, belief in literal 'transubstantiation' has remained a bone of contention for Protestants, even though authoritative Anglican and Roman theologians today share the more cognitive belief that there is a 'real presence' in the Host which simply defies definition.

Hilaire Belloc, recording his own approach to Bolsena by night, almost crows at his naughtiness; he heard a pony-cart coming up behind him, and was blowed if he wasn't going to hitch a lift on it.

This time there was no temptation of the devil; if anything the advance was from my side. I was determined to ride, and I sprang up beside the driver ... That was a good drive, an honest drive, a human aspiring drive, a drive of Christians, a glorifying and uplifted drive, a drive worthy of remembrance forever. The moon has shone on but few like it though she is old; the lake of Bolsena has glittered beneath none like it since the Etruscans ... It broke my vow to pieces; there was not a shadow of excuse for this use of wheels: it was done openly and wantonly in the face of the wide sky for pleasure.

And so it was in the highest of spirits that he dropped down at the lakeside inn and ordered a platter of fresh fried fish.

There is something admirably Gargantuan about Belloc's glee. My own lunch was more modest, and, although I was probably within yards of where he had broken his fast, I ate *al fresco* so that I could watch the holidaymakers at play in the lakeside shops and cafés. It was a fruit pie, a good one, even if I couldn't be as sure as Belloc that every ingredient was local.

Refreshed, I walked on to the nearby British and Commonwealth War Cemetery. It seems to have been a principle of the War Graves Commission that, where possible, a military cemetery should enjoy an uplifting view. Here, at San Antonio, a parade ground of Portland headstones, laid neatly on a sloping bluff, overlooked a wide arc of the lake, silken in the early afternoon.

I found a young family reading the inscriptions; the children shared their parents' striking blondness and, given the history, I took them for Germans, but they turned out to be Dutch and, having kept up with the event, I commiserated with them over their team's defeat by Spain in the World Cup Final a few weeks back.

"Thank you for your understanding," said the father, as if he were representing a grieving family. In fact he was speaking on behalf of an aggrieved nation.

I noticed the cemetery's gardener at work, and complimented him on the extraordinary array of roses. Every headstone had a rose planted at its foot. After surrendering Rome in June 1944, it was at Bolsena that the German army made its first stand against the Allies; there was a big tank battle on the open ground east of the lake. Almost 600 Commonwealth war dead are buried here, a third of them from South Africa. I wondered afterwards if that wasn't the connection with the family from Holland.

Writing when he did, Hilaire Belloc could hardly anticipate the carnage that two World Wars would inflict on these southern fields, but in a thoughtful paragraph he calls up the ghosts of his French and our British ancestors who fought over, and died, in this foreign land.

> Your fathers and mine coming down into this country to fight, as was their annual custom, must have had a plaguy time of it, when you think that they could not get across the Alps until summer-time, and they had to hack and hew, and thrust and dig, and slash and climb, and charge and puff, and blow and swear, and parry and receive, and aim and dodge, and butt and run for their lives at the end, under an unaccustomed sun ... they are dead now and we do not even know their names.

I was still tracking the lake's southern shores when I reached Montefiascone, where I stayed the night. There is something indefinably un-Italian about the town; its architecture is overdone, and extravagantly monumental. This may have something to do with its having been one of the summer retreats of the Popes, part of the old Papal States absorbed in 1870 into the newly unified Italy. It was as if this process had never quite been completed; or perhaps these lands had lain under Papal rule for so long that they were marked indelibly in the same way that the Roman Catholic Church teaches that the soul is stamped with Original Sin. Nothing was quite as I expected; even the girl at the reception in the *Hotel Altavilla* spoke faltering Italian. She turned out to be from Romania and had come to Italy to be with her boyfriend, and although she had played the cello for her country's State Orchestra, here she couldn't get a job teaching music.

"The townspeople in Montefiascone won't even let me play in their amateur orchestra," she said. "So I work in the hotel. It could be worse."

I sat in the piazza below the cathedral, watching the sun chase shadows round the third grandest dome in all Italy – after St Peter's, of course, and the Duomo in Florence – and, after that, two drunken youths fighting with bare fists. This was the only time I saw any kind of violence in Italy. Excessive drinking is somewhat part of the history of the town; its local Moscatello wine trades under the name of '*Est, Est, Est*', enigmatic until you know the story of the early 12th century Bishop Johannes Fugger of Augsburg, a mighty wine connoisseur who would reputedly send his steward on ahead to scout the inns with the best wine and chalk on their walls the word '*est*'. At Montefiascone the servant found such excellent wine that he wrote '*est, est, est*'. One thing led to another, and the Bishop was laid to rest here in the church of San Flaviano. The Latin inscription on his tomb recounts the story; so perhaps it is true. It might have appealed to Hilaire Belloc, another keen wine drinker, but he bypassed the town.

The best part of Montefiascone was leaving it; I departed early on August 7th by way of the Papal Palace and the gardens of Rocca dei Papi, and here on a hill above the cathedral stands a *belvedere* from whose upper loggia there is an unrivalled view back across the lake and forward to the distant hills of the *Campagna*, the countryside which surrounds Rome.

The old Roman road survives for long stretches from Montefiascone to Viterbo; paved in dark basalt slabs polished smooth by centuries of use. This is perhaps the best section of ancient road on the entire Via Francigena, and it retains a sense of its past by wending through hazel woods and beside *farro* wheat and barley fields; many, by the time I passed, already under the plough. The walls and towers of Viterbo are sighted from far away at the foot of a volcano that is, itself, long extinct; but the black earth round its skirts is still steaming. The city is surrounded by thermal springs and, approaching from the north, the Via Francigena passes one of these natural geysers, *Bagnaccio,* 'little bath'. Unaware of this, I didn't know whether my eyes were playing tricks on me when a field in the middle distance appeared to be occupied by bikini-clad women, all in a squatting position. It was only as I got closer that I could see that they were sitting and bathing in a thermal bath. So I took off my boots and socks, rolled up my trousers, and joined them. The alkaline water, at 40 degrees, washed over my tired feet like the first bite of a refreshing peppermint.

Viterbo's great city walls had overwhelmed Hilaire Belloc – "untouched, the bones of the Middle Ages ... like a range of cliffs" – and he could not make up his mind whether to enter the city; he did in the end, though, because he was Belloc, and curious, and hungry.

> It is all very well to neglect Florence and Pisa because they are some miles off the straight way, but Viterbo right under one's hand it is a pity to miss. Then I needed wine and food for the later day in the mountain.

I had no such compunction: I had made the short 17 kilometres to Viterbo before lunch, and intended to spend the afternoon as a tourist in this erstwhile city of the Popes which had for a time challenged Rome as the headquarters of the Western Christian Church. Five of the early Popes were elected in Viterbo and four had died here. The last time I myself had seen the city was on a cold winter's day in 1978 when every street reeked of rotting grape skins; they were brewing the two local liqueurs – Sambuca and Amaro dei Papi.

In the August sun of 2010, dressed quite differently from my 28-year-old self, I strolled into the glorious medieval Papal Palace to present my pilgrim passport for Giovanni Paulo to stamp, which he did with a mixture of enthusiasm and reverence that I knew I did not deserve.

"Viterbo is honoured that you have come all this way," he told me.

"You have had many more honourable guests," I said, at a loss. But the welcome I had received left a glow.

I entered the great hall where the Papal elections had been held, and found the holes made in the floor for the cardinals' tent-pegs still visible. The election here of Pope Gregory X in 1271 had a dramatic dénouement. The deliberations dragged on for two years without result, so the Captain of the townspeople, Raniero Gatti, tried to force a decision by removing the roof of the hall, and, when that didn't work, reducing the food supply to the Cardinals. That worked. It was Gregory X who in consequence made the rules under which conclaves are still held, and as a correspondent in Rome I covered two of these strange elections in the space of three months in 1978 – the year of the three Popes. It was extraordinary reporting an event that we could neither see, nor hear, and in which the participants were bound by an oath of silence, and out of which nothing came except puffs of smoke – black for an inconclusive vote when the ballot papers were burnt, and white for an election. The appearance on the afternoon of October 16th on the balcony of St Peter's, after 1978's second puff of white smoke, of Cardinal Karol Józef Wojtyła was one of the most astonishing stories I covered. Officially atheist, Communist Poland had produced the first non-Italian Pope since 1522. The world was stunned, and forever changed. Communism in East Europe was dealt an instant and systemic mortal blow. It changed me, too; I flew with the newly elected Pope in the Vatican press corps on his first momentous trip back to his homeland and, a little under a year later, I was transferred from Rome to Warsaw.

Walking quite by chance down one of the narrow streets in the old city, I looked into a courtyard to the terrace of a restaurant. There sitting at a table, shaded by an *ombrellone* from the hot sun, was Kees.

"I thought you would be in Rome by now," I said. He smiled as if encountering a long-lost friend, and invited me to join him for a beer.

"I fell ill at Bolsena and spent a day in bed," said Kees. To be sure he was unshaven, and his face was drawn. He looked worn out, and what came next was a little incoherent. "Also, I am afraid of finishing this walk; I don't know if I want to go back to work. Maybe I will keep going. Perhaps I will walk on to Bethlehem."

Up to now, we hadn't touched on religion, or religious motives.

How was I to gauge whether Kees was so deep into Christianity that he felt compelled to go all the way to its birthplace? I didn't want to ask; but I could tell him about the gruesome reality of the so-called Holy Land. Admittedly, I had only lived there for three years (as country manager for Reuters); I hadn't walked to it, nor would I wish to.

"It's very un-holy," I said. "The only genuine relics of Christianity in Israel are the Palestinian Christians, and they are being squeezed out by the fundamentalists on both sides. The shrines will leave you cold, and Bethlehem is behind barbed wire. The Sea of Galilee is worth a visit, but that's a long way to go to see a lake that looks pretty much like the one we have just walked by."

"Perhaps I will just go on as far as Bari," said Kees.

We talked about arriving in Rome, and he told me about another Dutch pilgrim he had met, a young woman who was walking from Canterbury. She was called Everdiene, and she was using satellite navigation. The afternoon wore into evening and I returned to the *Hotel Tuscia* to spruce up before heading out to observe the colourful evening *passeggiata* in the bustling Via Marconi. Here, dining at an open terrace, I plumped for the local speciality of worm-shaped pasta, *lombrichelli*, in a *piccante* sauce, and a deliciously fruity local red wine, watching the contented crowds walking by as the sun went down.

This pilgrim's departure from Viterbo that Sunday morning, August 8th, was just as ceremonious as his reception. I was waved off from the *Tuscia* by all the early morning staff, one of them even plunging a water-bottle into my rucksack. Viterbo, it seems to me, takes its pilgrims to heart. The clock on the imposing Mussolini-era Post Office pointed to seven as I headed towards the Porta Romana, and out down the Via Cassia, a *statale* once more.

But it was only 50 minutes of dangerous living, and justified by the day and time. I did, though, stay on constant alert for bicycles before turning down a quiet country lane towards Tobia. This isn't in the Lightfoot guide but it saved me a long detour west to Vetralla where the Via Francigena leads. The lane, appropriately named *Strada Valalta* – High

Valley Street – cut through volcanic rock, and one side entry was just like a canyon, with 15-metre high tufa rock walls on either side. The road to Tobia had more surprises to come – a signpost to 'Spiteful Kennel', and another to 'Amnesia Bar' – but the biggest surprise of all came out of my pocket. I had grown accustomed to seeing the world upside down, with the red arrow of my compass pointing with absolute sureness south instead of north. I took the compass out just to satisfy myself that I was indeed walking due south; to my astonishment the needle had swung back to normal. The arrow was now, with equal confidence, again pointing north. Some magnetic pulse transmitted through the volcanic rock around Viterbo had miraculously countermanded whatever chthonic force had reversed the needle on the *Chemin des Dames*. Nobody has ever explained to me the workings of that: how a compass can become spooked, and then, just as suddenly, unspooked.

After the hamlet of Tre Croci I exchanged tarmac for forest track, down through sunken lanes beneath large Mediterranean oaks, firs and chestnuts, leading out to long stretches of open country which meandered through groves of ripening hazelnut – all welcome shade. I was in the heartland of the ancient Etruscans, the civilisation that preceded the Romans, and the gentle going under foot afforded a good mental antechamber to Rome itself. It was no longer a distant goal; now I must focus on the reality of actually arriving there, a preoccupation that would come increasingly into play over the next few days. I was, meanwhile, reaching my day's limit; the Etruscan town of Capránica, built of dark basalt rock and perched high on a volcanic plug, looked inviting. But it had no hotels, and so after 26 pleasant but hot kilometres I settled for a bed and breakfast just outside town.

La Locanda Monticelli, directly on the Via Francigena, is a farmhouse which has gradually evolved and grown upwards from an ancient Etruscan cave. Over the centuries layer was added to layer to create today's multi-storey building. Level with the cave-cellar was an inviting pool, occupied when I arrived by a party of young modern Romans enjoying their Sunday in the country. I couldn't help but notice an alluring black girl at the poolside; she turned out to be an immigrant from Somalia, one of Italy's former African colonies, albeit a short-lived one. She was stretched out like an Etruscan goddess on the warm stones at the foot of the curling stairway to the pool. I thought of the frequent famines in her former country, recalling the migrants from the Horn of Africa I had seen in Calais, and again I reflected on the uneven fates that await us all.

I joined the youthful group; lazing all afternoon on a hammock and dipping in and out of the fresh, cool water; my back, coddled now while marching by a cotton shirt and protected from the sun by a neck scarf, didn't complain: it was long cured. Paolo, my host, cooked for me at sunset. An architect, he derived deep spiritual satisfaction from occupying a house whose foundations were laid by nature and excavated by people who lived here well over 2,000 years ago.

"We don't count for much in the end," he mused.

"I know," I said. "We are just part of a process. I think that is why I walk: it holds back time and, perhaps, also helps me understand how small we are."

The Monday morning of my last half-week on the road, August 9th, brought about a meeting in the town of Sutri which forced me to dig even deeper into why it is that I have to walk, and what, for that matter, impels anyone in an age of easy transport to walk long distances.

I was on the main road, leaving town, more or less opposite the impressive hulk of the Roman amphitheatre, when I spotted someone walking ahead of me. Like me, she was hugging the tarmac shoulder as oncoming cars whooshed past, but unlike me she was wearing the two primary colours of the Dutch flag – blue shorts and a red shirt. A plastic bag, straw sunhat and water bottle were hitched to her rucksack. I knew at once that this was the young compatriot Kees had talked about, and I made up the ground between us.

"Good morning," I said, coming alongside. "Let me go in front. I'll take the traffic for you."

I accepted her smile as a yes, and so we walked on in single file, without exchanging any further words, until we came to a provincial road to Bracciano. There, no longer under the threat of being mown down, we paused and greeted one another. Goodness knows what she thought of me; I saw instantly that she was most attractive, with generous lips, high cheek bones, and radiant blue eyes.

"You must be Brian," she said – she could only have got that from Kees – "I am Everdiene Geerling."

We got back into our stride. Everdiene was only my third walking companion in 70 days' slow progress across the European mainland, and she proved an ideal fellow pilgrim, both forthcoming and with a wide-ranging mind. Her job as an education consultant takes her round the world, wherever there are Dutch schools to advise or inspect. Long-distance walking had not entered her existence until she decided on a whim that she would take time off work and walk to Rome. She had started from Canterbury. Long-distance walks are something I do, and need; but, given the anti-social nature of the pastime, I could not help wondering whether Everdiene, who must have been in her thirties, wasn't carrying a broken heart – but I would not ask. Instead we chatted about her country, and about walking.

Everdiene located herself, as far as I could tell, on the liberal side of Dutch politics. For her, Wilders and his supporters were absolutely out of line in expecting Muslims to surrender obligingly to their adopted country's culture and language.

"I travel all over the world," she explained, "and I don't see too many Dutch people learning the languages of the countries where they work. Overseas, they tend to live in their little Dutch enclaves."

Setting aside politics; what, I asked, was it like to live for the road? Everdiene confessed that it was only now, after nearly three months, that at last she felt comfortable. She had got into the rhythm of walking, of getting up every day, and setting out for a new place to sleep; her life had thus become simplified.

"There is contentment inside me now. My mind has gone into a sort of numbed blank, and I feel as if I have become one with my road."

I was wondering what would follow; a revelation perhaps about what she was blanking out, and why she wasn't content before she set out. But it was in fact a question, which both excited me and challenged my own experience.

"What is the next stage?" Everdiene asked. "What happens after this contentment?"

I, too, had been walking for a long time, and as for contentment, I think it's fair to say that I had set out a contented soul, and for the most part remained so. I had loved virtually every day and almost every hour of my journey. I had only once thought of giving up; and now there remained just this slight nagging tug in me to finish: to be done, for a while, with the daily routine of walking up to 40,000 paces. Then in a flash I realised the answer to Everdiene's question; I was just as surprised by it, but also frightened by its implications.

"The next stage," I said, "it's quite simple. The next stage is when you cannot stop. When you have become so used to walking, so dependent upon the rhythmic tread of your footfall, the anticipation of the next bend in the road and the pleasure of a new view opening over the brow of a hill ... that it takes over and you just have to keep going."

"I hope we are stopping in time," said Everdiene.

I suddenly thought of Kees in the courtyard at Viterbo, talking about going on to Bari or the Holy Land, and I wondered if he would be able to stop, or indeed if he even wanted to stop.

Soon we overtook a group of Italian scouts from Brescia; they were walking to Rome from Viterbo, and making heavy weather of it. Several of them were already limping.

"*Coraggio!*" I said.

"It's all right for you two," one of them piped up cheerfully. "You're professionals!"

"We've been promoted," I told Everdiene, and translated the compliment. "They think we are professional walkers."

"No," she rejoined. "We've just had a lot of practice."

We reached Campagnano di Roma – in conversation our 26 kilometres over the gentle foothills of the Sabatini and Sabini Mountains had flown by – and Everdiene and I parted ways; she had shelter in a convent and I had booked into the *Benigni*, the only hotel in town open in August. I had no sooner settled in and taken a shower than Everdiene, underwhelmed by what was on offer at the convent – mats on a concrete floor – rejoined me and booked a room. Minutes later, Kees too walked in. Thus it was that the three of us, who had walked huge distances from England and Holland, often only a few kilometres or hours apart but each in our own little world, came together at the gates of Rome.

We spent the afternoon going our various ways in the centre of Campagnano, a town which was little more than a long main street bounded at one end by a baroque triumphal arch, agreeing to meet in the evening at the hotel for dinner. The *Benigni* was a good choice; the restaurant served my favourite *antipasti* – a selection of cold roasted and fried Mediterranean vegetables, *fagiolini, fagioli, cipolle, funghi, piselli, melanzane* – green beans, white beans, onions, mushrooms, peas and aubergines.

"This is our first and last supper," I said. "It's our celebration before arriving in Rome."

Kees, though, remained in a sunken mood. Instead of the sparkle in his eyes which had so struck me under the bright Tuscan sun, his features registered doubt, not celebration.

"Have you and Everdiene thought about re-entry?" he asked. The image of astronauts re-entering the earth's atmosphere struck me as being both apt and shocking. "Have you considered what happens to you after you have arrived?"

"You mean adjusting to normal life?" said Everdiene.

"Yes, that is the hard part. You are all wound up and suddenly you have nowhere to go." Kees had understood all too well. The problems start when you cannot stop. Now it was my turn.

"In a sense we have just been escaping," I said. "We've been on the run, and now we are about to be caught again, or at least caught up again in our work, our friends, and our families."

"That's just the point," replied Kees. "Take my advice and hold onto the road for as long as you can. Remember all those first steps at daybreak long after you have resumed catching the bus or tram back to work again."

This was the serious business over, and we sauntered up and down our three versions of the Via Francigena, separate and shared, recollecting funny moments, mishaps, interesting meetings, and hard sections. In all our versions, the Alps and Tuscany glowed; the plains of Lombardy induced, at our table, a chorus of exasperation.

Hilaire Belloc, in his own headlong march on Rome, had shot like a bullet from Viterbo, stopping only occasionally to admire the Campagna or to muse on the decline of Etruria and rise of Rome.

> All the night long, mile after mile, I hurried along the Cassian Way. For five days I had slept through the heat, and the southern night had become my daytime.

I am only now beginning to form a better understanding both of *The Path to Rome* and of the way Hilaire Belloc achieved his journey. His book, discursive, provocative, irritatingly hyperbolic, is enormous fun. He enjoyed writing it, and even into old age, he maintained that it was the only book he had ever written for love. "Why on earth did you write this book?" asks the Imaginary Reader. "For my amusement," replies the Author.

As for his walk, though, I am less sure. Belloc so assiduously bangs on about the "ceaseless journey", and its often self-inflicted discomforts, that I think he enjoyed writing about his journey to Rome far more than the experiences of actually walking it. It seems more like something he endured; perhaps even a penance. And it is a fact that after reaching Rome he never again went on such a long walk; indeed, he took up sailing. In Lucca he sums up his journey in terms of considerable hardship:

All my days of marching, the dirty inns, the forests, the nights abroad, the cold, the mists, the sleeplessness, the faintness, the dust, the dazzling sun, the Apennines – all my days came over me.

Everdiene and I had agreed to walk together the following day, August 10th; Kees, needing the space, would make his own way. We arranged to meet for breakfast at the bar in the piazza outside the hotel, the only one open for breakfast at seven o'clock. When she didn't appear, I fretted until I had called her on her mobile, reminding myself how lucky I had been not to have had, for most of my walk, someone else's timekeeping to worry about, and, indeed – as both Gail and Jon Harris would remind me – how lucky that other person had been! Peter had been a late sleeper, but that was a long way back; another century, it seemed. Everdiene's angelic smile when she strolled across – she had found the document she had mislaid at the bottom of her rucksack – dissolved the irritation of 15 lost minutes, and I treated her to a special breakfast of croissants and freshly squeezed orange juice.

We were now so close to Rome, and yet the country remained surprisingly rural. On its way from Campagnano to the next town, Formello, the Via Francigena winds through the pastures and woodland of the Parco di Veio, where wild horses and white *chianina* cattle grazed. In the Sorbo Valley, the Via Francigena waymarks had one last laugh at us; we took the wrong way ending up in a blind coomb by a cascading waterfall. Back on course, Formello itself proved to be the last redoubt of the true *Campagna*, its narrow streets and hilltop perch giving off an air of aloofness with which it managed to ignore being on the edge of a great metropolis. La Storta, where our paths would separate, is altogether different. It is already – 18 kilometres out – a suburb of Rome.

Field paths took us there round the side of a little hill; the last stretch was by road, down a busy *statale*. On arrival at La Storta, in token of our 24 pleasantly shared kilometres, I kissed Everdiene – she looked mildly surprised – fondly on both cheeks, and I went my way, knowing that we each needed space to prepare for Rome, to work out how to deal with re-entry. I checked into La Storta's only hotel, *La Cassia*, three concrete storeys alongside the main road, and I spent the afternoon in wanton self-indulgence, first a haircut, then my eyebrows plucked, and a complete manicure and pedicure, and finally a full body massage. I rewarded the new streamlined Brian Mooney with a bottle of red wine from the nearby Alban Hills and a hefty dish of pasta and prawns, and went to bed well content. I was ready – in body, if not in soul – for Rome.

Ah, but the excitement of arriving was too much, and I slept fitfully. Hilaire Belloc, as I found out later, had felt much the same.

But as I slept, Rome, Rome, still beckoned me, and I woke in a struggling light as though at a voice calling; and slipping out I could not but go on to the end.

I, too, was up and away from my concrete box on August 11th before six o'clock: it was still dark when I took breakfast – surprisingly tasty coffee and a fresh croissant – at the all-night bar of a petrol station. At first, the way into Rome is far from the romantic, magical end that a traveller could expect after walking all that distance. In truth, it is like the approach to any big city. From La Storta, the Via Francigena follows the side of the busy Via Cassia, which here is mercifully pave-mented, and then it leads to a section where there is only a hard shoulder as it joins the Via Trionfale and crosses Rome's great six-lane ring-road, with one last *farro* wheat field in sight. From a walker's viewpoint, the only triumphant thing at that stage was getting back onto a proper urban sidewalk without having been killed. So, following Belloc's foot-steps, I plodded on, a little less than triumphantly, down the Via Trionfale for a good hour or so through the evolving city, and then came at last to Rome's highest hill.

For Italy a modest 139 metres – though it would be a mountain back in Essex – Monte Mario had been in the 15th century the domain of Cardinal Mario Mellini. Now it is a public park; I entered the gates and walked up the steps and winding path to the top, little prepared for the view.

Laid out before me, as if presented on a golden platter, was the City of Rome. The eucalyptus trees on the slopes below were lit sharply by the morning sun, while the pines on the distant Pincian Hill and Borghese Gardens swam in the early haze. Apartment blocks, angled off one another along the haphazard lines of the city streets, filled the cityscape, while rising above them, above every church and roof and tower, rising even through the lines of the surrounding hills, arched the great dome of St Peter's. My destination may still have been four kilometres away, but I knew I had arrived – the way you know something for certain in a dream. I asked a lady who was exercising her dog to take a photograph, and she gladly obliged me with several; in one I am smiling from ear to ear. I don't think she believed me when I told her I had walked from London; but, then, how was I to believe it, either?

Hilaire Belloc would not have experienced the same view. A century ago, the Vatican City and St Peter's Basilica were still surrounded and hemmed in by old Rome; Via Conciliazione, the great avenue carved out of the old city tenements after the 1929 Lateran Pact in order to create an open vista of the Basilica, was not yet conceived. Belloc's first sighting of St Peter's was from beside the Tiber.

> Far on the right were white barracks of huge and hideous appearance; over these the Dome of St Peter's rose and looked like something newly built. It was of delicate blue, but made a metallic contrast against the sky.

I walked on into the reality of the city, and while crossing Piazza Risorgimento I phoned Gail; but through the twin agencies of insomnia and haste, my re-entry hadn't got off to a good start: I had arrived early. Gail was still on the other side of Rome checking into the hotel we had booked. I marked time with a sandwich and drinking a coke, watching the tourists lining up for the Vatican museum. Belloc also had to mark time at the end of his path; but he was doing things properly. He had not made his way directly to St Peter's but instead to the church of Santa Maria del Popolo where he was told he had to wait 20 minutes for Mass. So he went to a café on the Corso, where he called for coffee, bread and brandy.

After my own 20-minute pause for early elevenses, I walked through the great loggia into St Peter's Square, where as a young correspondent I had reported the funerals of two popes and the elections of two more. Thirty-two years on, twin giant television screens were mounted either side of the piazza, and the vast arena in front of the Basilica was heaving with crowds from all over the world, but this wasn't a welcome back for me. The screens were relaying the daily blessing by the German Pope Benedict from the summer Papal residence at Castel Gondolfo. My eyes raked the two identical images and dropped immediately to where Gail was standing, with her back to the Basilica, gazing, the wrong way as it happened, down Via Conciliazione. I stole up on her from behind. Soon afterwards, as if by serendipity, Kees and Everdiene followed each other into the square. All told, it was a joyful reunion, and, for Gail, a revelation. Hitherto she had been convinced that the only person mad enough to make this trip on foot was her husband.

The three pilgrims went into the Holy See's Pilgrim Office to have their pilgrim passports stamped and to receive their *Testimonium* – certificate of pilgrimage, today's equivalent of the precious parchment providing an earthly pardon or a plenary indulgence – for which medieval pilgrims would have striven so hard and endured so much discomfort and danger. We had had it far easier, but even so the modern-day Latin scroll attesting that we had completed our pilgrim journey to Rome seemed, after all those long miles, somehow flimsy and somewhat inadequate; perhaps we had secretly hoped for an indulgence.

There were too many people queuing at the security gates to get into St Peter's without a long wait. I wasn't going to join them. In the slender volume of St Luke, I had carried Simon Peter's story with me; in the Gospel account I had followed him from the shores of Galilee to the end of Jesus' journey on earth, and in three countries I had passed through gateways and by statues, chapels and churches erected in his honour, but I had not walked all this way to stand in line to visit his tomb.

In any case I had a date with the 'keeper of the keys' elsewhere, closer to home. After I had been snapped by a photographer for *The Times,* Gail and I crossed the Tiber and followed round the Vittorio Emanuele monument to a little street between the Forum and Colosseum, Via delle Sette Sale. We must have looked an odd couple amid the elegance of central Rome – the pilgrim in tattered shirt and darned trousers, with big walking boots and bulging yellow rucksack, Gail in pretty summer dress and straw hat. We climbed the steps to the Basilica of San Pietro in Vincoli, 2,115 kilometres (or in Saxon miles, 1,322) from its sister church in Coggeshall.

I walked slowly between the Doric pillars of the nave and descended to the small crypt below to inspect St Peter's chains, displayed in a glass-fronted tabernacle beneath the high altar. I saluted them, and attempted a prayer of thanks for the unfettered freedom I had enjoyed over the last 76 days. I recalled that Archbishop Sigeric had come here, too. On arrival in Rome he had made an elaborate procession around a great many of its churches and basilicas before presenting himself to Pope John XV at the Lateran Palace for a midday meal – and, of course, to collect his pallium.

"So then," said Gail, with that expression of animated curiosity I knew so well. We were now outside, standing between the columns of the portico at the top of the steps. The last time we had stood together like this was by the ancient oak on the outskirts of Coggeshall. "So where to now?"

"Simple," I replied. "I know a really great place where we can have pizza for lunch."

"That's a long way for a pizza," declared Gail.

SIXTEEN
ENVOI

OVER THE NEXT FEW WEEKS, THE THREE PILGRIMS kept in touch by
email:

Hi Everdiene

I hope you are finding 're-entry' OK. I find the adjustment very strange
and sometimes rather hard. It was great meeting up with you and sharing
a few days and that wonderful moment of arrival. I am sorry we seemed
just to buzz off but I was being summoned by a photographer. Here are
some photos with a few more to follow.

Stay in touch – Brian

Hi Brian

Thanks for the pictures. It is a good memory trying not to forget what a great
travel we made. My family and friends are more proud than I am, but I realise
it is not very common to do this. I don't know when and where, but once I
will do this again. Maybe walking back from Rome to Canterbury.
I really enjoyed it sharing some days with you. And indeed, what a wonderful
moment of arrival. Attached is a photo of you calling me. Please let me know

when your article and all the photos will be published in *The Times*.

On the one hand I like it to be at home, on the other hand it is strange not walking anymore. I like the normal things such as shopping, cooking and watering the plants, but it takes also a lot of time to do it. Waking up, packing your bag, only shopping if you see a shop and you need something for the day and walking is much easier. I am happy that I have more than a week to get used of it. And I am stiffer than when I walked. Every morning when I get out of my bed I move like an old lady. I hope that will become better.

And of course, we stay in touch!

Regards – Everdiene

Hi Everdiene

There is a piece in today's *Times*, with your name in it!

Kind Regards – Brian

Hi Brian

I bought *The Times* of Saturday, but it was the international edition and I couldn't find your article. On the website I could download it, so I got it. I liked the article, so did my friends and family. We are looking forward to your book.

Last week I started to work again. I was more tired than after walking 30 kilometres. I hope you still enjoy your free days.

Kind Regards – Everdiene

Dear Everdiene

How good to hear from you again. I am still feeling that something big is missing in my life – so much so that I am seriously thinking of walking back to London from Rome next year!
The strangely painful withdrawal from the Via Francigena seems to be part of the journey. It seems to me that we are meant to miss it.
Good luck at work and please contact me when you are next in London.

Kind Regards – Brian

Dear Brian

I recognise that feeling of missing something big in my life. I also think about where my next walk will go to. And walking back is one of the serious options (also Assisi and Naples or Bari are possible). Unfortunately next year is not possible at all. My employer will not be happy with that idea.
I don't know if I told you about the Austrian guy I met. He has walked for five years now. He has no home and no job anymore. Walking made him much happier than a 'normal' life. After a year of being away he walked back home to his parents' house. That was his home now for a few weeks or months. And after these weeks or months he walked again. I understood his reasons. Now I am back home and have to work again I understand him even more. On the other hand it is also good to be back. I really appreciate it for keeping me posted. And I'll let you know when I am in London.

Kind Regards – Everdiene

Dear Kees

Here are some photos. Keep in touch.

Best wishes – Brian

Hey Brian

Nice pictures, reminding me a very good time. It shows we were really human beings. Now back in daily life, yes a hard time. I really need some patience for myself to find out how daily life is working.
Yes, keep in touch good old friend.

Kees

Hi Kees

There is a piece in today's *Times* with your name in it!

Best, Brian

Brian

So you are making money with my name! I can see that daily life is taking us back. Here I am landing, and starting to work trying to keep in touch and trying to stay connected to the space and silence that I felt on the trip.

All Best – Kees

The messages petered out; the pilgrims returned to their other lives.

Hilaire Belloc had ended the account of his journey with a burst of hilarious doggerel; the last four lines a vivid self-portrait:

Drinking when I had a mind to,
Singing when I felt inclined to;
Nor ever turned my face to home
Till I had slaked my heart at Rome.

A century on, the three fellow pilgrims concluded that they had slaked their hearts every step of their way to Rome.

Appendix

Daily Stages of the author's walk from Coggeshall to Rome:

Date	Leg	Kms	Miles
28 May	Coggeshall – Pleshey	32.8	20.5
29 May	Pleshey – Loughton	43.2	27
30 May	Loughton – City of London	24	15
31 May	City of London – Cobham	51.2	32
1 June	Cobham – Charing	48	30
2 June	Charing – Capel	43.2	27
3 June	Capel – Guines	24	15.0
4 June	Guines – Wisques	36	22.5
5 June	Wisques – Amettes	32	20.0
6 June	Amettes – Arras	42	26.3
7 June	Arras	–	–
8 Jun	Arras – Bapaume	30	18.8
9 Jun	Bapaume – Peronne	26	16.3
10 June	Peronne – Ham	31	19.4
11 June	Ham – Coucy-Le-Château	36	22.5
12 June	Coucy-Le-Château – Braye	30	18.8
13 June	Braye – Reims	48	30.0
14 June	Reims	–	–
15 June	Reims – Ay	30	18.8
16 June	Ay – Châlons-en-Champagne	30	18.8
17 June	Châlons-en-Champagne – Vitry-le-François	33	20.6

18 June	Vitry-le-François – St Dizier	30	18.8
19 June	St Dizier – Donjeux	42	26.3
20 June	Donjeux – Chaumont	41	25.6
21 June	Chaumont – Langres	40	25.0
22 June	Langres – Champlitte	39.4	24.6
23 June	Champlitte – Gy	42	26.3
24 June	Gy – Besançon	34.5	21.6
25 June	Besançon	–	–
26 June	Besançon – Ornans	25	15.6
27 June	Ornans – Pontarlier	35	21.9
28 June	Pontarlier – Sainte-Croix	23.5	14.7
29 June	Sainte-Croix – Chavornay	32	20.0
30 June	Chavornay – Lausanne	30	18.8
1 July	Lausanne – Villeneuve	5	3.1
2 July	Villeneuve – Martigny	27.5	17.2
3 July	Martigny – Orsières	20	12.5
4 July	Orsières – Grand St Bernard	25	15.6
5 July	Grand St Bernard – Aosta	29	18.1
6 July	Aosta	–	–
7 July	Aosta – Saint Vincent	36	22.5
8 July	Saint Vincent – Pont St Martin	28	17.5
9 July	Pont St Martin – Ivrea	23.1	14.4
10 July	Ivrea – Santhià	36	22.5
11 July	Santhià – Vercelli	27	16.9
12 July	Vercelli – Mortara	32	20.0
13 July	Mortara – Garlasco	23	14.4
14 July	Garlasco – Pavia	26	16.3
15 July	Pavia	–	–
16 July	Pavia – Miradola Terme	30	18.8
17 July	Miradola Terme – Piacenza	36	22.5
18 July	Piacenza – Fidenza	40	25.0
19 July	Fidenza	–	–
20 July	Fidenza – Fornovo di Taro	37	23.1

21 July	Fornovo – Berceto	28	17.5
22 July	Berceto – Pontremoli	28	17.5
23 July	Pontremoli – Aulla	24	15.0
24 July	Aulla – Sarzana	17	10.6
25 July	Sarzana – Marina di Pietrasanta	32	20.0
26 July	Marina di Pietrasanta	–	–
27 July	Marina di Pietrasanta – Lucca	36	22.5
28 July	Lucca – Ponte a Cappiano	31	19.4
29 July	Ponte a Cappiano – Gambassi	37	23.1
30 July	Gambassi – Graciano d'Elsa	28.5	17.8
31 Jul	Graciano d'Elsa – Siena	25	15.6
1 Aug	Siena – Ponte d'Arbia	29.5	18.4
2 Aug	Castel Fabiano	–	–
3 Aug	Ponte d'Arbia – San Quirico	27.2	17.0
4 Aug	San Quirico – Radicófani	30	18.8
5 Aug	Radicófani – Acquapendente	28	17.5
6 Aug	Acquapendente – Montefiascone	37	23.1
7 Aug	Montefiascone – Viterbo	17	10.6
8 Aug	Viterbo – Capránica	26	16.3
9 Aug	Capránica – Campagna di Roma	25.5	15.9
10 Aug	Campagna di Roma – La Storta	25	15.6
11 Aug	La Storta – Roma	18	11.3
TOTALS		**2,115**	**1,322**